U.S. Immigration and Migration
Biographies

U.S. Immigration and Migration

Biographies

Volume 1
A–J

James L. Outman,
Roger Matuz, and
Rebecca Valentine

Lawrence W. Baker,
Project Editor

U.X.L
A part of Gale, Cengage Learning

GALE
CENGAGE Learning™

Detroit • New York • San Francisco • New Haven, Conn • Waterville, Maine • London

GALE
CENGAGE Learning™

U.S. Immigration and Migration: Biographies

James L. Outman, Roger Matuz, Rebecca Valentine

Project Editor
Lawrence W. Baker

Editorial
Sarah Hermsen, Diane Sawinski

Permissions
Lori Hines

Imaging and Multimedia
Dean Dauphinais, Lezlie Light, Mike Logusz

Product Design
Pamela A. E. Galbreath, Kate Scheible

Composition
Evi Seoud

Manufacturing
Rita Wimberley

For permission to use material from this product, submit your request via Web at http://www.gale-edit.com/permissions, or you may download our Permissions Request form and submit your request by fax or mail to:

Permissions Department
Gale
27500 Drake Rd.
Farmington Hills, MI 48331-3535
Permissions Hotline:
248-699-8006 or 800-877-4253, ext. 8006
Fax: 248-699-8074 or 800-762-4058

Permission for front cover photographs are as follows (clockwise from top left): Arnold Schwarzenegger (Corbis Corpo- ration); Kalpana Chawla (AP/Wide World Photos); and Alexander Graham Bell (Corbis Corporation).

While every effort has been made to ensure the reliability of the information presented in this publication, Gale does not guarantee the accuracy of data contained herein. Gale accepts no pay- ment for listing; and inclusion in the publication of any organization, agency, institution, publication, service, or indi- vidual does not imply endorsement by the editors or publisher. Errors brought to the attention of the publisher and verified to the satisfaction of the pub- lisher will be corrected in future editions.

LIBRARY OF CONGRESS CATALOGING-IN-PUBLICATION DATA

Outman, James L., 1946–

U.S. immigration and migration. Biographies / James L. Outman, Roger Matuz, Rebecca Valentine ; Lawrence W. Baker, editor.

p. cm. — ([U.S. immigration and migration reference library])

Includes bibliographical references and index.

ISBN 0-7876-7733-7 (set : hardcover : alk. paper) — ISBN 0-7876-7568-7 (v. 1) — ISBN 0-7876-7668-3 (v. 2)

1. United States—Emigration and immigration—Juvenile literature. 2. United States—Emigration and immigration— Government policy—Juvenile literature. 3. Immigrants—United States—Biography—Juvenile literature. 4. Immigration advocates—United States—Biography—Juvenile literature. 5. Immigration opponents—United States—Biography—Ju- venile literature. I. Title. II. Title: US immigration and migration. Biographies. II. Matuz, Roger. III. Valentine, Rebecca. IV. Baker, Lawrence W. V. Title. VI. Series.

JV6465.O88 2004
304.8'73'0922—dc22   2004003552

Printed by EPAC Monterrey MX, 4th Printing. 09/2009

Printed in Mexico
4 5 6 7 15 14 13 12 11 10 09

Contents

Volume 1

Volume 2

Reader's Guide

The U.S. Constitution, signed in 1789, gave Congress the right to create laws involving immigration and citizenship. When the first Congress assembled, it created a loose idea of what it meant to be a citizen of the United States: all "free white persons" who had lived in the country for a couple of years were eligible. But the concept of citizenship was still vague. The naturalization process—the set of rules for becoming a citizen—was initially quite simple. The young nation actively sought immigrants to bring their professional skills and labor and to take part in expanding the borders of the nation from the Atlantic Ocean to the Pacific Ocean. There were initially no immigration agencies or border patrols—no passports or green cards. But not everyone was allowed to become a citizen or afforded the same rights. Issues of race for non-whites and Hispanics as well as a historical preference for the northwestern European immigrants led to inequalities and discrimination from the start.

Legislations and policies have continually added to or changed the original vague requirements, rights, and responsibilities of citizenship and immigration. Through the Fourteenth and Fifteenth Amendments after the American Civil War (1861–65), the concept of the "free white persons" eligible to become citizens was amended to include African Americans. Women's citizenship generally was dependent on their husband or father's citizenship until 1920. Until 1943, most Asians were not included in the definition of someone who could become a citizen.

American sentiment toward immigrants has always gone back and forth between positive and negative for a number of reasons. During good economic times when labor is needed, immigrants usually receive better treatment than during economic downturns when people fear the competition for employment. When mass migrations from particular areas begin, there is often hostility in the United States toward the latest group to arrive. They are often perceived as different and as a threat to "American values," leaning more toward Western European traditions. Immigration has almost always been at the center of political controversy in the United States. In fact, the first anti-immigrant government policies began to arise within only a few years of the signing of the Constitution.

Immigration restrictions brought about by nativist (favoring the interests of people who are native-born to a country, though generally not concerning Native Americans, as opposed to its immigrants), racist, or anti-immigrant attitudes have had a very major impact on the U.S. population, dictating who entered the country and in what numbers. The Chinese, for example, were virtually stopped from immigrating by the Chinese Exclusion Act of 1882 until it was repealed in 1943. Many families were separated for decades because of the severity of U.S. restrictions. Immigration from many other countries was significantly reduced by the immigration quota (assigned proportions) systems of 1921 and 1924.

Most immigrants, since the first English settlers landed at Jamestown, have had to pay tremendous dues to settle in North America. There has been a long-held pattern in which the latest arrivals have often been forced to take on the lowest-paying and most undesirable jobs. However, many historians of immigration point out that the brightest and most promising professional prospects of the nations of the world have immigrated to the United States. A daring spirit and the ability to overcome obstacles have always been, and continue to be today, qualities common to the immigrants coming into the nation.

The United States differs from many other countries of the world in having a population made up of people descended from all of the world's nations. Immigration controversy continues to confront the United States in the early twenty-first century, posing difficult questions from concerns about regulating entry and controlling undocumented immigration, to providing public services and a decent education to recently arrived immigrants. In the early years of the twenty-first century, the U.S. Marines intercepted refugees from the civil uprising in Haiti and sent them back to their country, where they feared for their lives. When does the United States provide refuge and what makes the nation deny others who are in need? These concerns are not likely to be resolved in the near future. The value of studying the historical and cultural background of immigration and migration in the nation goes well beyond understanding these difficult issues.

Why study immigration and migration?

As a chronicle of the American people's roots, the history of immigration and migration provides a very intimate approach to the nation's past. Immigration history is strongly centered on the people of the United States rather than the presidential administrations or the wars the nation has fought. Learning about the waves of immigration and migration that populated the continent and seeing the American culture as the mix of many cultures is central to understanding the rich diversity of the United States and appreciating it as a multicultural nation.

The two-volume *U.S. Immigration and Migration: Biographies* presents the life stories of fifty individuals who either played key roles in the governmental and societal influences on U.S. immigration and migration or are immigrants who became successful in the United States. Profiled are well-known figures such as German-born physicist Albert Einstein; Scottish-born industrialist Andrew Carnegie; Czech-born Madeleine Albright, the first female U.S. secretary of state; and English-born comedic actor Charlie Chaplin. In addition, lesser-known individuals are featured, such as Kalpana Chawla, the first female astronaut from India; Mexican-born Antonia Hernández, a lawyer and activist for Latino causes; and folk singer Woody Guthrie, whose songs focused on the plight of victims of the Great Depression and the Dust Bowl of the 1930s—migrants who left the Midwest in search of a better life in the West.

U.S. Immigration and Migration: Biographies also features sidebars containing interesting facts about people and events related to immigration and migration. Within each full-length biography, boldfaced cross-references direct readers to other individuals profiled in the set. Finally, each volume includes photographs and illustrations, a "U.S. Immigration and Migration Timeline" that lists significant dates and events related to immigration and migration as well as the biographees, and an index.

U.S. Immigration and Migration Reference Library

U.S. Immigration and Migration: Biographies is only one component of the three-part U.S. Immigration and Migration Reference Library. The other two titles in this set are:

- *U.S. Immigration and Migration: Almanac* (two volumes) presents a comprehensive overview of the groups of people who have immigrated to the United States from the nations of Africa, Europe, Asia, and Latin America, as well as those who migrated within the country to unexplored lands or to newly industrialized cities. Its seventeen chapters include information on groups or clusters of groups of immigrants from other nations and cultures: Pre-Columbian; Spanish; English; Scotch and Scotch-Irish; French and Dutch; Africans; German; Irish; Scandinavian; Chinese, Japanese, and Filipino; Jewish; Italian and Greek; Eastern European; Arab; Asian Indian, Korean, and Southeast Asian; Mexican; and other Latino and Caribbean groups. Internal migration is also covered, including westward expansion, forced migration, and industrialization and urbanization. The *Almanac* also contains more than 150 black-and-white photographs and maps, "Fact Focus" and "Words to Know" boxes, a "Research and Activity Ideas" section, a timeline, and an index.

- *U.S. Immigration and Migration: Primary Sources:* This volume tells the story of U.S. immigration and migration in the words of the people who lived and shaped it. Eighteen excerpted documents provide a wide range of perspectives on this period of history. Included are excerpts from presidential vetoes; judicial rulings; various legislative acts and treaties; personal essays; magazine articles; party platforms; and works of fiction featuring immigrants.

- A cumulative index of all three titles in the U.S. Immigration and Migration Reference Library is also available.

Acknowledgments

Thanks to copyeditor Theresa Murray; proofreader Amy Marcaccio Keyzer; the indexers from Synapse, the Knowledge Link Corporation; and typesetter Jake Di Vita of the Graphix Group for their fine work. Additional thanks to Julie Burwinkel, media director at Ursuline Academy, Cincinnati, Ohio, and Janet Sarratt, library media specialist at John E. Ewing Middle School, Gaffney, South Carolina, for their help during the early stages of the project.

Comments and suggestions

We welcome your comments on *U.S. Immigration and Migration: Biographies* as well as your suggestions for topics to be featured in future editions. Please write to: Editor, *U.S. Immigration and Migration: Biographies,* U•X•L, 27500 Drake Road, Farmington Hills, Michigan, 48331-3535; call toll-free: 800-877-4253; fax to 248-414-5043; or send e-mail via http://www.gale.com.

U.S. Immigration and Migration Timeline

c. 13,000 B.C.E. The first immigrants arrive on the North American continent and gradually migrate in groups throughout North and South America. Neither the timing of the first migrations nor their origins are known.

c. 400 C.E. The Anasazi culture emerges in the Four Corners region of present-day Arizona, New Mexico, Utah, and Colorado. The Anasazi, thought to be the ancestors of the Pueblo, Zuni, and Hopi Indians, were known for their basketry and pottery as well as their elaborate mansions built into high cliff walls.

c. 700 People of the moundbuilding Mississippian culture build the city of Cahokia near present-day East St.

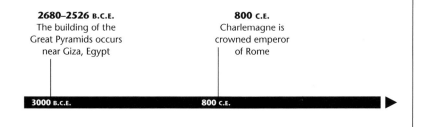

2680–2526 B.C.E.
The building of the
Great Pyramids occurs
near Giza, Egypt

800 C.E.
Charlemagne is
crowned emperor
of Rome

3000 B.C.E.   800 C.E.

Louis, Illinois, about five square miles wide, and containing about a hundred mounds situated around central plazas.

1000   Norse explorer Leif Eriksson sets out from Greenland and apparently sails to Vinland, in present-day Newfoundland, Canada.

1492   Navigator Christopher Columbus arrives in the Caribbean while searching for a route to Asia on an expedition for the kingdom of Spain. He returns to Hispaniola (the island which today is home to Haiti and the Dominican Republic) with settlers the following year.

1565   Spanish explorers and settlers establish Saint Augustine, Florida, the oldest permanent European settlement in the United States.

1607   The Jamestown settlers from England arrive in Virginia and establish a colony.

1618–1725 From five to seven thousand Huguenots flee the persecution in France and sail to America to settle in the British colonies.

1619   A Dutch warship brings twenty African slaves to Jamestown, Virginia, the first Africans to arrive in the British colonies.

1620   The Pilgrims and other British colonists aboard the *Mayflower* land in Plymouth Harbor to found a new British colony.

1624   The first wave of Dutch immigrants to New Netherlands arrives in what is now New York. Most settle at Fort Orange, where the city of Albany now stands.

1016
Viking Canute
the Great begins
rule as king of
England

1492
The Moors
and the Jews
are expelled
from Spain

1618
The Thirty Years'
War begins

1000   1200   1400   1600

1630–40 In the Great Migration from England to New England, about twenty thousand men, women, and children, many of them Puritans, migrate.

1649 An Act Concerning Religion (The Maryland Toleration Act) is issued, allowing the English colony of Maryland to be a refuge for English Catholics who were often persecuted for their beliefs during the English civil war. The act sets the stage for future religious freedoms.

1718 The vast territory of Louisiana becomes a province of France; the European population of the colony numbers about four hundred.

1769 Two Spanish expeditions—one by land and one by sea—leave Mexico to colonize Alta California, the present-day state of California.

1774 English-born scientist **Joseph Priestley** discovers oxygen. Twenty years later, he leaves for America with his family, and soon thereafter establishes the first Unitarian Church in Philadelphia, Pennsylvania.

1784 The Treaty of Fort Stanwix is enacted; the United States agrees to give Native Americans control of the western territory in an attempt to protect native lands from further takeovers by Europeans. However, European settlers ignore the act and it is never enforced by either the British or the U.S. government.

1789 English immigrant **Samuel Slater** brings secret designs of early textile machinery to the United States. He later builds a textile mill in Pawtucket, Rhode Island, the first of many that Slater will own and operate in New England.

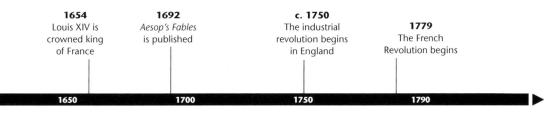

1654
Louis XIV is
crowned king
of France

1692
Aesop's Fables
is published

c. 1750
The industrial
revolution begins
in England

1779
The French
Revolution begins

1650   1700   1750   1790

1790 Congress passes an act providing that "free white persons" who have lived in the United States for at least two years can be naturalized (become citizens) in any U.S. court. Along with non-white males, this also excludes indentured servants, slaves, children, and most women, all of whom are considered dependents.

1804 Meriwether Lewis and William Clark set out on their overland trip across the continent to the Pacific Ocean, forging a path never before explored by European Americans.

1808 Congress prohibits the importation of slaves into the United States, but the slave trade continues until the end of the American Civil War in 1865.

1808 German immigrant **John Jacob Astor** organizes the American Fur Company in Oregon.

1815–45 About one million Irish Catholics immigrate to the United States.

1825 A group of Norwegians immigrate to the United States, eventually settling in Illinois, where they begin the Fox River settlement. This serves as the base camp for future Norwegian immigrants to the United States.

1827 Haitian-born **John James Audubon** publishes the first volume of his *Birds in America* series of illustrations.

1830s Many tribes from the Northeast and Southeast are forcibly moved to Indian Territory (present-day Oklahoma and Kansas). Southern tribes to be removed include the Cherokee, Chickasaw, Choctaw, Creek, Seminole, and others. In the North, the Delaware, Miami, Ottawa, Peoria, Potawatomi, Sauk and Fox, Seneca, and Wyandot tribes are removed. The government is not prepared to provide supplies for so many

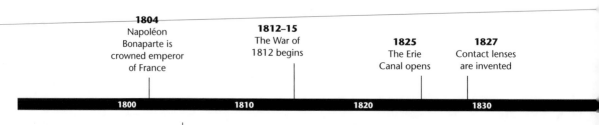

1804
Napoléon Bonaparte is crowned emperor of France

1812–15
The War of 1812 begins

1825
The Erie Canal opens

1827
Contact lenses are invented

| 1800 | 1810 | 1820 | 1830 |

Indians along the trails and in new homes, causing great suffering and death for the Native Americans.

1830s The mass migration of Germans to the United States begins.

1835 French immigrant **Alexis de Tocqueville**'s book *On Democracy in America* is first published, becoming a best-seller. It will remain a unique study of everyday American society during a period of rapid growth marked by a steady immigration of Europeans to the United States.

1836 The Mexican province of Texas declares its independence from Mexico. Texas will become a state in 1845.

1836–60 The Jewish population of the United States grows from fewer than 15,000 to about 160,000. Most of the Jewish immigrants during this period are from Germany.

1841 The first wagon trains cross the continent on the Oregon Trail.

1845 The potato crop in Ireland is hit with a mysterious disease, beginning the Irish potato famine. By the winter of 1847, tens of thousands of people are dying of starvation or related diseases. An estimated one to one and a half million Irish Catholics leave Ireland for the United States over the next few years.

1846 Swiss naturalist **Louis Agassiz** arrives in Boston, Massachusetts, to great acclaim; he will become a professor at Harvard University, bringing his enthusiasm for natural-history research to American students.

1848 Thirteen-year-old **Andrew Carnegie** and his family leave Germany for the United States. He will grow up

1831
Nat Turner leads
slave rebellion

1835–42
The Seminole
War is fought

1841
William Henry
Harrison is the first
U.S. president to die
in office

1846
The Smithsonian
Institution is
founded

1830   1835   1840   1845

to be one of the most successful immigrants to ever come to America.

1848 After the Mexican-American War, the United States acquires the Mexican provinces of New Mexico, Arizona, California, and parts of Nevada, Colorado, and Utah. Between 80,000 and 100,000 Mexicans suddenly find themselves living in the United States. Those who choose to stay in their homes automatically become citizens of the United States.

1848 Gold is discovered in the foothills of northern California's Sierra Nevada Mountains. In the next few years, hundreds of thousands of people from all over the United States and around the world migrate to California hoping to strike it rich.

1848–1914 An estimated 400,000 Czechs immigrate to the United States from Austria-Hungary.

1850 **Millard Fillmore** becomes U.S. president after the sudden death of Zachary Taylor. Fillmore, known for his anti-immigrant prejudice, will suffer an overwhelming loss in the presidential election of 1856.

1850s Having escaped slavery, **Harriet Tubman** becomes a "conductor" on the Underground Railroad, a secret network of houses where escaping slaves could safely be hidden on their way to Canada.

1850s Anti-immigrant associations, such as the American Party (also known as the Know-Nothing Party), the Order of United Americans, and the Order of the Star-Spangled Banner, are on the rise. Their primary targets are Catholics, primarily Irish Americans and German Americans.

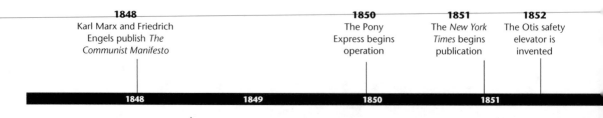

1848
Karl Marx and Friedrich Engels publish *The Communist Manifesto*

1850
The Pony Express begins operation

1851
The *New York Times* begins publication

1852
The Otis safety elevator is invented

1848   1849   1850   1851

1851–1929 More than 1.2 million Swedish immigrants enter the United States.

1855 Castle Island, operated by the State of New York, becomes the first central immigrant-processing center in the United States.

1855 The anti-immigration Know-Nothing Party reveals its platform. A year later, former president Millard Fillmore is this party's candidate in the presidential election; he loses.

1862 Congress passes the Homestead Act to encourage people to settle west of the Mississippi River. Under this act, a person can gain ownership of 160 acres simply by living on the land and cultivating it for five years.

1864–69 Thousands of Chinese laborers work on the first transcontinental railroad in the United States, cutting a path through treacherous mountains.

1866–1914 More than 600,000 Norwegians immigrate to the United States.

1867–1914 About 1.8 Hungarians immigrate to the United States.

1868 The Fourteenth Amendment of the Constitution provides citizenship rights to African Americans.

1869 The first transcontinental railroad in the United States is completed.

1869 German-born engineer and bridge designer **John Augustus Roebling** dies, never seeing his famous Brooklyn Bridge completed.

1870 The Fifteenth Amendment gives African American citizens the right to vote.

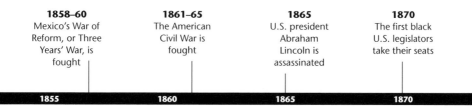

1858–60
Mexico's War of Reform, or Three Years' War, is fought

1861–65
The American Civil War is fought

1865
U.S. president Abraham Lincoln is assassinated

1870
The first black U.S. legislators take their seats

1855   1860   1865   1870

1870 Polish serfs are given their freedom and begin to emigrate. Up to two million Poles will immigrate to the United States between 1870 and 1914.

1870–1920 About 340,000 Finns immigrate to the United States.

1872 Hungarian immigrant **Joseph Pulitzer** buys the struggling *St. Louis Post,* which begins his career as a newspaper publisher.

1874 As a member of the Knights of Labor, Irish immigrant **Mary Jones** travels to Pennsylvania to provide support for the coal miners who had been on strike for over a year. During this time, Jones earns the nickname "Mother Jones" for her ability to boost the morale of her fellow strikers.

1876 Scottish native **Alexander Graham Bell** receives a patent for an "electric speaking telephone," thought to be the most valuable single patent ever granted.

1877 At Bear Paw, Montana, Colonel Nelson Miles leads an assault on the Nez Perce tribe. **Chief Joseph** tries to negotiate a peaceful end to the suffering endured by his people, who had been driven from their tribal homeland.

1880–1920 About 35 million people, mainly from southern and eastern Europe, arrive on U.S. shores.

1880–1920 About 4 million people leave Italy for the United States, making Italians the single largest European national group of this era of mass migration to move to America.

1880–1924 About 95,000 Arabs immigrate to the United States, most from the area known as Greater Syria—present-day Syria, Lebanon, Jordan, Palestine, and Israel.

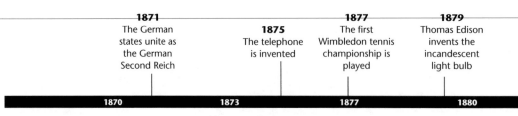

1871
The German states unite as the German Second Reich

1875
The telephone is invented

1877
The first Wimbledon tennis championship is played

1879
Thomas Edison invents the incandescent light bulb

1870   1873   1877   1880

1881–1914 About 2 million Eastern European Jews arrive in the United States.

1882 The Chinese Exclusion Act prohibits the naturalization of Chinese immigrants for ten years and prohibits Chinese laborers from entering the country. For the Chinese already in the country, it denies hope of gaining citizenship and for many Chinese men it meant that their wives or families would not be able to join them. The act, the first major restriction on immigration in the United States, is extended twice and becomes permanent in 1902.

1884 **Helen Hunt Jackson** finishes *Ramona,* her novel inspired by the struggles of Native Americans who are enduring oppression and forced relocation by the U.S. government.

1885–1924 About 200,000 Japanese people immigrate to Hawaii.

1886 More than a million people turn out to see the **Statue of Liberty** unveiled. Designed by French sculptor Frédéric Auguste Bartholdi, the torch-bearing statue becomes a symbol of American freedom.

1889 **Jane Addams** and a traveling companion, teacher Ellen Gates Starr, found Hull House, a community and social center dedicated to helping the working poor and immigrants in Chicago, Illinois, during the time of American industrialization.

1890 Canadian-born businessman **James J. Hill** reorganizes his railroad building company as the Great Northern Railway Company. The company lays tracks connecting Minnesota to Washington State, opening up the Pacific Northwest to settlers and railroad workers who

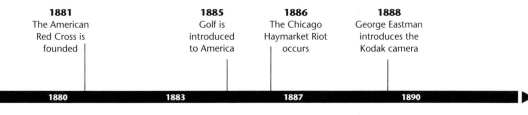

1881
The American
Red Cross is
founded

1885
Golf is
introduced
to America

1886
The Chicago
Haymarket Riot
occurs

1888
George Eastman
introduces the
Kodak camera

1880   1883   1887   1890

were willing to establish their farms and homes along the railroad's path.

1890   The Superintendent of the United States Census issues a statement that the American frontier has closed—that is, it has become populated and is therefore no longer a frontier.

1891   The Immigration and Naturalization Service (INS) is created as the department that administers federal laws relating to admitting, excluding, or deporting aliens and to naturalizing the foreign-born who are in the United States legally. It remains in operation until 2003.

1892   The federal government takes over the process of screening incoming immigrants at the Port of New York and creates an immigration reception center at Ellis Island, one mile southwest of Manhattan. Before it closes in 1954, more than 16 million immigrants will pass through Ellis Island.

1900   In this one year, one-tenth of Denmark's total population immigrates to the United States.

1903   The last five lines of the poem "The New Colossus" are engraved on a plaque and affixed to the Statue of Liberty. **Emma Lazarus**, the poem's author and an advocate of Jewish rights, had died in 1887 and did not live to see her work displayed on the statue.

1905   German-born **Albert Einstein** publishes a series of papers, including one based on a concept known as Einstein's "special theory of relativity."

1907   The Dillingham Commission, set up by Congress to investigate immigration, produces a forty-two-volume report. The commission claims that its studies show that people from southern and eastern Europe have a

1891	**1898**	**1904**	**1910**
The escalator is invented	The Spanish-American War is fought	The movie camera is created	The Mexican Revolution begins

| 1890 | 1895 | 1900 | 1905 |

higher potential for criminal activity, are more likely to end up poor and sick, and are less intelligent than other Americans. The report warns that the waves of immigration threaten the "American" way of life.

1907 As anti-Asian immigrant sentiment rises in the United States, Congress works out the "Gentlemen's Agreement" with Japan, in which the United States agrees not to ban all Japanese immigration as long as Japan promises not to issue passports to Japanese laborers for travel to the continental United States.

1910 To enforce the Chinese Exclusion Act, an immigration station is built at Angel Island in the San Francisco Bay. Any Chinese people arriving in San Francisco go through an initial inspection upon arrival; many are then sent to Angel Island for further processing and thousands are held there for long periods of time.

1910–1920 Between 500,000 and 1,000,000 African Americans migrate from the southern United States to the cities of the North.

1912 Jane Addams publishes *Twenty Years at Hull-House,* in which she writes of her experiences as owner of a house primarily designed to help immigrants trying to adjust to a completely different way of life.

1913 California passes the Alien Land Laws, which prohibit Chinese and Japanese people from owning land in the state.

1914 Swiss-born silent movie star **Charlie Chaplin** appears in his first production, *Kid Auto Races at Venice.*

1917 Congress creates the "Asiatic barred zone," which excludes immigration from most of Asia, including China, India, and Japan, regardless of literacy.

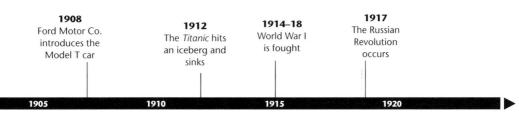

1908
Ford Motor Co. introduces the Model T car

1912
The *Titanic* hits an iceberg and sinks

1914–18
World War I is fought

1917
The Russian Revolution occurs

1905   1910   1915   1920

1920 Jamaican-born **Marcus Garvey** organizes the first of several international conventions, adopting a document titled the "Declaration of Rights of the Negro People of the World." It is a concise statement of Garvey's philosophy of black pride, unity, and immigration to Africa.

1920s–30s More than 40,000 Russians come to the United States in the first few years after the Russian Revolution of 1917. Many Russians go into exile in other European cities. In the 1930s, those in exile in Europe begin fleeing the rising Nazi movement. More than a million people who had been born in Russia but were living elsewhere in Europe immigrate to the United States in the 1930s.

1921 Congress passes the Emergency Quota Act, which stipulates that each nation has an annual quota (proportion) of immigrants it may send to the United States, which is equal to 3 percent of that country's total population in the United States in 1910. Because the majority of the U.S. population was from northwestern Europe in 1910, this method favors northwestern Europeans over other immigrants.

1921 In *Ozawa v. United States,* the U.S. Supreme Court rules against an upstanding twenty-year Chinese immigrant resident of the United States who had applied to become a U.S. citizen on the grounds that he was not "white."

1924 Congress passes the Immigration Act of 1924 (National Origins Act), which restricts the number of immigrants even beyond the Emergency Quota Act of 1921. Under the new act, immigration is decreased to a total equaling 2 percent of the population in 1890. Under

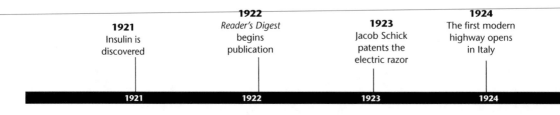

1921 Insulin is discovered

1922 *Reader's Digest* begins publication

1923 Jacob Schick patents the electric razor

1924 The first modern highway opens in Italy

1921 1922 1923 1924

this act, each country may only send 2 percent of its 1890 population in the United States per year. The new act skews the permitted immigration even further in favor of Western Europe, with the United Kingdom, Germany, and Ireland receiving more than two-thirds of the annual maximum quota. This legislation ends the era of mass migrations to the United States.

1924   The Oriental Exclusion Act prohibits most Asian immigration, including the wives and children of U.S. citizens of Chinese ancestry.

1924   Congress creates the Border Patrol, a uniformed law enforcement agency of the Immigration Bureau in charge of fighting smuggling and illegal immigration.

1925   One out of every four Greek men between the ages of fifteen and forty-five have immigrated to the United States.

1927   The first of a trilogy of novels by Norwegian-born writer **O. E. Rölvaag** is published. The writings chronicle the lives of immigrants in Minnesota and South Dakota.

1927   Lithuanian native **Al Jolson** stars in the role of Jack Robin in the first successful sound movie, *The Jazz Singer.*

1928   The Notre Dame football team defeats Army, 12-6. Before the game, Notre Dame's coach, Norwegian immigrant **Knute Rockne**, gives his famous locker-room speech that includes the phrase, "Win one for the Gipper."

1931   Hungarian immigrant **Bela Lugosi** plays the leading role in the Universal Studios film *Dracula,* the first talking horror movie.

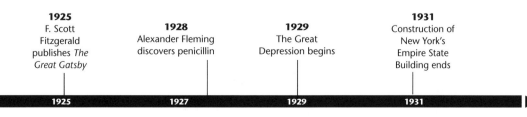

1925
F. Scott Fitzgerald publishes *The Great Gatsby*

1928
Alexander Fleming discovers penicillin

1929
The Great Depression begins

1931
Construction of New York's Empire State Building ends

1925   1927   1929   1931

1934 The Tydings-McDuffie Act sets the date and some of the terms of independence for the Philippines on July 4, 1946. Since the United States had acquired the Philippines from Spain in 1898, Filipinos had entered the United States as nationals (people who live in a country legally, are loyal to the country and protected by it, but are not citizens). The act takes away status of Filipinos as U.S. nationals, reclassifying them as aliens, and restricts Filipino immigration by establishing an annual immigration quota of 50.

Late 1930s Woody Guthrie begins his career as a folk singer, known primarily for providing a voice for those displaced by the Great Depression and the Great Dust Storm.

1938 Italian native **Enrico Fermi** receives the Nobel Prize in physics. The Fermi family travels to Sweden, attends the ceremonies, then boards a ship to the United States.

1938 **Henry Kissinger** comes to the United States as a child refugee from Nazi Germany.

1939 U.S. president Franklin D. Roosevelt appoints Austrian native **Felix Frankfurter** to the U.S. Supreme Court. The Senate unanimously confirms the decision to appoint Frankfurter, who, as a boy, had immigrated to New York with his family to escape Austria's persecution of its Jewish inhabitants.

1941 A top-secret study on nuclear fission, called the Manhattan Project, is established in 1941. Enrico Fermi is one of those working on the project.

1942 The United States, heavily involved in World War II, needs laborers at home and turns to Mexico. The U.S. and Mexican governments reach an agreement called

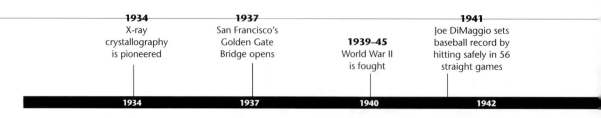

1934	**1937**		**1941**
X-ray crystallography is pioneered	San Francisco's Golden Gate Bridge opens	**1939–45** World War II is fought	Joe DiMaggio sets baseball record by hitting safely in 56 straight games
1934	1937	1940	1942

the Mexican Farm Labor Supply Program, or the *bracero* program. The program permits Mexicans to enter the country to work under contract as farm and railroad laborers. The program continues for twenty-two years and brings 4.8 million Mexicans to work on U.S. farms and in businesses.

1942   During World War II, President Franklin D. Roosevelt signs Executive Order 9066, which dictates the removal and internment of Japanese Americans. More than 112,000 Japanese Americans living along the Pacific coast are taken from their homes and placed in ten internment camps for the duration of the war.

1943   Congress repeals the Chinese exclusion acts. Immigration from China resumes. Most of the new immigrants are females, the wives of Chinese men who have been in the United States for decades.

1945   As World War II ends, more than 40,000 refugees from Europe flee to the United States. Because the quota system does not provide for them, they are admitted under presidential directive.

1945   The War Brides Act allows foreign-born spouses and adopted children of personnel of the U.S. armed forces to enter the United States. The act brings in many Japanese, Chinese, and Korean women, among other groups.

1948   The first U.S. refugee policy, the Displaced Persons Act, enables nearly 410,000 European refugees to enter the United States after World War II.

1950   The Internal Security Act forces all communists to register with the government and denies admission to any foreigner who is a communist or who might engage in subversive activities.

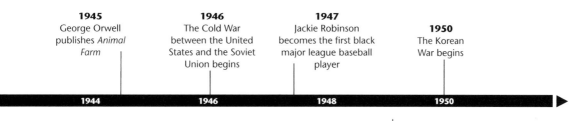

1945
George Orwell publishes *Animal Farm*

1946
The Cold War between the United States and the Soviet Union begins

1947
Jackie Robinson becomes the first black major league baseball player

1950
The Korean War begins

1944   1946   1948   1950

1951 Chinese immigrant **An Wang** founds Wang Laboratories to develop, produce, and market applications using his memory cores and other inventions.

1952 Congress overrides President Harry S. Truman's veto of the Immigration and Nationality Act, which upholds the quota system set in 1921–24 but removes race as a bar to immigration and naturalization and removes discrimination between sexes. The act gives preference to immigrants with special skills needed in the United States, provides for more rigorous screening of immigrants in order to eliminate people considered to be subversive (particularly communists and homosexuals), and allows broader grounds for the deportation of criminal aliens.

1953 The television program *Make Room for Daddy,* starring comic actor **Danny Thomas**, debuts on the ABC network.

1954 As jobs in the United States become harder to find, Mexican workers are viewed as unwanted competition by many. Under Operation Wetback, a special government force locates undocumented workers and forces them to return to Mexico. In one year alone, about one million people of Mexican descent are deported.

1959 The Cuban Revolution initiates a mass migration from Cuba to the United States—more than one million Cubans will immigrate after this year.

1960 Romanian and Jewish immigrant **Elie Wiesel**'s memoir *Night* is published. The book, which describes Wiesel's experiences in the Nazi concentration camps, will sell more than five million copies throughout the world and will be translated into thirty languages.

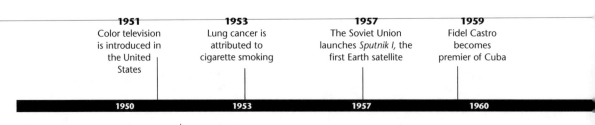

1951	**1953**	**1957**	**1959**
Color television is introduced in the United States	Lung cancer is attributed to cigarette smoking	The Soviet Union launches *Sputnik I,* the first Earth satellite	Fidel Castro becomes premier of Cuba

| 1950 | 1953 | 1957 | 1960 |

1960–80 The Filipino population in the United States more than quadruples, from 176,130 to 781,894.

1960s Between 4 and 5 million African Americans have migrated from the South to the North since the turn of the century.

1962 Hawaiian voters elect World War II hero **Daniel K. Inouye** as their senator. He becomes the first American of Japanese descent to serve in the U.S. Congress.

1962 Comic actor Danny Thomas dedicates the St. Jude's Children's Research Hospital, in Memphis, Tennessee.

1963 Civil rights activist **Yuri Kochiyama** meets Malcolm X and joins his group, the Organization for Afro-American Unity.

1963 **Daniel Patrick Moynihan** and fellow professor Nathan Glazer write *Beyond the Melting Pot,* a book challenging the belief that immigrants to the United States mix with other cultures and form an "American" identity.

1965 In a new spirit of immigration reform, Congress repeals the national-origins quotas and gives each Eastern Hemisphere nation an annual quota of 20,000, excluding immediate family members of U.S. citizens. The Eastern Hemisphere receives 170,000 places for immigrants and the Western Hemisphere 120,000. (In 1978, Congress creates a worldwide immigration system by combining the two hemispheres.)

1966–80 About 14,000 Dominicans per year enter the United States, most seeking employment they cannot find at home.

1968 Japanese native **Yoko Ono** meets Beatle John Lennon at an exhibit of her artwork; they marry within a year.

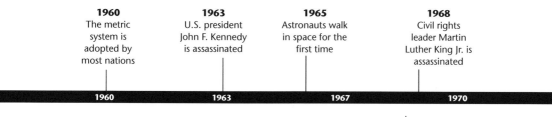

1960	**1963**	**1965**	**1968**
The metric system is adopted by most nations	U.S. president John F. Kennedy is assassinated	Astronauts walk in space for the first time	Civil rights leader Martin Luther King Jr. is assassinated
1960	1963	1967	1970

1970 The campaign against grape growers, led by union leader **César Chávez**, finally succeeds; after a successful grape boycott, a group of California growers signs an agreement with the United Farm Workers, giving grape pickers higher wages.

1972–81 Sailboats carrying Haitians begin to arrive on the shores of Florida. More than 55,000 Haitian "boat people"—and perhaps more than 100,000—arrive in this wave.

1973 Henry Kissinger, U.S. secretary of state and a major influence in U.S. foreign policy, wins the Nobel Peace Prize.

1975 Saigon, the South Vietnamese capital, falls to the communist North on April 30; at least 65,000 South Vietnamese immediately flee the country.

1975–81 About 123,600 Laotian refugees enter the United States.

1976 Daniel Patrick Moynihan is elected as a U.S. senator from New York and serves for twenty-four years.

1977 Palestine native **Edward Said** is elected to the Palestine National Council (PNC) and begins his work to seek a peaceful agreement between Palestinians and Israelis.

1977 **Josie Natori** leaves a successful career in finance to design a line of sleepwear using materials and design work from her native Philippines. She generates $150,000 worth of orders in only a few months.

1979 In the aftermath of the Vietnam War, the Orderly Departure Program (ODP) is established to provide a safe alternative for Vietnamese people who are fleeing the country in large numbers, often risking their lives in

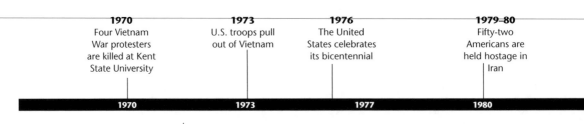

1970
Four Vietnam War protesters are killed at Kent State University

1973
U.S. troops pull out of Vietnam

1976
The United States celebrates its bicentennial

1979–80
Fifty-two Americans are held hostage in Iran

1970   1973   1977   1980

overcrowded old boats. Under the ODP, refugees are allowed to leave Vietnam directly for resettlement in one of two dozen countries, including the United States. There are about 165,000 admissions to the United States under the ODP by 1989, and new arrivals continue into the 1990s.

1980   More than 125,000 Cubans flee to the United States during the Mariel Boat Lift.

1980–86   Tens of thousands of Cambodian refugees enter the United States annually.

1981–2000   The United States accepts 531,310 Vietnamese refugees.

1982   Peru native **Isabel Allende** wins international acclaim for *La casa de los espíritus*. Three years later, the novel is published in English as *The House of the Spirits*.

1982   In *Plyler v. Doe,* the U.S. Supreme Court rules that the children of illegal immigrants have the same rights as everyone else, especially the right to an education.

1983   Chinese-born architect **I. M. Pei** receives the prestigious Prizker Architecture Prize and uses the $100,000 award to establish a scholarship fund for Chinese students to study architecture in the United States.

1984   Austrian immigrant **Arnold Schwarzenegger** stars in the successful futuristic film *The Terminator.*

1984   New York governor **Mario Cuomo** delivers a memorable keynote address at the Democratic National Convention. The speech includes the story of his immigrant family's efforts to make a good life in America and raises awareness of the need for political programs to help the less fortunate.

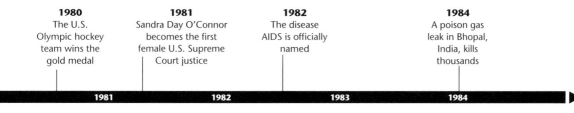

1980
The U.S. Olympic hockey team wins the gold medal

1981
Sandra Day O'Connor becomes the first female U.S. Supreme Court justice

1982
The disease AIDS is officially named

1984
A poison gas leak in Bhopal, India, kills thousands

1981   1982   1983   1984

1985 Mexican native **Antonia Hernández** becomes president of the Mexican American Legal Defense and Educational Fund (MALDEF), vowing to ensure equal opportunity to all Latinos. She works to support bilingual education and challenge anti-immigrant laws.

1986 The Immigration Reform and Control Act (IRCA) provides amnesty (pardon to a group of people) to more than 3 million undocumented immigrants who had entered the United States before 1982, allowing them to become legal residents. The measure outlaws the knowing employment of undocumented immigrants and makes it more difficult for undocumented immigrants to receive public assistance.

1988 Congress passes the Amerasian Homecoming Act, which brings thousands of children—most are the offspring of American servicemen and Asian mothers—to the United States.

1989 **Le Ly Hayslip** becomes nationally famous in the United States when her first book, *When Heaven and Earth Changed Places,* is published. The book chronicles her experiences as a girl growing up during the Vietnam War.

1991–93 Some 43,000 Haitians try to reach the United States by boat. Many of their boats are intercepted by U.S. officials and those emigrants are taken to Guantánamo Bay, a U.S. naval base in Cuba.

1993 **John Shalikashvili**, a Polish-born member of the U.S. Army, is chosen to become chairman of the Joint Chiefs by President Bill Clinton.

1994 In an effort to stop undocumented workers from illegally crossing the border, the government adopts Operation Gatekeeper, an extensive border patrol system

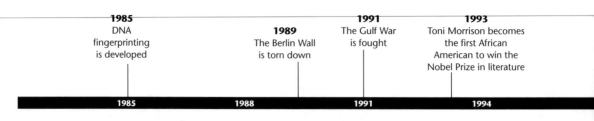

1985
DNA fingerprinting is developed

1989
The Berlin Wall is torn down

1991
The Gulf War is fought

1993
Toni Morrison becomes the first African American to win the Nobel Prize in literature

1985   1988   1991   1994

at Imperial Beach at the border between Mexico and southern California. The number of border agents is increased and new hi-tech equipment is put to use, costing billions of dollars over the next few years. Illegal immigration moves further inland where the climate is more severe, proving to be deadly in some cases.

1994 The United States enters a Wet Feet–Dry Feet agreement with Cuba under which, if fleeing Cubans trying to reach the United States are caught at sea, U.S. authorities will send them back to Cuba. If the Cubans make it to U.S. shores, they will be admitted to the country.

1994 California citizens vote in favor of Proposition 187, a law designed to stop immigrants without visas from receiving public benefits from the state; a judge later blocks the state from putting the proposition into effect.

1996 Congress passes the Illegal Immigration Reform and Immigrant Responsibility Act (IIRIRA). The IIRIRA creates a huge increase in funding for border patrol personnel and equipment. This act creates harsher penalties for illegal immigration, restricts welfare benefits to recent immigrants, and makes the deportation process easier for U.S. administrators. The IIRIRA also tries to make it harder for foreign terrorists to enter the United States.

1996 The bombing of the Oklahoma Federal Building at the hands of a terrorist (a U.S. citizen) in 1995 raises new fears about terrorism. The Anti-terrorism Act is passed, making deportation automatic if an immigrant commits a deportable felony (a grave crime), even if the immigrant has been in the United States

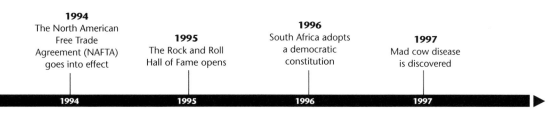

1994
The North American Free Trade Agreement (NAFTA) goes into effect

1995
The Rock and Roll Hall of Fame opens

1996
South Africa adopts a democratic constitution

1997
Mad cow disease is discovered

1994 1995 1996 1997

since early childhood. By 2003, 500,000 people had been deported under the terms of this act.

1997 Czech native **Madeleine Albright** assumes the role of U.S. secretary of state during the administration of Bill Clinton. She becomes the highest-ranking woman in the U.S. government at that time, and the first woman in U.S. history to hold that title.

1997 The Border Patrol initiates Operation Rio Grande, strengthening the Texas-Mexico border with more agents to deter people from crossing.

1998 California passes Proposition 227, a referendum that bans bilingual classroom education and English as a second language (ESL) program, replacing them with a one-year intensive English immersion program.

2000 The Immigration and Naturalization Service estimates the number of undocumented immigrants in the country at about 7 million, up from the estimate of 5.8 million in 1996. About 70 percent of the undocumented immigrants are from Mexico.

2001 Congress passes the USA PATRIOT Act ("Uniting and Strengthening America by Providing Appropriate Tools Required to Intercept and Obstruct Terrorism"). The bill calls for increased border patrol and tightened provisions for screening and restricting immigrants. It grants sweeping new powers to federal police agencies and permits indefinite detention of immigrants and aliens in the country for minor immigration status violations.

2001 Within weeks of the September 11 terrorist attacks on New York and Washington, D.C., approximately 1,200 immigrants are arrested by federal government agents as part of an anti-terrorist campaign. Most are from Saudi

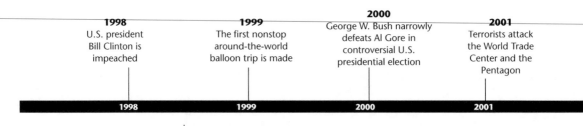

1998 U.S. president Bill Clinton is impeached	1999 The first nonstop around-the-world balloon trip is made	2000 George W. Bush narrowly defeats Al Gore in controversial U.S. presidential election	2001 Terrorists attack the World Trade Center and the Pentagon
1998	1999	2000	2001

Arabia, Egypt, and Pakistan. Many are held without charges and without access to attorneys or their families. Many are deported. None are charged with terrorism.

2002　The Homeland Security Department requires the annual registration of temporary male immigrants from twenty-four predominantly Arab or Muslim countries as well as North Korea. People from the following countries are required to register: Afghanistan, Algeria, Bahrain, Eritrea, Iran, Iraq, Lebanon, Libya, Morocco, North Korea, Oman, Pakistan, Qatar, Saudi Arabia, Somalia, Sudan, Syria, Tunisia, United Arab Emirates, and Yemen. The following year, five more countries are added to the list: Bangladesh, Egypt, Indonesia, Jordan, and Kuwait. Of the 83,519 people who register with immigration officials in 2002, 13,799 are put in deportation proceedings. Others complain of terrifying or humiliating interrogations and harsh conditions. Immigrant and civil liberties groups protest the policy.

2002　Conservative talk-show host and former presidential candidate **Patrick J. Buchanan** publishes *The Death of the West: How Dying Populations and Immigrant Invasions Imperil Our Country and Civilization,* in which he warns that immigration and low birth rates would result in white people being a minority in the United States, where they once constituted an overwhelming majority.

2003　The explosion of space shuttle *Columbia* takes the life of **Kalpana Chawla,** the first female astronaut from India, and the lives of her six fellow crew members.

2003　Actor Arnold Schwarzenegger is elected governor of California.

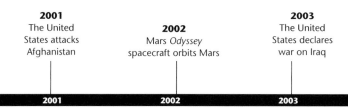

2001
The United States attacks Afghanistan

2002
Mars *Odyssey* spacecraft orbits Mars

2003
The United States declares war on Iraq

2001　　　　2002　　　　2003　　　　2004

U.S. Immigration and Migration
Biographies

Jane Addams

Born September 6, 1860
Cedarville, Illinois

Died May 21, 1935
Chicago, Illinois

Founder of Hull-House and
of modern social work

hicago, Illinois, 1890. "Hog Butcher for the World," poet Carl Sandburg (1878–1967) called it, in his 1916 poem, "Chicago." "Tool Maker, Stacker of Wheat, / Player with Railroads and the Nation's Freight Handler; / Stormy, husky, brawling, / City of the Big Shoulders." In 1890, Chicago was all these things, and more. It was the new home of thousands of Italians and Lithuanians, Poles and Bohemians, Germans and Greeks, immigrants from southern and eastern Europe recently arrived in America with pockets full of dreams and little else. Chicago was also the new home of a well-educated, sophisticated, and independent young woman. Despite her uncertain health, she did not feel like settling for the conventional life of a housewife in her all-American hometown of Cedarville, Illinois. Her dreams were about compassion and social justice, about helping to save struggling people whose lives were threatened by the mercilessness of industrial America at the turn of the twentieth century. She, too, put her stamp on the City of the Big Shoulders. Her name was Jane Addams.

The genius of Addams was her ability to take direct action and ease the suffering of factory workers and their fami-

"Teaching in a Settlement requires distinct methods, for it is true of people who have been allowed to remain undeveloped and whose facilities are inert and sterile, that they cannot take their learning heavily."

Jane Addams. *Library of Congress.*

lies. She dealt not only with immigrants but also with natives of the United States who came to the big city in search of work and money. Addams met their problems head-on and took the house she lived in and turned it into a community and social center called Hull-House. By so doing, Addams founded the field of social work in the United States. She later branched out to become a force in education, labor relations, women's rights, civil rights, and civil liberties. She won the Nobel Prize for Peace in 1931, the first American woman to do so.

Cedarville

Jane Addams was born into a large family in Cedarville, Illinois, west of Chicago. Her mother died when she was two years old. Her father, John Addams, was the prosperous owner of a mill that ground wheat into flour, a local political leader, and a friend of President Abraham Lincoln (1809–1865; served 1861–65). John Addams had been among the founders of the Republican Party, founded in 1852, which led the opposition to slavery before the American Civil War (1861–65). He remarried in 1868. His daughter Jane was almost the baby of the family—she was the eighth of nine children. Jane absorbed her father's sense of responsibility to work for social improvement. What she did not absorb was the usual idea, in the middle of the nineteenth century, of what a proper daughter of a Republican leader in a small midwestern town ought to do with her life after her education.

Jane Addams was an excellent student in school. She had ambitions to attend one of the East Coast colleges for women that had been founded recently, and from there perhaps become a medical doctor. Her parents disapproved of Jane's traveling so far east for college, and they preferred that she become educated with the idea of becoming a better wife. Instead of going east, Jane stayed near home, attending Rockford Female Seminary (later Rockford College for Women, and now Rockford College). Her father was a trustee, or overseer, of Rockford. Addams graduated first in her class in 1881, still thinking about attending medical school.

A grand tour

Addams spent the next six years focusing on her future. She enrolled in the Women's Medical College in

Philadelphia, Pennsylvania, but had to drop out because of pain from a lifelong curvature of her spine. After undergoing corrective back surgery, Addams spent a year strapped into a brace that left her almost immobile. Afterwards, she spent a year and a half touring Europe. Shortly after she returned home, her beloved father died suddenly. She spent two years at home thinking about what to do with her life, then embarked on another trip to Europe. While in London, she visited an institution called Toynbee Hall, a settlement house that had been established to help ease some of the social difficulties experienced by poor working people in England's capital city. The original idea for settlement houses was to have people from universities move to a working-class neighborhood to help relieve the poverty that existed and to learn about the plights of the poor. The visit was the turning point in Addams's life.

On her second European tour, Addams was struck by the wide range of social problems encountered by workers affected by the Industrial Revolution, a period of industrial growth that introduced the mass production of goods in factories instead of in homes or in smaller individual workshops as had previously been the case. In that era, governments did not address issues arising from the growth of industrial cities, such as inadequate housing or poverty brought on by unemployment. Poor and uneducated workers were on their own. The result was often widespread suffering of whole families who lacked the resources to solve their problems. London's Toynbee Hall was an example of how such problems could be addressed on a local scale. Residents of Toynbee Hall offered counseling, advice, and education in ways of coping with the change from living in a rural village to living in a large city.

In 1889, Addams and a traveling companion, teacher Ellen Gates Starr (1859–1940), went to Chicago to establish a settlement house like Toynbee Hall. They found a large house that had been built by Chicago real estate developer Charles J. Hull (1820–1889) on the corner of Halsted and Polk Streets. Addams and Starr moved into the house, according to the *Nobel e-Museum* web site, to "provide a center for a higher civic and social life; to institute and maintain educational and philanthropic (charitable) enterprises and to investigate and improve the conditions in the industrial districts of Chicago."

Hull-House

Addams and Starr made Hull-House a place where families could turn for help. A person could get a hot lunch, leave a child in day care, learn English, or get medical care or legal advice. By its second year, Hull-House hosted two thousand people a week. It had added kindergarten classes for toddlers and evening classes for adults. It had an art gallery, a gymnasium, a music school, and an employment bureau where men and women could look for jobs.

At the center of the project was Addams. She had always believed that women could play bigger roles than housewives, and she attracted like-minded young women to help her set up new programs for the working poor in the neighborhood. Addams's reputation quickly spread throughout the city (and eventually, throughout the world). Even though women could not yet vote, Addams was elected to the Chicago Board of Education and became chairperson of its School Management Committee.

As Addams continued to work to improve the lives of the working people around her—both immigrants and native-born Americans—Addams became convinced that political changes were needed in addition to volunteer charity work. She started campaigning for laws to limit the hours and ages at which children could work, to require children to attend school, and to inspect factories for unsafe conditions. She became the voice of the working poor, representing their cause to the city government by lobbying for, or promoting, street paving, public parks, and playgrounds in poorer neighborhoods. She encouraged workers to form labor unions, associations that worked for better wages and working conditions. In 1912, Addams seconded the nomination of former president Theodore Roosevelt (1858–1919; served 1901–9) at the convention of the Progressive Party. She campaigned for Roosevelt during the election, but his bid for reelection failed.

Addams's observations of immigrants at Hull-House

The people who received assistance from Hull-House included both native-born Americans who had moved from farms or small towns to Chicago, looking for work, and immigrant families. Addams took special note of the problems facing immigrants. Addams set up Hull-House during a period of large-scale immigration into the United States from southern and eastern Europe. At the time, most immigrants came from a rural background in some of the poorest regions of Europe. They had grown up with a way of life that had changed little for hundreds of years. Suddenly, they were in an urban environment, unable to speak the language and utterly unused to the urban industrial culture developing in the United States.

Addams was a sensitive observer of the newly arrived and struggling families. She noticed, for example, that the role of parent and child was often reversed, with teenaged children showing their parents how to function in the new society. In one case, an Italian woman was used to baking her own bread every day, but not at home. In Italy, it had been done in a community oven. In Chicago, the woman had no idea how to operate the oven in her household and had to depend on her daughter to show her.

Addams also noted that young women submitted to their parents' expectations for their lives. They often were required to assume the social roles that might have been appropriate for young women in a rural village of Russia or Italy—primarily limited to staying at home to tend to children and performing household tasks—but that seemed completely out of touch with Chicago around the year 1900. Young city women in the United States were expected to bring in money by working outside the home. (Addams may have seen something of her own reluctance to settle for a conventional woman's role in the experiences of young immigrant women.)

In her memoir, *Twenty Years at Hull-House,* published in 1910, Addams noted how the role of fathers was changed, even crushed, by the immigrant experience. She told of a father from Bohemia (now part of the Czech Republic) whose daughter took classes at Hull-House. The father was often drunk. He eventually committed suicide in the midst of a strong reaction against too much alcohol. Only after his death did Addams learn from his widow that in Europe, he had been a highly skilled goldsmith who had made his wife, now a widow, a beautiful wedding ring. In America, in Chicago, he had been forced to find a job shoveling coal in the furnace room of a factory. The wife had usually been able to calm her husband's fits of frustration and anger by handing him a bit of metal to work on at home. "This story threw a flood of light upon the dead man's struggle and on the stupid maladjustment [inability to adjust to human demands] which had broken him down," Addams wrote in *Twenty Years at Hull-House.* "Why had we never been told? Why had our interest in the remarkable musical ability of his child, blinded us to the hidden artistic ability of the father? We had forgotten that a long-established occupation may form the very foundations of the moral life, that the art with which a man [found comfort] may be the salvation of his uncertain temperament."

Twenty Years at Hull-House served as a diary for Addams and as a handbook for workers at institutions similar to Hull-House. Her book also served as a document of American industrialized society in the era, and was widely read. Other books followed about every two years.

Addams grew from a young woman intent on helping the workers of Chicago to one who played a role on the na-

tional stage. At the start of World War I (1914–18), she was determined to promote international peace. She opposed America's entry into the European war, and in 1915 she helped found the Women's Peace Party. She traveled to Europe to campaign for a quick, peaceful solution to the war between England and France on one side and Germany and Austria on the other. She favored establishing a permanent international peacekeeping organization. After World War I,

Addams became an assistant to Herbert Hoover (1874–1964), a businessman placed in charge of organizing delivery of emergency food aid to the defeated nations in Europe after the war ended. (Hoover was elected president in 1928.)

The causes promoted by Addams in international affairs met with mixed success. The United States eventually entered World War I on the side of Britain and France in 1917. The League of Nations, an international organization similar to the United Nations, was organized much as had been proposed by President Woodrow Wilson (1856–1924; served 1913–21), as a means of preventing any future world war. But the U.S. Senate never agreed to join the League. In 1919, Addams was elected first president of the Women's International League for Peace and Freedom, a private group devoted to promoting peace, including U.S. membership in the League of Nations.

In 1926, Addams suffered a heart attack, and she never fully recovered her health. On December 10, 1931, she was awarded the Nobel Peace Prize, the first American woman so honored. On the same day, Addams was admitted to a hospital in Baltimore, Maryland. Four years later, she was diagnosed with cancer and died on May 21, 1935. Her funeral service was held in the courtyard of Hull-House in Chicago.

—James L. Outman

For More Information

Books

Addams, Jane. *Twenty Years at Hull-House*. New York: Macmillan, 1910. Reprint, Boston: Bedford/St. Martin's, 1999.

Eliot, George. *The Mill on the Floss*. New York: Harper & Bros., 1860. Reprint, New York: Knopf, 1992.

Elshtain, Jean Bethke. *Jane Addams and the Dream of American Democracy: A Life*. New York: Basic Books, 2002.

Hovde, Jane. *Jane Addams*. New York: Facts on File, 1989.

Periodicals

Kornblatt, Mark, and Pamela Renner. "'Saint' Jane." *Scholastic Update* (February 23, 1990): p. 10.

Levinsohn, Florence Hamlish. "A Tribute to a Life of Caring; Halsted Street's Living Memorial to Jane Addams." *Chicago* (November 1986): p. 304.

Web Sites

Carl Sandburg Chicago Poems. http://carl-sandburg.com (accessed on March 4, 2004).

Holli, Melvin G. "Hull House and the Immigrants." *Illinois Periodicals Online*. http://www.lib.niu.edu/ipo/iht1010323.html (accessed on March 4, 2004).

"Jane Addams Biography." *Nobel e-Museum*. http://www.nobel.se/peace/laureates/1931/addams-bio.html (accessed on March 4, 2004).

Luft, Margaret. "About …." *Jane Addams Hull House*. http://www.hullhouse.org/about.asp (accessed on March 4, 2004).

Louis Agassiz

Born May 28, 1807
Motier-en-Vuly, Switzerland

Died December 14, 1873
Cambridge, Massachusetts

Naturalist and teacher

> "The book of Nature is always open.... Strive to interpret what really exists."

Louis Agassiz (pronounced AG-uh-see) was the leading naturalist of the nineteenth century, advancing the study of nature through scientific observation. Born in Switzerland, he emigrated to the United States in middle age after his reputation was already well established. Agassiz was famed for his studies of glaciers, the moving rivers of ice that led Agassiz to formulate the notion of an "Ice Age" in the distant past. As a professor at Harvard University, Agassiz taught generations of students engaged in the scientific study of nature, which he regarded as evidence of God. On that basis, he led opposition to the new theory of evolution brought forth by English naturalist Charles Darwin (1809–1882).

Youth in Switzerland

Jean Louis Rodolphe Agassiz was born into a comfortably well-off family in Switzerland. His father was a minister, and the family was deeply religious. Young Agassiz developed a reverence for the natural world as God's creation that he retained all his life. Agassiz's parents thought he should study

Louis Agassiz. *Library of Congress.*

medicine and become a doctor, and he was willing to follow this course. He did not dislike medicine, but he had always been drawn to the natural world and everything in it. Slowly but surely that interest would grow into a life's passion.

In 1824, Agassiz went to the University of Zurich, and two years later he moved to Heidelberg, Germany, to further his medical studies. What really increased with the move was his desire to be a naturalist. He decided to go to the University of Munich to take advantage of its fame in natural history.

Agassiz produced and published his first scholarly work while at Munich when he was just twenty-one years old, a volume titled *The Fishes of Brazil*. Two eminent scientists connected with the university, J. B. von Spix (1781–1826) and K. F. von Martius (1794–1868), returned in 1821 from an extended tour through the country of Brazil, in South America, with a vast collection of data about the fish they had found there. Von Spix died in 1826, and von Martius turned the fish collection over to Agassiz. The young Agassiz transformed the raw data into an important, respected collection with color illustrations, the most comprehensive book of its kind at the time.

The time spent at Munich was key for Agassiz in several ways. He completed his medical degree, but at the same time *The Fishes of Brazil* gave him a reputation as a naturalist. On a personal level, this period marked the beginning of a life-long friendship and collaboration with Joseph Dinkel, who produced the illustrations for much of Agassiz's work. (In the era before photography, detailed, life-like drawings were a key part of books published by naturalists.)

In 1831, Agassiz was once again ready to make a move, this time to Paris, the leading center for study of the natural sciences at the time. There he was befriended by Baron Georges Cuvier (1769–1832), a brilliant and eminent scientist who had long been working on a massive project for identifying fossil fishes. (A fossil is a remnant, impression, or trace of an organism of past geologic ages that has been preserved in the earth's crust, as in a rock.) Cuvier turned over his research to Agassiz, who threw himself whole-heartedly into the project. He spent a portion of each day at the Museum of Natural History in Paris, and eventually visited all the natural history collections in Europe. In 1839, the result of all this research began appear-

Baron Georges Cuvier.
Library of Congress.

ing as *Researches on Fossil Fishes*, a massive work that was published in five large volumes. Previously, only eight fossil fish types had been identified. Agassiz's work identified 340 types, and his book included 1,290 illustrations.

Different types of animals

Cuvier was working on a master plan for a system of classifying animals. In Cuvier's plan, which Agassiz adopted and later enhanced, different classes of animals (such as birds, fish, and mammals) existed because God intended them to be exactly what they were and had created them that way. The system rejected the new theory of evolution, which concluded that differences in animal life were a result of changes over time in response to a creature's environment. For instance, Cuvier believed that a fish was a fish because God intended it to be a fish, and a reptile was a reptile because God intended it to be a reptile; the evolutionists thought reptiles had developed, or "evolved," from a fish and grown legs to adapt to living on land. In Cuvier's view—and later in Agassiz's view as well—God populated the seas with fish and the land with reptiles and mammals, and there was no link between them. Agassiz, with his firm religious beliefs, further believed that similarities between different classes of animals were the result of what God had in mind when making that kind of animal. Further, he theorized that, when a similar type of creature was to be found in widely separate parts of the world, this was an indication of a separate creation at that location, rather than evidence that animals migrated from one place to another.

These thoughts put Agassiz in direct conflict with evolutionists such as Charles Darwin, who pointed to similarities in animals as evidence of a direct link between different types of animals. In Darwin's view, different creatures had had a common ancestor but changed over a long period of

Evolution versus Creation

The 1800s were a sort of "golden age" of natural history. In Europe and America, curiosity about the natural world and the desire to catalog every last bit of life on Earth was highly popular. Hunting for fossils—those traces of ancient skeletons found engraved in stones—was a popular hobby, along with rock-hunting and insect collecting. Serious, established scientists like Charles Darwin were able to thrive in this general atmosphere.

After many years of field research and expeditions, Darwin published a book titled *On the Origin of Species by Means of Natural Selection, or the Preservation of Favoured Races in the Struggle for Life* in 1859. In it, he argued that changes to creatures (evolution) occurred very gradually over millions of years through a process he called natural selection. This meant that when some accidental variation occurred in a species that was favorable for its survival, that variation would be passed on within the species. Life forms that failed to adapt to changes became extinct, or died out; life forms that did evolve survived. Furthermore, and most radical for his time, Darwin asserted that the many different species of life evolved from one single life form. The most controversial example was the evolution of human beings from a much earlier form of ape.

Evolution proponent Charles Darwin. *Photo Researchers, Inc.*

Many people at the time (and continuing into the twenty-first century), including many scientists like Agassiz, opposed the idea of evolution because it conflicted with the creation story in the Bible. They insisted that natural-history observations should be interpreted within the framework of religious faith. In their view, all the forms of life existed because God created them that way, according to his divine plan.

Darwin tried to ignore the religious debate surrounding his work, and insisted that it be judged on its scientific merit only, but the debate between evolutionists and creationists still remains controversial in the twenty-first century.

time, adjusting to their environment and evolving into something else through "natural selection." Natural selection was Darwin's theory that the strongest, best adapted specimens were better able to withstand challenges posed by the environment or predators, and that their traits, such as size or shape, were passed on to their offspring, resulting in the gradual change, or evolution, of an entire species. Agassiz argued that studying animals and plants was really about trying to understand God's divine plan for all life.

In Paris, Agassiz married Cecile Braun, the sister of his close friend Alexander Braun (1805–1877), a botanist (scientist who specializes in the study of plants). Cecile was an accomplished natural-history artist and contributed illustrations for Agassiz's fish studies. The newlyweds moved to Neuchâtel, Switzerland. There, Agassiz became a professor of natural history and would embark on his most distinguished scientific work.

Claim to fame

With Agassiz's reputation and enthusiasm as a lure, Neuchâtel soon became an important center for students interested in studying natural history. Agassiz was a talented and dedicated teacher and attracted brilliant students to his side. He took great pleasure in being a mentor, or guide, to young and ambitious scientists. He also shared his knowledge in the wider community, offering informal lectures and leading nature walks for the children of the city. Agassiz was an early proponent of "hands-on" learning, believing that outdoors was the best possible classroom for the study of nature. This approach is common practice in the twenty-first century, but it was new and revolutionary at Agassiz's time.

Since Agassiz was in Switzerland, the land of the Alps (the highest mountain chain in Europe), it was natural that his thinking would turn to glaciers. The modern concept of a glacier is a sheet of ice slowly moving or spreading out over land—a slow-moving river of ice. But the movement of glaciers is not obvious at first glance, and in Agassiz's time, the study of glaciers was new.

Agassiz was introduced to glacial theory by a scientist friend, Jean de Charpentier (1786–1855). Agassiz soon made a

giant leap forward by concluding that glaciers not only moved, but that a large portion of Europe, from the North Pole stretching and spreading over the continent, had at one time been covered by glaciers. He referred to this period of glaciers and extreme cold as the "glacial epoch" and sometimes borrowed a friendlier term used by a fellow scientist: the "Ice Age." True to his hands-on philosophy, he set out on a series of field expeditions to test his theory by direct observation.

To prove his theory that glaciers moved, Agassiz devised a simple experiment. At the Aar glacier in Switzerland, he drove a straight line of stakes across the ice sheet. Over months, the stakes advanced from their original placements, and the straight line of stakes became a U shaped formation, showing not only glacial movement but that the middle of a glacier moves more quickly than the edges. Over the next few years, the notion that Earth had undergone at least one Ice Age, an extended period of extreme cold and glacial activity, became more widely accepted. Geologists began to under-

Louis Agassiz spent a great deal of time studying glaciers. *Susan D. Rock.*

stand how much of Earth's landscape had been carved and polished by glaciers.

For Darwin and other evolutionists, the new information on glaciers helped explain how plants and animals that were undeniably similar showed up in widely separated areas. They concluded that glaciers sometimes cut in between areas, and when the glaciers retreated or melted, half of the former habitat might be on the other side of a large lake or a mountain from the other side. Agassiz clung to his strict belief in the "divine plan."

America!

In the middle of the nineteenth century, the United States was a lure for many Europeans for a variety of reasons. For Agassiz, North America seemed like a huge new area to explore for new forms of fish and other plant life. Agassiz arrived in Boston in 1846 to great acclaim. He traveled throughout the East Coast giving lectures and became convinced that America offered unlimited and exciting work for a naturalist. An offer of a professorship at Harvard University helped him make a quick decision to make America his permanent home.

Agassiz brought energy to his new post. He led major exploration trips that included studies of the Great Lakes, the Rocky Mountains, and Florida. He also introduced new methods of education; Agassiz is sometimes called America's first "university builder" because of the fresh teaching methods he introduced. Students reacted enthusiastically to Agassiz's new approach. The combination of his great knowledge and his ability to attract eager young minds to his work soon helped put the United States into the forefront of natural-history research.

Agassiz helped found Harvard University's museum of natural history and the National Academy of Sciences. His last major achievement, just a few months before his death, was establishing a teacher-training institute that emphasized teaching natural history by the "direct-experience" method.

Agassiz died in Cambridge, Massachusetts, on December 14, 1873.

—James L. Outman

For More Information

Books

Bolles, Edmund B. *The Ice Finders: How a Poet, a Professor, and a Politician Discovered the Ice Age*. Washington, DC: Counterpoint, 1999.

Lurie, Edward. *Louis Agassiz: A Life in Science*. Chicago: University of Chicago Press, 1960.

Peare, Catherine Owens. *A Scientist of Two Worlds: Louis Agassiz*. Philadelphia: Lippincott, 1958.

Robinson, Mabel Louise. *Runner of the Mountain Tops; The Life of Louis Agassiz*. New York: Random House, 1939. Reprint, Detroit: Grand River Books, 1971.

Periodicals

"Creationists: Of Two Minds About Science." *Discover* (March 1987): p. 6.

Lee, Jeffrey A. "Louis Agassiz." *Focus* (Winter 2002): p. 30.

Web Sites

Agassiz, Elizabeth Cabot Cary. "Louis Agassiz: His Life and Correspondence." Electronic book via *Project Gutenberg*. http://ibiblio.org/gutenberg/etext04/agass10.txt (accessed on March 4, 2004).

"Louis Agassiz (1807–1873)." *University of California, Berkeley, Museum of Paleontology*. http://www.ucmp.berkeley.edu/history/agassiz.html (accessed on March 4, 2004).

Madeleine Albright

Born May 15, 1937
Prague, Czechoslovakia

Czech refugee from World War II who became the first female secretary of state

"The success of American foreign policy ... will make the difference between a future characterized by peace, rising prosperity and law, and a more uncertain future in which our economy and security are always at risk, our peace of mind is always under assault and American leadership is increasingly in doubt."

Madeleine Albright.
AP/Wide World Photos.

M adeleine Albright was the daughter of Jewish parents in Czechoslovakia at a time when Germany controlled the country and hunted down Jews for eventual murder as undesirable people. Her family smuggled her out of the country to England. She made her way to the United States, where she eventually became U.S. ambassador to the United Nations and, later, the first woman secretary of state.

Early life in Czechoslovakia

Madeleine Albright was born Maria Jana Korbel on May 15, 1937, in Prague, Czechoslovakia. Her father, Josef Korbel (1909–1977), was a diplomat for the Czech government. When Germany seized control of Czechoslovakia in 1939, Josef and his wife Anna fled with their daughter to the safety of London to avoid arrest in Prague at a time when the German government was discriminating against Jewish citizens.

After the end of World War II (1939–45), the family returned to Czechoslovakia, but when communists took control of the government, the family again fled, this time to the

United States. Josef had been working as chairman of a special United Nations commission. (The United Nations is an international organization, composed of most of the nations of the world, created to preserve world peace and security.) He took the opportunity to ask for political asylum, or permission to live in the United States for fear of being persecuted by the government. In 1948, at the age of eleven, Maria came with her family, which now included another son and daughter, to settle in Denver, Colorado, where Josef became a professor at the University of Denver. It was upon moving to the United States that her mother rechristened Maria as Madeleine.

Not until she was confirmed as secretary of state in 1997 did the full story of Madeleine Albright's background come to light. Michael Dobbs (1950–), a reporter researching an article for the *Washington Post,* learned in an interview with one of Albright's cousins in Czechoslovakia that the Korbel family had been Jewish. He also learned that three of Albright's grandparents, along with several other relatives, had died in concentration camps during the Holocaust. (The Holocaust was the period between 1933 and 1945 when Nazi Germany, led by dictator Adolf Hitler [1889–1945], systematically persecuted and murdered millions of Jews and other innocent people.)

Albright had been brought up as a Roman Catholic. She was told that her family members had died during the war and that her family had left Czechoslovakia because her parents were political activists. Albright later defended her parents' decision to change their children's religion, saying, "My parents did everything in their power to make a good life for their children. They were very protective of us…. What they gave us children was the gift of life, literally. Twice, once by giving us birth and the other by bringing us to America to escape what, clearly now, would have been a certain death. So I am not going to question their motives…. I have been proud of the heritage that I have known about and I will be equally proud of the heritage that I have just been given."

Journalism background

Albright attended Wellesley College in Massachusetts on a scholarship, majoring in political science and graduating with honors in 1959. At wellesley, she developed an interest in journalism and became editor of the school newspaper. Three days after graduating from Wellesley, she married Joseph Medill Patterson Albright (1937–), heir to a large newspaper fortune.

Her initial career plan was to be a journalist. After graduating, she began working at the *Rolla Daily News* in Rolla, Missouri, but soon moved to Chicago, Illinois, when her husband accepted a new job at the *Chicago Sun-Times*. She tried to get a job at another newspaper, but was discouraged by the editor, who addressed her as "honey" and said, "You may want to be a reporter, but you can't be on a competing paper and you can't be on the paper your husband works on, so why don't you find another career?"

Looking back on the incident, Albright later commented, "And I didn't fight it. I would fight it now, of course—but I think I'm better at what I do now than I would have been as a journalist."

Albright focused instead on raising her family. But this was interrupted by the premature birth of her twin daughters, Anne and Alice. Unexpectedly, Albright changed her focus. She independently studied Russian to occupy herself at the hospital until her daughters could come home. (She already knew French, Polish, and Czech.) When her husband got a new job as the city editor of *Newsday,* a newspaper published in the suburbs of New York City, the Albrights moved to Long Island, New York, and there Albright resumed her formal education. She earned a language certificate in Russian in 1968 and in that same year earned a master's degree in international affairs from Columbia University in New York City. She then began working on a doctorate degree in international relations at Columbia. When the family moved again, this time to Washington, D.C., Albright commuted to Columbia to finish her degree, which she earned in 1976.

Albright enters politics

It was at this time that Albright entered into Democratic politics, working as a coordinator and later as chief legislative assistant for the unsuccessful 1976 presidential campaign of Edmund Muskie (1914–1996), a U.S. senator from Maine. In 1978, Zbigniew Brzezinski (1928–), one of her professors at Columbia, chose Albright to work on his staff at the White House, where she stayed until President Jimmy Carter (1924–; served 1977–81) was defeated for reelection in 1980.

Albright spent from 1981 to 1982 on a Woodrow Wilson fellowship at the Smithsonian Institution Woodrow Wilson International Center for Scholars, researching and writing *Poland: The Role of the Press in Political Change*. During this time, in 1982, her husband left her; the couple divorced the next year.

After completing her fellowship, Albright joined the faculty of Georgetown University as a professor of international affairs. She taught a variety of courses including international studies, U.S. and Soviet foreign policy, and the politics of central and eastern Europe. She served as the director of the Women in Foreign Service program at Georgetown's School of Foreign Service, and she helped to develop other programs to help women pursue opportunities in foreign service.

While at Georgetown, Albright continued her involvement in politics. She was an advisor to former vice president Walter Mondale (1928–) and U.S. representative Geraldine Ferraro (1935–) of New York in their unsuccessful 1984 campaign for the presidency and vice presidency. Four years later, she was an advisor to Massachusetts governor Michael Dukakis (1933–) in his 1988 campaign for president, which also failed.

After the 1988 election, Albright became president of the Center for National Policy, a Democratic nonprofit research organization that works to promote discussion and research of domestic and international issues.

Throughout her years at Georgetown University, Albright often hosted discussions on foreign policy in her home. There, many of the top minds in international affairs gathered to discuss foreign-policy issues. Albright herself had by this time become a prominent figure in international affairs.

In 1992, Albright worked on the presidential campaign of Arkansas governor Bill Clinton (1946–) as a senior foreign-policy advisor. After his election, he appointed her as the U.S. ambassador to the United Nations. Albright became the second woman ever to represent the United States at the United Nations. At the time she was the only woman on the Security Council, which carries on much of the crucial work of the United Nations. Clinton also elevated her position to that of a member of his cabinet, the group of people who head government departments and report directly to the president. At the United Nations, Albright dealt

Madeleine Albright listens as Palestine Liberation Organization (PLO) leader Yasser Arafat talks on the phone with U.S. president Bill Clinton. © *Reuters NewMedia Inc./Corbis.*

with several important issues, drawing both praise and criticism. Her decision to attend the Fourth World Conference on Women, held in Beijing, China, was criticized by some who had hoped she would boycott the conference as a way of sending a message to China about government violations of human rights. Albright defended her participation by saying U.S. relations with China should not center on just one issue. Albright supported resolutions to expand the effort of the United Nations to maintain peace in the east African country of Somalia. She worked to gain support for the North American Free Trade Agreement (NAFTA), which eliminated most tariffs, or taxes, on trade among Canada, the United States, and Mexico.

While Albright was representing the United States at the United Nations, a civil war broke out in Yugoslavia, resulting in many civilian deaths. She urged President Clinton to take an active role in ending the conflict, as a means to promote democracy throughout the world.

First female secretary of state

In 1996, when Warren Christopher (1925–) resigned as secretary of state, President Clinton nominated Albright to replace him. She became the first woman to ever hold the position of secretary of state and the highest-ranking woman in the U.S. government. Albright took over the post in 1997 and immediately began traveling overseas, seeking to make her presence known in the international community. She soon came to be respected and admired by world leaders.

As secretary of state, Albright continued to deal with the issue of the war in Yugoslavia. Relations with China cooled over issues of trade and human rights. The United States also pushed to include more countries in the North Atlantic Treaty Organization (NATO), the organization established after World War II to prevent the Soviet Union from invading Western Europe. The Middle East continued to demand the attention and energy of Albright and the Clinton administration.

Palestinian men and boys in the West Bank throw stones at Israeli soldiers.
Reuters/Corbis-Bettmann.

In 1997, Albright made her first official trip to the Middle East, hoping to assist Israelis and Palestinians negotiate a peace settlement to end their half-century-old struggle for control over land in Palestine. Sensing no progress in the discussions, Albright left, resolving not to return until the two sides were ready to agree to work toward an agreement. She came back to the Middle East in 2000, the last year of the Clinton presidency, to help Clinton reach a resolution, but this attempt also was unsuccessful.

Albright became the first U.S. secretary of state to visit Ho Chi Minh City, the capital of Vietnam, since communist forces took over South Vietnam in 1975. She also was the first secretary of state to visit North Korea. As at the United Nations, Albright, intent on promoting democratic governments, often advocated military involvement by the U.S. armed forces.

Albright left office in 2001 upon the completion of Clinton's term as president. She returned to the faculty of Georgetown University. In 2003, her memoir, *Madam Secretary,* was published.

—*James L. Outman*

For More Information

Books

Albright, Madeleine. *Madam Secretary: A Memoir.* New York: Miramax, 2003.

Blood, Thomas. *Madam Secretary: A Biography of Madeleine Albright.* New York: St. Martin's Press, 1997.

Dobbs, Michael. *Madeleine Albright: A Twentieth-Century Odyssey.* New York: Henry Holt and Co., 1999.

Lippman, Thomas W. *Madeleine Albright and the New American Diplomacy.* Boulder, CO: Westview Press, 2000.

Periodicals

"An American in North Korea." *The Economist* (October 28, 2000): p. 37.

Cooper, Matthew. "The Lady Is a Hawk." *Newsweek* (December 16, 1996): p. 24.

Gibbs, Nancy. "The Many Lives of Madeleine." *Time* (February 17, 1997): p. 52.

Weymouth, Lally. "As I Find Out More, I'm Very Proud." *Newsweek* (February 24, 1997): p. 30.

Web Sites

Albright, Madeleine. "Archive of Speeches, Proclamations and Other Statements, 1997–2000." *U.S. State Department.* http://usinfo.state.gov/usa/womenusa/archive.htm (accessed on March 4, 2004).

Albright, Madeleine. "Commencement Speech at Harvard University." *The United States Agency for International Development.* http://www.usaid.gov/multimedia/video/marshall/albright.html (accessed on March 4, 2004).

Isabel Allende

Born August 2, 1942
Lima, Peru

Writer of novels and memoirs

"I knew exactly what was happening in my country, I lived through it, and the dead, the tortured, the widows and orphans, left an unforgettable impression on my memory."

Isabel Allende. *Getty Images.*

Beginning in the 1980s with the international success of her first novel, *The House of the Spirits,* Isabel Allende became the best-known contemporary female writer from South America. In her novels and autobiographical works, Allende draws on her experiences to weave together tales of families as well as the effects of social and political pressures. Her writings also feature richly described settings, sometimes with elements of fantasy.

Influenced by grandparents

Isabel Allende was born in Lima, Peru, in 1942 to Chilean parents. At that time, her father, Tomás, was serving in Peru as a diplomat for the government of Chile. He was a first cousin of Salvador Allende Gossens (1908–1973), who later became president of Chile. Isabel Allende and her mother, Fransisca, maintained close ties with the Allende family even after Tomás abandoned his wife and daughter when Isabel was two years old. Mother and daughter returned to Santiago, Chile, to live with Fransisca's parents.

Allende's mother met another diplomat. He took the family on assignments to Bolivia, the Middle East, and Europe. The family was in Lebanon in 1958 when civil war erupted. Allende was sent home to her grandparents. She was fifteen years old, and it was then that her maternal grandparents most influenced her life. Allende's grandmother was a wonderful storyteller, and her grandfather was a strong-willed person who expected Allende to be able to support herself. Together they inspired Allende's imagination and instilled in her the discipline needed to be a writer. After she completed school, Allende began working as a secretary for the Food and Agricultural Organization, an association of the United Nations.

Shortly after turning twenty years old in 1962, Allende married Miguel Frias, an engineer. They would have two children, Paula and Nicolás. In the mid-1960s, Allende became a regular columnist for a magazine called *Paula,* as well as a reporter for another magazine, *Mampato.* She also worked for a television station as an interviewer.

Isabel Allende in front of a picture of her uncle, the late president of Chile, Salvador Allende Gossens. *AP/Wide World Photos.*

Why Allende Begins Writing Her Books on January 8

The House of the Spirits started Isabel Allende on her literary career. The book began as a letter she started writing to her dying grandfather on January 8, 1981. To continue to honor her grandfather and to draw on the good fortune of what began as a letter, Allende would begin all her subsequent books on January 8, the day she began writing the letter. She told interviewer Barbara Mujica in *Américas* magazine that it is "too easy to put off writing. There's always something better to do, like play with the grandchildren, for example, so I need the discipline of always beginning on the same day. And once I begin, I don't start any other project until I finish the first one."

A letter becomes a novel

When Allende's uncle, Chilean president Salvador Allende Gossens, was overthrown and assassinated in a coup, or a military takeover of government, in 1973, Allende's life changed. So, too, did life in Chile. The country became a military dictatorship under the ruthless command of General Augusto Pinochet Ugarte (1915–). His regime used violence to strictly enforce their laws and power. Allende joined church-sponsored groups to help provide aid to needy families and to help victims of the military dictatorship. Those activities put her life in danger. She later told *Publishers Weekly* interviewer Amanda Smith that the brutal government takeover affected her deeply: "In that moment, I realized that everything was possible—that violence was a dimension that was always around you."

Allende and her family fled Chile in 1974, settling in Caracas, Venezuela. Despite having a strong reputation as a journalist, Allende could not immediately find work as a writer in Venezuela. She turned to teaching before finally landing a job as a reporter for Venezuela's leading newspaper, *El nacional* (*The National*). Upon learning that her grandfather was dying back in Chile, Allende began writing a letter to him on January 8, 1981. Her grandfather died before the letter was mailed, but Allende kept writing, forming a story based on her family history. What began as a letter was soon transformed by Allende into a novel. Published first in Spain in 1982, *La casa de los espíritus* won international acclaim. The praise and popularity were repeated in the United States in 1985 when the novel was published in English as *The House of the Spirits*.

Drawing on Allende's personal experience, the novel tells of an extended family caught up in political turmoil in Chile. "Because of my work as a journalist," Allende wrote in her "Sobreda con de los espiritos" essay, "I knew exactly what was happening in my country, I lived through it, and the dead, the tortured, the widows and orphans, left an unforgettable impression on my memory. The last chapters of *La casa de los espíritus* narrate those events. They are based on what I saw and on the direct testimonies of those who lived through the brutal experience of the repression." Along with detailed descriptions of events, setting, and characters, Allende weaves fantastic events into the story. This blending of realistic detail and fantasy elements is called "magic realism," a technique used by several famous Latin American authors.

Happiness and tragedy

Allende continued to combine personal experiences and imaginary events in her next few works of fiction. *De amor y de sombra* (1984; translated as *Of Love and Shadows*, 1987) features a journalist whose investigation into a murder points to ruthless political motives for the killing. *Eva Luna* (1988) concerns a scriptwriter who becomes involved with a filmmaker. The unnamed country where the two characters live resembles Chile. However, because the country is unnamed, the events could happen anywhere.

During a period of great personal change in her life, Allende completed a collection of short stories, *Cuentos de Eva Luna* (1990; published as *The Stories of Eva Luna,* 1991), and a novel, *El Plan infinito* (1991; published as *The Infinite Plan,* 1993). While composing these works, Allende also taught creative writing at several colleges in the eastern United States as well as at the University of California, Berkeley.

Allende was divorced from her first husband in 1987. The following year, while she was visiting stores and colleges on a book tour, Allende met a lawyer named William Gordon. He

 Allende and Success

In the spring 1999 issue of *NPQ: New Perspectives Quarterly,* Isabel Allende spoke about the popularity of her books in the United States.

First, I have a very good translator who helps convey the spirit of each book while also adapting it to the new culture. She says things like, "This sentence will not sound good in English. It's very sentimental." In Latin culture, for example, we talk about destiny. In America, "destiny" is a loaded word. You say "luck" or "fate." So, by the choice of words my translator adapts my work to the culture.

I also think that the mixture of honest emotion, feminism, politics and the bringing of other cultures into the book fascinates Americans. People in the U.S. are touched by the raw and explicit emotion of my books. Because ... this is a culture in which people deny or withhold their emotions.

Selected English Language Works of Isabel Allende

The House of the Spirits. New York: A.A. Knopf, 1985.

Of Love and Shadows. New York: Knopf, 1987.

Eva Luna. New York: Knopf, 1988.

The Stories of Eva Luna. New York: Atheneum, 1991.

The Infinite Plan. New York: HarperCollins Publishers, 1993.

Paula. New York: HarperCollins Publishers, 1995.

Aphrodite: A Memoir of the Senses. New York: HarperFamingo, 1998.

Daughter of Fortune: A Novel. New York: HarperCollins, 1999.

Portrait in Sepia. New York: HarperCollins Publishers, 2001.

City of the Beasts. New York: HarperCollins, 2002.

My Invented Country: A Nostalgic Journey through Chile. New York: HarperCollins, 2003.

had read and greatly admired her novel *Of Love and Shadows.* He met Allende at a publicity stop in San Jose, California. After that meeting they began dating and soon married. The couple settled in the San Francisco area.

A book-related event had turned into a happy encounter for Allende, but a few years later she learned of a tragedy at another book-related event. During a party celebrating the Spanish-language publication of *The Infinite Plan,* Allende received a phone call informing her that her daughter, Paula, was gravely ill. Paula had recently married a Spanish man and was performing volunteer work for poor children at a Catholic school in Madrid, Spain, when she contracted an illness. She lapsed into a coma from which she never recovered, dying over a year later in December 1992.

Along with visiting her daughter regularly during her illness, Allende kept a diary about her own daily life and reflected on her past, including family incidents and political events. She had wanted to read the entries to Paula during recovery. Instead, the diary was later published as *Paula* in 1995. In an interview with Barbara Mujica in *Américas* magazine, Allende recalled, "My mother told me: 'Write or you'll die,' and I started to think that as long as I wrote, Paula would stay alive. It was a way of defying death. My mother saw the end way before I did. Life is full of signs and premonitions, if only we knew how to read them. I had a lot of trouble coming to terms with the truth."

Invented and adopted countries

After the publication of *Paula,* Allende continued to work as a writer and teacher. Her later books include *Afrodita: Cuentos, recetas y otros afrodisíacos* (1997; published as

Aphrodite: A Memoir of the Senses, 1998), *Daughter of Fortune: A Novel* (1999), *Portrait in Sepia* (2001), *City of the Beasts* (2002), and *My Invented Country: A Nostalgic Journey through Chile* (2003). *City of the Beasts* is a young adult novel about a boy spending the summer in Chile with his grandmother while his mother is in Texas for treatment of cancer. The boy's grandmother has been hired to write an article on the Beast, a real or imagined animal that has been terrorizing a jungle area. "The story is a struggle between good and evil, filled with surprises and adventure," wrote Angela J. Reynolds in *School Library Journal.* "Put this title on your 'If You Liked Harry Potter' lists," she added.

My Invented Country: A Nostalgic Journey through Chile is a memoir inspired by the terrorist attacks on the United States on September 11, 2001. The attacks led Allende to consider her life in her adopted country, the United States, and similar feelings she had experienced twenty-eight years earlier, when the Allende government was overthrown in Chile. Allende calls Chile "my invented country" because she was never able to fully settle there. Allende had lived in Chile for only part of her childhood, was forced to take exile as an adult when Chile became a military state in 1973, and returned for visits only after she turned forty-five years old—beginning in 1988, when Chile was free from military dominance. Allende concludes that she lost a country in 1973, but gained a new one, affirmed in 2001 by sharing in the grief and aftermath of violence. In 2003, Allende became a naturalized citizen of the United States.

—*Roger Matuz*

For More Information

Books

Allende, Isabel. "Writing as an Act of Hope." In *Paths of Resistance.* Edited by William Zinsser. Boston: Houghton Mifflin, 1989, pp. 39–63.

Correas de Zapata, Celia. *Isabel Allende: Life and Spirits.* Houston: Arte Público Press, 2002.

Levine, Linda Gould. *Isabel Allende.* New York: Twayne Publishers, 2002.

Zinsser, William, ed. *Paths of Resistance: The Art and Craft of the Political Novel.* New York: Houghton Mifflin, 1989.

Periodicals

Mujica, Barbara. "The Life Force of Language." *Américas* (November-December 1995): pp. 36–43.

Reynolds, Angela J. *"City of the Beasts"* (book review). *School Library Journal* (December 2002): p. 58.

Skafidas. Michael. "Pinochet's Ghost." *NPQ: New Perspectives Quarterly* (Spring 1999): pp. 22–26.

Smith, Amanda. "Interview with Isabel Allende." *Publishers Weekly* (May 17, 1985).

Web Sites

Isabel Allende. http://www.isabelallende.com/ (accessed on March 4, 2004).

John Jacob Astor

Born July 17, 1763
Waldorf, Germany

Died March 29, 1848
New York, New York

First American immigrant millionaire

John Jacob Astor was one of the first examples of what became a great American myth: poor boy sails from Europe to the United States and ends up a millionaire thanks to hard work. But in Astor's case, it was not myth: He did sail from London to Baltimore, Maryland, before he was twenty years old, with very little money in his pocket. When he died, he was thought to be the richest man in the United States. The usual version of his life describes how Astor made a fortune buying and selling animal furs, especially beaver skins, to be turned into men's hats; then he made profitable investments in real estate, or land, development in New York City, where his name is enshrined in the well-known luxury hotel called the Waldorf-Astoria. Less famous is his role as an international drug dealer who also made a small fortune lending money to the U.S. government.

"Rogues do their work at night. Honest men work by day. It's all a matter of habit, and good habits in America make any man rich. Wealth is a result of habit."

The jolly butcher's son

Astor was born in the small German village of Waldorf, near the German university city of Heidelberg. As noted

John Jacob Astor. *National Portrait Gallery.*

in the *Dictionary of American Biography,* Astor's father, a butcher in the town, was once described as "jovial, good-for-nothing … much more at home in the beer-house than at his own fireside." John Jacob was the youngest of three sons, and at age seventeen he left Waldorf to join an older brother who was living in London. He paid for his trip by taking a job on a boat carrying timber down the Rhine River.

Astor spent three years in London, working with his brother in a musical instrument shop, learning English and saving money for the trip across the Atlantic Ocean to join his other brother, who was already in New York. Astor decided to wait out the American Revolutionary War (1775–83) in England. In 1783, after England signed a peace treaty with the newly independent United States, Astor bought the lowest-price ticket on a ship sailing to Baltimore. He had about twenty-five dollars in his pocket, and seven flutes, which he planned to sell once he got to New York. The trip had a small hitch at the end: Astor's ship got stuck in ice near Baltimore, and he spent two months aboard the ship until the ice melted in the spring of 1784. While waiting on the ship, Astor got to know another German passenger who had had experience acquiring furs from Native Americans. This chance acquaintance apparently set Astor on his first successful money-making venture: the fur trade.

A bride and three hundred dollars

After arriving in Baltimore, Astor made his way to New York to join his older brother in March 1784. Accounts of his first activities in New York differ, but within two years, Astor owned a small shop in Manhattan where he was in the business of buying and selling furs trapped in the American wilderness, primarily by Native Americans who sold the furs to white traders. Astor had recently married Sarah Todd, whose family gave her a wedding gift of three hundred dollars. This amount was a significant sum of money in 1786 and enough to help the couple establish a business.

Astor was about five feet nine inches tall. Newspaper stories about him later in life described him as slightly overweight, boxy in shape. He was said to speak with a heavy German accent and write without much regard to correct spelling or grammar.

Success with furs

Astor was eventually highly successful as a trader in furs, which meant buying animal skins either from Native Americans or from white "mountain men" who ventured into the wilderness of the Rocky Mountains and the Pacific Northwest to find and trap animals. Astor then sold the furs he had bought to manufacturers of fur coats or fur hats. For the most part, Astor hired others to negotiate directly in the purchase of furs, although he occasionally ventured out himself, once going as far as Mackinaw in Michigan.

In building his fortune, Astor took full advantage of being in the right place at the right time. He entered the fur business just before furs, and in particular fur hats for men, became enormously popular. He also entered the business just when the United States was on the brink of rapidly expanding into the interior of the North American continent, well beyond the narrow strip of territory east of the Appalachian Mountains that English immigrants had begun colonizing

John Jacob Astor shown buying fur from Native Americans. *© Bettmann/ Corbis.*

with early settlements in Virginia and Massachusetts. In 1796, the United States and Britain signed a treaty known as the Jay Treaty (after American negotiator John Jay [1745–1829]), which resulted in British withdrawal from military forts in the so-called Northwest Territory (the area around the Great Lakes). The treaty also opened new opportunities for Americans to trade with Canada (which in 1796 was British territory). The effect of the treaty for Astor was to enable him to expand his fur-trading business rapidly.

Astor traveled to London in 1799 in an effort to supplement his growing fur business with trade overseas. While in London, Astor obtained a license from the British East India Company, which controlled trade with India. This license enabled Astor's ships to trade in any port controlled by the company. Although he was already a well-established businessman by then, Astor traveled at the lowest possible cost in a travel class called steerage. Steerage class entitled him to a small bunk bed deep inside the ship. It was the same sort of ticket he had used to travel to the United States from London fifteen years earlier. It was characteristic of Astor for his lifetime to *make* tremendous amounts of money but to *spend* as little as possible.

In April 1803, President Thomas Jefferson (1743–1826; served 1801–9) signed a treaty with France to acquire a vast stretch of wilderness west of the Mississippi River. The next year, Jefferson sent Captains Meriwether Lewis (1774–1809) and William Clark (1770–1838) on an expedition to explore the new territory. Their demanding trip blazed a wilderness path that eventually made it possible for Astor to make a fortune by expanding his fur-trading business westward into the areas newly acquired from France. More directly, it enabled Astor to complete with the Northwest Company, a well-established English company already trading in furs from the American West.

Astor's contribution was not in blazing a new path through the wilderness. Instead, his contribution was in having a grand vision of how to earn a business fortune from the fur trade and in acquiring the political influence and financial resources to make it happen. Even before the Lewis and Clark expedition, Astor had built his small shop into a prosperous business, and his fortune had grown from the $25 he had when he arrived as an immigrant to around $250,000. In 1808, Astor organized the American Fur Company, with him-

self as its sole owner. His business plan was to establish a fortress in Oregon, where the Columbia River drains into the Pacific Ocean. There, Native American and white fur trappers could bring their furs to sell to Astor. In turn, ships owned by Astor would carry the furs to China, across the Pacific Ocean, where they could be sold. While in China, Astor could purchase Chinese tea and other goods that the same ships could bring back to the East Coast of the United States. It was a huge, even magnificent, global trading plan, and eventually Astor made it succeed.

The first step was establishing a fur-trading post in Oregon, which Astor called Astoria. Set up in 1811, the plan almost immediately fell victim to fighting between the United States and Britain in the War of 1812 (1812–14). Threatened with an imminent British military occupation of Astoria, Astor's representative sold the outpost to the Northwest Company, Astor's Canadian-owned main competitor in the fur trade, at a significant loss. It seemed that

Fort Astoria, John Jacob Astor's fur-trading post in Oregon, in 1813. *Library of Congress.*

the War of 1812 had sunk Astor's scheme before it could get off the ground.

But the war actually proved to be a business boon for Astor in another area. The U.S. government needed to borrow money to finance its operations, and Astor was willing to be a lender, although at a great cost to the government (and eventually to the U.S. taxpayers whose taxes paid off the loans). In 1814, at the end of the war, Astor and other investors bought government bonds for about eighty-two cents on the dollar (meaning that the government promised to pay back one dollar in exchange for a loan of eighty-two cents—an interest rate of nearly 22 percent).

Over the next twenty years, Astor's good business judgment enabled him to build one of the great fortunes of early American history—thanks in part to his influence over government policy. For example, in 1816, Astor persuaded Congress to pass a law that barred noncitizens of the United States from engaging in the fur trade, except as employees of American companies. The law was designed to help Astor acquire the trading posts of his main competitor, the Canadian-owned Northwest Company, which were located along the upper (northern) Mississippi River. During the winter of 1821–22, Astor persuaded the Congress to close government trading posts set up in 1796 to trade with Native Americans in the West, thereby giving Astor even more control over the Western fur trade. Five years later, in 1827, Astor bought the Columbia Fur Company, his main competitor in trading furs in the northwest. Buying his competitor left Astor with just one major competitor, the Rocky Mountain Fur Company, which bought furs trapped south of Astor's territory. Although he controlled the fur trade over a vast territory, Astor did not thrive in competition with Rocky Mountain Fur Company. Astor's company suffered losses from attacks by Native Americans. Rocky Mountain's fur trappers were regarded as better than Astor's, and their ability to trade furs with Native Americans was also regarded as superior.

Astor began to lose interest in his fur business. By June 1834, he had sold the business entirely. It was good timing, since the demand for furs as fashionable clothing was beginning to decline during the same period. Astor had made a significant fortune from the business, however, and went on to make even more money buying property in New York City.

There were two related business practices during Astor's early success that have long detracted from Astor's story as one of the first, and most successful, rags-to-riches immigrants to the United States. These business practices involve alcohol and the drug opium.

When Astor entered the fur trade, many Native Americans were living a nomadic (wandering) existence in the wilderness of North America as they had been for countless generations before the arrival of immigrants from Europe. Their lives were largely focused on hunting or trapping animals, which they used for food and clothing (such as leather and fur). Europeans had little of obvious value to trade for these mainstays of Native American life. Although colorful beads are famous as essentially worthless items exchanged with Native Americans for valuable furs, the trading of alcoholic beverages also played an important role. Native Americans had no experience drinking alcohol, and many proved to be highly susceptible to alcohol abuse. In effect, they would trade weeks or months of effort acquiring furs for a few hours of the sensation of drunkenness. Alcoholism, as addiction to alcohol is called, eventually devastated the lives of many Native Americans in the nineteenth and twentieth centuries.

Later, when Astor expanded his enterprise to include trade with China, some part of his success was connected to trading in the addictive narcotic, or pain-relieving, drug opium. In the nineteenth century, China was a largely self-contained society that had something Europeans wanted (silk and tea), but the Chinese were generally uninterested in buying the manufactured goods Europeans could sell in exchange. An exception was opium, the addictive drug closely related to heroin. Opium comes from seeds of a poppy plant grown in India and Turkey and present-day Afghanistan. Britain, by virtue of its control over India in the early nineteenth century, controlled much of the international trade in opium, with China as its biggest market despite strong opposition by the Chinese government.

The East India Company was positioned as the main business that carried out British trade with Asia. Astor obtained a license to ship merchandise by ship to the ports controlled by the East India Company. He began by selling furs in China, returning with silk and tea, and also sold opium in China for at least a decade after 1800. At the time Astor was engaged in the drug trade, it was not as clear to people as it became in the twenty-first century how devastating addictive drugs based on opium can be on a country. A large and profitable international drug trade with China continued for much of the nineteenth century; when the Chinese government objected, the British government went to war twice to guarantee the right of British merchants to sell the drug in China. Some part of Astor's fortune thus came from his profits as an international drug dealer.

Develops land in New York City

By 1834, Astor had retired from the fur business entirely and focused on buying and developing land in Manhattan. At the time, the island was not as densely packed as it became over the next century. Astor could see that the island of Manhattan was already a major American port, that its land was limited, and that, as a major port, there were great advantages to being located on the island, especially in the decades before bridges or tunnels replaced ferries as the connection between Manhattan and the mainland or with Long Island. As with the fur trade, Astor's timing was perfect. Astor had entered the New York real estate (property) business on the eve of a rapid expansion of the city as a major destination for Europeans immigrating to the United States. He preserved and built on his fur fortune by buying land and building apartment houses, putting him in an excellent position to take advantage of the rising demand for living space. His fortune grew significantly during the last fourteen years of his life, partly as a result of buying back houses he had sold to people at a fraction of their value when families fell on hard times and could not afford to repay their mortgages, or home loans, used to acquire the houses. Astor's name became highly unpopular in the popular imagination, as reflected in newspaper articles after he died that were highly critical of his conduct.

Astor died in 1848, in New York, at age eighty-four. He was described at the time as the richest man in America, with a fortune estimated at $20 million (worth about $375 million in 2002). Unlike other self-made millionaires who arrived in the United States with practically nothing, Astor was disinclined to give away his money. He contributed about $400,000 (about 2 percent of the total) to found the Astor Library, which was consolidated with other libraries in 1895 to form the New York Public Library. Astor's small charitable gift later stood in marked contrast to another poor immigrant-turned-millionaire, **Andrew Carnegie** (1835–1919; see entry in volume 1), who made libraries a particular focus of his effort to give away as much of his fortune as he could after he sold his steel business.

At the time of Astor's death, the *New York Tribune* criticized him for focusing his whole life solely on making money. Whatever the opinion of newspapers at the time of his death, Astor's fortune passed intact to only one of his sons, William (1792–1875), as his other son was mentally impaired. The Astor family became one of New York's leading social stars throughout the nineteenth century and into the twentieth. When the luxury passenger ship *Titanic* hit an iceberg and sank in the North Atlantic in 1912, an heir of John Jacob Astor, John Jacob Astor IV (1864–1912), went down with the ship. He was the wealthiest passenger to drown in the famous shipping disaster.

In the twenty–first century, there are few reminders in New York of the man thought to be the richest American at the time of his death. A short block in Manhattan is named Astor Place, and the Waldorf-Astoria Hotel occupies an entire square block of some of the world's most expensive real estate. The subway station that stops at Astor Place, in Greenwich Village, is decorated with molded figures of beavers—a symbol of the basis of the fortune made by a butcher's son from Waldorf, Germany.

—*James L. Outman*

For More Information

Books
Haeger, John Denis. *Astor: Business and Finance in the Early Republic*. Detroit: Wayne State University Press, 1991.

Irving, Washington. *Astoria, or, Anecdotes of an Enterprize Beyond the Rocky Mountains*. Edited by Richard D. Rust. Lincoln: University of Nebraska Press, 1982.

Madsen, Axel. *John Jacob Astor: America's First Multimillionaire*. New York: John Wiley, 2001.

Periodicals

Baida, Peter. "'Poor Jacob!'" *Forbes* (October 26, 1987): p. 345.

Bujalski, Scott James. "John Jacob Astor: America's First Multimillionaire." *Corporate Counsel* (April 2001): p. 75.

Web Sites

Hubbard, Elbert. "John J. Astor." *Little Journeys to the Homes of Great Business Men.* Online version from *Encyclopedia of the Self.* http://authorsdirectory.com/b/jastr10.htm (accessed on March 5, 2004).

"John Jacob Astor." *The Astor's Beechwood.* http://www.astorsbeechwood.com/JohnJacobAstor.html (accessed on March 5, 2004).

"John Jacob Astor." *Dictionary of American Biography* base set. American Council of Learned Societies, 1928–36. Reproduced in *Biography Resource Center.* Detroit: Gale, 2003.

John James Audubon

Born April 26, 1785
Les Cayes, Haiti

Died January 27, 1851
New York, New York

Illustrator and painter of
North American birds

In the early 1800s, most of the land that now makes up the United States had not yet been explored. What sort of landscape it contained—mountains? lakes? deserts?—could only be guessed at by European settlers on the East Coast. What animals and birds might make their homes there was also a mystery. The opportunity for ordinary people who might be interested in observing and describing the natural wonders of the continent was wide open; interested amateurs could make significant contributions to scientific knowledge of the region. That is exactly the opportunity that John James Audubon saw and seized. He captured the beauty of birds through his painting, contributing to the nation's understanding and appreciation of its rich wildlife in a series of paintings collectively called *Birds of America*.

"Proud of its beautiful form, and prouder still of its power of flight, [the whooping crane] stalks over the withering grasses with all the majesty of a gallant chief. With long and measured steps he moves along, his head erect, his eye glistening with delight."

John James Audubon. *Getty Images.*

A two-time immigrant at a tender age

John James Audubon was born in Haiti, an island in the Caribbean Sea. His father was a French naval officer and had made a fortune in Haiti as a merchant and planter. His Haitian mother, whom his father did not marry, died soon after his birth. Several years later, Audubon's father decided to return to France, and to the wife he had left there, taking his young son with him. Luckily for the boy, his stepmother was very lenient with him, perhaps more than was strictly good, and Audubon grew up in his new country rather spoiled and carefree.

As Audubon grew older, his father became concerned over his lack of useful education and took matters into his own hands. The young Audubon was sent for naval training, but he resisted learning anything. His father's next idea was to send him to Paris to study art; this did not last long and was also unsuccessful. Finally, in 1803, Audubon was sent to America to live on a farm his father owned near Philadelphia, Pennsylvania. The father's agent in charge of the farm could both look after him and guide him in the management of the property. So, at the age of eighteen, Audubon immigrated to his second foreign land.

A life's mission takes shape

Audubon was no better a student of farm management than he had been of anything else. He spent most of his time following his favorite pursuits—fishing, hunting, and drawing birds. It was around this time that he had the idea of inserting wires into the bodies of birds he had killed so that they could be posed in different ways for his sketches. He also made the first known "banding" experiment in America (see box). He tied silver thread to the legs of several baby birds. The following spring, two of these birds returned and nested near their birthplace. It was also during his period on the farm that he became engaged to a young neighbor, Lucy Bakewell.

The years from 1807 to about 1820 were a series of business failures for Audubon, perhaps, in part, because his heart was not in it. A move to Kentucky to operate a general store ended in the store's failure. He married Bakewell in 1808, but Audubon's fortunes did not improve. More business enterprises followed, but all ended in failure. Whether it was tending store or running a sawmill, Audubon could not buckle down and make it prosper. He would always spend more time hiking through the woods, sketching birds that he saw, than promoting his business ventures. At the end of this

Tracking Birds: Banding

Bird banding is an important tool for studying the movement, survival, and behavior of birds. Placing a band on a bird's leg makes it possible to study the life span, nesting habits, migration, and social structure of different species of birds. It is helpful in tracking population gains or declines.

The first record of banding a bird's leg is traced to the year 1595, when a falcon belonging to King Henry IV (1366–1413; reigned 1399–1413) of England was lost in France. The falcon had a metal band attached to its leg. The next day, the bird was discovered 1,350 miles away, on the island of Malta in the Mediterranean Sea.

A gray heron that had been banded by Duke Ferdinand (1610–1670) of Tuscany (Italy) in 1669 was found by his grandson in 1728, showing that the heron lived at least 60 years.

John James Audubon provided the first record of banding in North America. In 1803, he tied silver threads to the legs of some young phoebes (small grayish-brown birds) near Philadelphia. The next spring, several returned to the same area to nest.

In 1899, Hans Mortensen, a Danish school teacher, began a new system of banding, using aluminum rings inscribed with his name and address and placed on the legs of several birds of different species, including storks and hawks. In 1902, Paul Bartsch (1871–1970), a scientist whose hobby was the study of birds, organized the first scientif-

A Western sandpiper bird receives a band on its leg. © *Roy Corral/Corbis.*

ic banding in North America. One hundred black-crowned night herons in the District of Columbia were banded with metal strips inscribed "Return to Smithsonian Institution." This is the basic model followed ever since.

In the twenty-first century, the U.S. Department of the Interior and the Canadian Wildlife Service work together on the North American Bird Banding Program to assure that all data from banded birds is recorded in a useful way and is available to share among scientists. There is also a Bird Banding Laboratory, which can give banders permission to use radio transmitters to track individual birds. Scientists are also beginning to use satellite transmitters on birds, so that they can be tracked anywhere on Earth.

period of his life, Audubon was bankrupt and was briefly jailed for debt. (In the nineteenth century, people who borrowed money and could not pay it back were often jailed, just as if they had stolen the money.)

He determined to forget about business as a likely pursuit, and he decided to try to earn money by drawing portraits. He was pleasantly surprised to discover that people would pay five dollars for a simple sketch of their own faces. However, the income was not steady enough to support a family. In 1820, he found work as a taxidermist in a new museum in Cincinnati, Ohio. (Taxidermists preserve animals for displays in museums.) Audubon found this skill useful when he painted birds. His paintings are so lifelike that it might seem as if he photographed birds while they were still alive, rather then painted them. In fact, Audubon preserved dead birds, with special techniques that he developed to preserve their lifelike poses.

Around this time it occurred to Audubon to publish the paintings of birds that he had been collecting in a book. Finally, his life made sense to him. His one sustaining and lasting interest was in his drawings of birds. Perhaps if he could build on this passion, it would lead to success. He began to take journeys specifically to explore for new birds for his collection. He traveled both the Ohio and the Mississippi Rivers, sketching all the while. In 1824, he was ready for the next big step.

Birds of America meets with success in Europe

Audubon began to actively search for someone to publish *Birds in America*. He met with some resistance. For one thing, friends of Alexander Wilson (1766–1813), another illustrator of birds, used their influence to block Audubon's attempt to publish a competing work. Audubon decided to follow advice he had been given to look for a publisher in Europe. By 1826, he had gathered enough money to make the journey overseas with his drawings.

Audubon received welcome and encouragement in Edinburgh, Scotland. Then it was on to London, where he reached an agreement with Robert Havell Jr. (1793–1878) for publication. The undertaking was much more complicated than just printing and binding a book. Audubon supervised as Havell's men took the original drawings and printed and colored them. He also did his own promotional work, traveling, giving lectures, and holding exhibitions at which he would sell subscriptions for the completed work. Each subscriber received four title sheets, one for each of the projected volumes. Volume I held prints 1 to 100; volume II prints 101 to 200; volume III prints 201 to 300; volume IV prints 301 to 435. The prints were 40 inches by 30 inches, with each bird shown life-size and in its natural habitat. Although Audubon considered himself an artist, he also included an essay on each bird. Each essay contained a detailed description of its plumage, or feathers, and his observations on the bird's habitat, nest-building, and feeding habits. When complete and properly bound in leather, the full set weighed nearly two hundred pounds. The entire printing project took almost twelve years to complete. The first volume appeared in 1827 and the last volume in 1838.

At age fifty-three, Audubon was finally a success. Upon his return to the United States, he was proclaimed the country's leading naturalist, a scientist who studies the natural world of plants and animals.

One of John James Audubon's drawings from *Birds of America* shows two snowy owls in a tree.
American Museum of Natural History.

The Audubon family moved to a 35-acre estate on the Hudson River in upper Manhattan, in New York City. Audubon's next bird project was already under way. It would be a smaller version of the *Birds of America* collection. Audubon undertook a journey to the southern states and Florida, still searching for new specimens to add to his work. On this trip, he met and befriended John Bachman (1790–1874). Bachman would become a useful partner, since he could provide a more scientific slant to balance Audubon's artistic contribution. The two men decided to begin work on a collection of American mammals. Audubon had completed about half of the drawings for this volume when his eyesight began to fail. As his health began to fail generally, he kept to himself on his estate. He was becoming senile, and a stroke made his condition worse.

When he died in 1851 he was not especially rich, except in reputation and acclaim. His work is still considered an impressive achievement, and it set the standard for depictions of wildlife. His legacy endures in the National Audubon Society, which works to protect birds and their natural habitats.

—*James L. Outman*

For More Information

Books

Audubon, John James. *Audubon Reader: The Best Writings of John James Audubon*. Edited by Scott R. Sanders. Bloomington: Indiana University Press, 1986.

Brown, Colin, and Cyril Walker. *John James Audubon: American Birds*. New York: Gramercy, 1999.

Foshay, Ella M. *John James Audubon*. New York: H. N. Abrams, 1997.

Streshinsky, Shirley. *Audubon: Life and Art in the American Wilderness*. New York: Villard Books, 1993.

Periodicals

Gilbert, Bil. "An Odd Fish Who Swam Against the Tide." *Smithsonian* (January 1999): p. 112.

Grovier, Katherine, "Birds of Paradise: A New Edition of James Audubon's Work Illuminates a Lost Canadian World." *Time International* (January 25, 1999): p. 52.

Web Sites

Audubon, John James. "Birds of America." *The Audubon Society*. http://www.audubon.org/bird/BoA/BOA_index.html (accessed on March 8, 2004).

Audubon, John James. "Birds of North America, Audubon's Watercolors." *Nature.net*. http://www.nature.net/birds (accessed on March 8, 2004).

"John James Audubon's Birds of America." *California Academy of Sciences*. http://www.calacademy.org/exhibits/audubon (accessed on March 8, 2004).

Alexander Graham Bell

Born March 3, 1847
Edinburgh, Scotland

Died August 2, 1922
Baddeck, Nova Scotia, Canada

Inventor of the telephone

It is possible that Alexander Graham Bell is the world's best-known inventor. He is well known for inventing the telephone. This device would completely change how people communicated: Soon it became possible to talk instantly with anyone in the world with access to a telephone. Bell also worked in many other fields, including aviation, the design and manufacture of aircraft. He invented the hydrofoil, a craft that skims above the surface of the water.

> "All really big discoveries are the results of thought."

Born into a family of speech experts

Alexander Graham Bell was born in Edinburgh, Scotland, in 1847 to a family of experts in human speech. His grandfather, Alexander Bell, taught elocution, the art of speaking clearly, and his father, Alexander Melville Bell (1819–1905), was also an expert in elocution and the physiology of speech. (Physiology is a branch of biology that studies the functions of living matter, such as body organs. The physiology of speech involves the study of the mouth, tongue, throat, and voicebox, for example.) It was thus not a surprise

Alexander Graham Bell.
AT&T Bell Laboratories.

that the young Bell entered into the same field as his elders. Bell's mother was Elisa Grace Symonds Bell, a painter who was mostly deaf.

Bell's first job after graduating from the University of Edinburgh and University College in London was to assist his father on a project he called "visual speech"—teaching deaf people to speak by imitating the movements of the lips of the teacher. (Children learn how to speak by imitating sounds they hear; the deaf cannot do this.)

In 1870, the Bell family moved to Canada, and shortly afterwards Bell got a job teaching in Boston, Massachusetts, at a school for the deaf, the first public school established especially for deaf children. He also took in private students and later became a professor of speech at Boston University, in 1873. Bell was a leader in the field of teaching the deaf. He organized conventions for other teachers of the deaf and founded the American Association to Promote the Teaching of Speech to the Deaf.

Over the next three years, Bell conducted experiments with a variety of devices in connection with his work with the deaf. He received financial support from, among others, Gardner Hubbard (1822–1897), whose daughter was one of Bell's students and also his future wife. Hubbard was interested in Bell's idea for sending more than one telegraph message over the same wires at the same time. At the time, the Western Union company had a monopoly on, or complete control over, sending telegrams, the written messages created by alternating short and long tones ("dots" and "dashes") over wires. At the time, the telegraph was the fastest way of communicating over long distances. Bell persuaded Hubbard and other investors that it might be possible to send several messages at the same time by generating different tones (comparable to musical notes), one for each message.

His work on what was called a "harmonic telegraph" gave Bell the further idea that a whole range of messages could be sent over wires and made to simulate the human voice. Bell called this version of his work an "electronic speaking telegraph," which eventually became known as the telephone. The underlying idea was that electrical impulses sent over wires could make an object at the other end move or make a sound, much as the telegraph invented by Samuel F. B. Morse (1791–1872).

The telephone

Bell's work with the telegraph led directly to the telephone. He started by developing a way to send more than one message at a time over a single telegraph wire by using different harmonics, or tones (like notes on a musical scale). From this work, Bell got the idea of sending the sounds of a voice by developing what he called a "harmonic telegraph." In other words, if it were possible to send different musical notes over a telegraph wire, why not send the whole range of sounds that create a human voice?

To help in his work, Bell hired an assistant, Thomas A. Watson (1854–1934), whose job was to make the actual equipment suggested by Bell. The telephone was not the result of years and years of experimentation. Bell and Watson first managed to transmit a single musical note on June 2, 1875. Only eight months later, a lawyer for Bell filed a patent application in Washington, on February 14, 1876. (A patent is granted by the government to the first person to come up

The Impact of Bell's Invention

The telephone became one of the most significant and widespread inventions of the modern era. In the period since Bell obtained a patent on the instrument, telephones have spread everywhere and made a major impact on the way people relate to one another and do business.

Within three years of its invention, there were about five thousand telephones in use, all on private lines.

with a new invention; for a specific period of time, a patent gives the inventor the right to insist on payment from anyone else who uses the patented device or process.) On the same day that Bell applied for his patent, another inventor, Elisha Gray (1835–1901), filed a document indicating that he intended to apply for a similar patent. But Bell was there first. On March 7, 1876, the patent office granted Bell a patent for an "electric speaking telephone," thought to be the most valuable single patent ever granted. Bell had turned twenty-nine years old just four days earlier.

The story of Bell's first demonstration of the telephone is famous. Experimenting with the device, Bell spilled acid on himself and, perhaps unthinking, said into the instrument: "Mr. Watson, come here. I want you." The message was recorded as the first message transmitted by telephone, on March 10, 1876. A little over a year later, in April 1877, Bell succeeded in conducting a conversation between Boston and New York City. In July 1877, the Bell Telephone Company was established to promote use of the invention on a wide scale.

Bell's patent for the telephone was challenged by many other inventors who claimed to have already developed the same technology. Bell's claim to have been the first to invent the telephone was upheld in about six hundred cases, victories that enabled Bell to claim the exclusive, or sole, right to use his technology in building a communications network.

Bell was able to pursue both his invention and its business success. In 1884, a company formed by Bell built a telephone line linking Boston and New York. The next year, Bell and his colleagues organized the American Telephone and Telegraph Company (AT&T), which was destined to dominate the U.S. telephone business for a century.

Although the telephone became a dominant means of communication, success was not immediate. Bell demonstrated his invention throughout the United States and in Europe. In Europe, messengers were used to send notes back and forth

for quick communication, and the relative high cost of telephones and the low wages of messengers kept this system in use far longer than in the United States, where the telephone caught on more quickly. Initially, the cost of connecting telephones between two offices was about a year's wages for a messenger. Moreover, investors in the telegraph system were not eager to see a competing system succeed. Nevertheless, the ability to talk to someone over a great distance was so at-

Bell and the Deaf

Alexander Graham Bell always had a special relationship with the deaf. His mother, Elisa, was deaf, and even as a child, Bell tried to communicate with her by transmitting the vibrations of his voice through her skin. Most people shouted into a funnel-like device that Mrs. Bell held in her ear.

After moving to Boston, Bell began teaching deaf students, one of whom, Mabel Hubbard, he married in 1877. Another of his students was Helen Keller (1880–1968), who was blind and deaf from age two. Keller achieved worldwide fame with an inspiring victory over her disabilities, graduating from Radcliffe College, a part of Harvard University. Bell and Keller remained lifelong friends.

Bell's work with the deaf began with a technique called "visible speech," a technique developed by Bell's father that used illustrations to show the deaf how to place their tongue and lips to form words. It is a technique still used in the twenty-first century.

tractive that the telephone soon outpaced telegraphy as the preferred means of instant communication.

Bell won about ten thousand dollars from the government of France as a reward for his invention, and he used the money to start the Volta Laboratory in Washington, D.C. The laboratory worked on numerous inventions in the 1880s, including production of the first successful phonograph record. (The phonograph record is a vinyl cylinder used before the invention of the compact disc to record and play back sounds, especially music.) With profits from that invention, Bell established the Volta Bureau to study deafness, which had been Bell's first interest.

A lifetime of inventions

There is no doubt that Bell's invention of the telephone would have ensured him a place in history even if he had retired immediately after his first conversation. In fact, however, Bell was an inventive genius who was involved in many other fields. Bell was instrumental in founding *Science* magazine, which became the official publication of the American Association for the Advancement of Science, in 1880. He contributed many articles to it. He also was president of the National Geographic Society, an organization devoted to exploring the earth, from 1896 to 1904.

After 1895, Bell focused his genius on aviation. He worked on a kite capable of carrying a person and being steered. He designed a successful hydroplane, a high-speed boat that skims over the water. He also designed the aileron, the device at the rear of an airplane wing that alters the wing's shape and enables the plane to turn in different directions while flying.

Recognition and honors

Bell was widely recognized as one of the leading inventors of the late nineteenth century. He became wealthy as a result of his patent on the telephone and was a major contributor to a series of institutions that supported scientific research.

Universities including Harvard (in the United States), Oxford (in England), Heidelberg (in Germany), and Edinburgh (in Scotland) awarded him honorary degrees. In 1917, the governor general of Canada opened a memorial in his honor near the house where he lived after leaving Scotland for Canada on his way to the United States. (Bell became a U.S. citizen in 1882.)

Bell owned a large estate in Nova Scotia. He died there during a summer vacation, on August 2, 1922.

—James L. Outman

For More Information

Books

Bruce, Robert V. *Bell: Alexander Graham Bell and the Conquest of Solitude.* Boston: Little Brown, 1973. Reprint, Ithaca, NY: Cornell University Press, 1990.

Costain, Thomas B. *The Chord of Steel: The Story of the Invention of the Telephone.* Garden City, NY: Doubleday, 1960.

Mackay, James A. *Alexander Graham Bell: A Life.* New York: J. Wiley, 1997.

Waite, Helen Elmira. *Make a Joyful Sound: The Romance of Mabel Hubbard and Alexander Graham Bell.* Philadelphia: Macrae Smith, 1961.

Periodicals

Bruce, Robert V., and Ira Block. "Alexander Graham Bell." *National Geographic* (September 1988): p. 358.

Gordon, John Steele. "The Death of a Monopoly: AT&T Protected Its Interests with the Fiercest Vigilance—and Thereby Helped Bring Itself Down." *American Heritage* (April 1997): p. 16.

John, Richard R. "The Politics of Innovation." *Daedalus* (Fall 1998): p. 187.

Keller, John J. "Bell's Baby: Alexander Graham Bell's Proudest Invention Wasn't the Telephone." *The Wall Street Journal* (May 18, 1992): p. R16.

Web Sites

Alexander Graham Bell National Historic Site of Canada. http://fortress.uccb.ns.ca/parks/agbpla_e.html (accessed on March 9, 2004).

Casson, Herbert N. *The History of the Telephone.* http://casson.thefreelibrary.com/History-of-the-Telephone (accessed on March 9, 2004).

Farley, Tom. *Tom Farley's Telephone History Series.* http://www.privateline.com/TelephoneHistory/History1.htm (accessed on March 9, 2004).

Pat Buchanan

Born November 2, 1938
Washington, D.C.

Presidential advisor, newspaper columnist,
presidential candidate,
anti-immigrant crusader

S ome Americans take pride in describing the United States
as a nation of immigrants, and there is no doubt that
since 1620 the character of the North American continent
has been drastically changed as a result of people arriving
from Europe, Africa, and Asia. But the celebration of the nation of immigrants has often been countered by a strong
backlash against new arrivals. It happened in the middle of
the nineteenth century, with the secretive Know Nothing
Party, and it happened again at the end of the twentieth century with the repeated presidential aspirations of Pat
Buchanan, a well-known conservative (supporting traditional
values) newspaper columnist and presidential advisor.

Buchanan's efforts to achieve the White House, while
never close to successful, illustrated a thread running through
American politics, in which those born in the United States
have blamed foreign sources for their own economic unhappi-
ness. In the case of Buchanan, he blamed two main targets: in-
expensive goods imported from Asia, which he has said creates
worries about job security, and illegal immigration from Mexico, which he has vowed to stop by erecting a wall along the

"Uncontrolled
immigration threatens to
deconstruct the nation
we grew up in and
convert America into a
conglomeration of
peoples with almost
nothing in common."

Pat Buchanan. *Corbis.*

57

Mexican-American border. Buchanan's political positions have also emphasized the importance of religion in public life, a set of strict moral values, and an emphasis on minimizing government interference with business. In repeated campaigns for the presidency, Buchanan has demonstrated there is a small but steady core of Americans sympathetic to his viewpoint.

Early years

Patrick Joseph Buchanan was born in Washington, D.C., the son of a well-off insurance company executive who gave his sons boxing lessons as preparation for life. The Buchanan brothers led a rowdy existence that included occasional visits by the police department for disruptive behavior, fighting, and using their father's car without permission. While a senior attending Georgetown University in Washington, Buchanan was accused of assaulting the police officers who confronted him during a traffic stop. He was spared a jail sentence, but was forced to take a year off from Georgetown, which he spent working for his father. It was, perhaps, a measure of a combative personality that he later redirected into writing and politics.

After graduating from Georgetown, Buchanan went to Columbia University's School of Journalism, determined to redirect his forceful personality. Soon after graduating, he was hired by the *St. Louis Post-Dispatch* newspaper to write editorials, a job Buchanan felt gave him a suitable outlet for his argumentative tendencies. Buchanan was one of the youngest members of the paper's editorial staff. His work was well regarded and he was soon promoted.

Buchanan's newspaper career started in 1962, at the beginning of one of the most controversial decades in modern American history. President John F. Kennedy (1917–1963; served 1961–63) was the first Roman Catholic to be elected to the White House and the first Democrat elected since 1948. Throughout the South, African Americans were campaigning for equal civil rights, using tactics of nonviolent marches and sit-ins led by the Rev. Martin Luther King Jr. (1929–1968). The United States was just beginning a long, steady buildup of military forces in Vietnam. For the young editorial writer working for a conservative newspaper in St. Louis, many of these developments were highly distasteful. Buchanan authored many editorials highly critical of King's civil rights movement, while supporting a strong anticommunist foreign policy towards the Soviet Union (a country made up of fifteen republics, the largest of which was Russia, that in 1991 became independent states). Buchanan was influenced by J. Edgar Hoover (1895–1972), the long-time director of the Federal Bureau of Investigation (FBI), who strongly suspected that American communists sympathetic to the Soviet Union were influencing the civil rights movement.

Getting into politics

In 1966, Buchanan quit his job at the *Post-Dispatch,* frustrated that it would be years before he could expect to succeed his boss on the editorial page. Instead, he went to work for former vice president Richard Nixon (1913–1994), the unsuccessful Republican candidate for president in 1960 who was planning to run again in 1968. Buchanan got a job writing speeches for Nixon and his eventual vice presidential running mate, Maryland governor Spiro Agnew (1918–1996), during their successful 1968 campaign. After Nixon became president, he hired Buchanan to serve on his staff as a speech writer and to help plan a strategy for reelection in 1972.

Pat Buchanan in 1968, as a speechwriter for the Republican ticket of Richard Nixon and Spiro Agnew.
Library of Congress.

Buchanan's political career thus became closely linked to one of the most controversial politicians ever to occupy the White House. Nixon was the only president to resign from office in the face of almost certain impeachment by the U.S. House of Representatives. (To be impeached means to be accused of serious wrongdoing while in office. In Nixon's case, he was accused of involvement in planning a burglary at the headquarters of the opposition Democratic Party in June 1972, at the Watergate office complex in Washington, D.C., and then helping to cover up the burglary. His involvement and participation in the cover-up ran contrary to his oath of office, which required him as the president to uphold the law.)

Nixon resigned from office in 1974, to be succeeded by Vice President Gerald Ford (1913–; served 1974–77). (In 1973, Ford had succeeded Agnew as vice president, after Agnew resigned in light of accusations of earlier wrongdoings as a Maryland government official.) Buchanan worked for President Ford briefly, but he decided to return to the *Post-Dispatch* when Ford decided not to appoint him to be the U.S. ambassador to South Africa. At the time, South Africa was going through a bloody struggle between the minority white rulers and the majority of black Africans pressing for a voice in government. As a vocal critic of the civil rights movement in the United States, Buchanan was not considered suited to represent the United States in a country whose government was widely regarded as racist.

A second career in journalism, and back to politics

Buchanan left the White House to start a second career in journalism, first as a syndicated newspaper columnist (in which his stories are printed in many papers across the country) and later as the host of television talk shows. Buchanan gained a reputation as one of the most conservative commentators on politics. He was the host of a long-running program on CNN called *Crossfire* (1982–95) and also of a program called *Capital Gang* (1988–92). Buchanan gained a reputation as a leading representative of highly conservative politics.

In 1985, Buchanan briefly interrupted his television journalism career to become director of communications for President Ronald Reagan (1911–; served 1981–89) for two years. His time working in the White House gave Buchanan a record of practical experience, as well as exposure on television as a journalist, which put him in a unique political position to run for office later.

Buchanan reentered the political scene in 1992, running against President George Bush (1924–; served 1989–93) for the Republican nomination as president. Buchanan never seriously challenged Bush, but in the New Hampshire primary election (held to choose candidates for the Republican party's annual convention and in 1992 held to make the renomination of Bush official), Buchanan won 37 percent of the vote. The result was widely regarded as symbolic of discontent by some conservative Republicans with the generally moderate policies of the first President Bush. The high percentage demonstrated the existence of a core of conservative voters sympathetic with Buchanan's viewpoint, as well.

Buchanan tried to gain the Republican nomination again in 1996, when his chief opponent was former U.S. senator Bob Dole (1923–) of Kansas. Buchanan failed to gain the nomination, but some Republican Party leaders were surprised at the depth of public support for his conservative views. In 2000, Buchanan abandoned his efforts to be nominated as a Republican and instead mounted a presidential campaign as the candidate of the Reform Party. He came in a distant fourth, with less than half a million votes (out of over 103 million votes cast). The number represented less than one half of one percent of the total votes cast.

Buchanan returned to journalism, where he appeared regularly on radio and television and in newspapers. He started a new magazine entitled *The American Conservative* in 2002.

Buchanan and immigration

In 2002, Buchanan published a book titled *The Death of the West: How Dying Populations and Immigrant Invasions Imperil Our Country and Civilization*. In his book, Buchanan warned that white Americans would soon become a minority in the United States for the first time, due partly to illegal immigration from Mexico and other countries of Central America and partly to the fact that white women in the United States had relatively fewer babies than women of other races. In Buchanan's view, the relative decline of the number of Americans with European ancestors raised a danger to the civilization of the United States.

In his book, Buchanan declared that there was a great chasm, or division, in American society: "This chasm in our country is not one of income, ideology, or faith," he wrote, "but of ethnicity and loyalty." On the morning of September 11, 2001, four teams of terrorists seized control of civilian jet planes. Hijackers forced two of the planes into each of the twin towers of the World Trade Center in New York City, bringing the two skyscrapers crashing to the ground. A third team of terrorists intentionally flew their plane into the Pentagon, the building in Virginia that houses the headquarters of the U.S. military. The fourth plane crashed in a field in Pennsylvania, brought down by passengers who realized the hijackers intended to hit a government building in Washington and forced the plane down before it could reach its target. After the terrorist attacks on September 11, Buchanan declared that "suddenly we awoke to the realization that among our millions of foreign-born, a third are here illegally, tens of thousands are loyal to regimes [governments] with which we could be at war, and some are trained terrorists sent here to murder Americans. For the first time since [U.S. general and future president] Andrew Jackson [1767–1845] drove the British out of Louisiana in 1815, a foreign enemy is inside the gates, and the American people are at risk in their own country."

Buchanan asserted in his book that "in 1960, only sixteen million Americans did not trace their ancestors to Europe. Today [he wrote in 2002], the number is eighty million. No nation has ever undergone so rapid and radical a transformation." In Buchanan's view, such a large inflow of immigrants threatened the cultural and political standards long established in the United States. Many of the newcomers, he asserted, had little interest in adapting to American ways; they were interested solely in achieving economic success while maintaining their traditional cultural habits and beliefs.

In the twenty-first century, he said, immigration from Mexico in particular has taken on a new aspect. While earlier immigrants from Europe planned to move to the United States permanently, immigrants from Mexico plan on working only temporarily in the United States. Moreover, some Mexicans view immigration as a form of *la reconquista*, ("reconquest" in English) to reverse the result of the 1848 war with Mexico. As a result of that war, the United States took control of Texas and other Mexican territory, including territory now occupied by California, New Mexico, and Arizona.

In Buchanan's opinion, large-scale immigration, especially from Mexico, threatens the very nature of the United States. "We are not descended from the same ancestors [as we once were]," Buchanan asserted. "We no longer speak the same language. We do not profess the same religion.... Common principles of government are not enough to hold us together…. Americans no longer agree on values, history or heroes."

Although Buchanan was dramatically rejected by voters in his presidential campaign of 2000, receiving less than one half of one percent of the votes cast, he did emerge as a spokesman for Americans who believe that cultural factors including religion are an essential element in defining what the term "American" should mean. His argument had many similarities to issues raised more than 150 years earlier, when some Protestants objected that the large-scale immigration of Catholics from Ireland (who may have included some of Buchanan's own ancestors) was fundamentally changing what they perceived as the essentially Protestant character of the United States.

Buchanan's concerns addressed a basic issue surrounding migration to the United States: at what stage should it be finished? If American society celebrates its past as a "nation of immigrants," should the celebration stop when the immigrants are found coming from places besides western Europe? Or has it always been part of the character of human beings to roam the earth to find better opportunities? In prehistoric times those opportunities came in the form of more plentiful herds of animals to hunt; in a modern industrial society, they come in the form of better-paying jobs. Whether immigration to the United States has an endpoint is a question to which there may not be a right or wrong answer.

—*James L. Outman*

For More Information

Books

Brown, Mary Elizabeth. *Shapers of the Great Debate on Immigration: A Biographical Dictionary.* Westport, CT: Greenwood Press, 1999.

Buchanan, Patrick J. *The Death of the West: How Dying Populations and Immigrant Invasions Imperil Our Country and Civilization.* New York: St. Martin's Press, 2002.

Castles, Stephen, and Mark J. Miller. *The Age of Migration: International Population Movements in the Modern World.* New York: Guilford Press, 1993.

Harris, Nigel. *The New Untouchables: Immigration and the New World Worker.* New York: I. B. Tauris, 1995.

Miller, Mark J., ed. *Strategies for Immigration Control: An International Comparison.* Thousand Oaks, CA: Sage Periodicals Press, 1994.

Solomon, Barbara M. *Ancestors and Immigrants; a Changing New England Tradition.* Cambridge: Harvard University Press, 1956. Reprint, Boston: Northeastern University Press, 1989.

Periodicals

Jacoby, Tamar. "Too Many Immigrants?" *Commentary* (April 2002): p. 37.

Klinkner, Philip A. "The Base Camp of Christendom." *The Nation* (March 11, 2002): p. 25.

McNicoll, Geoffrey. "The Death of the West: How Dying Populations and Immigrant Invasions Imperil Our Country and Civilization" (book review). *Population and Development Review* (December 2002): p. 797.

Web Sites

Benedetto, Richard. "Profile of Patrick Buchanan." *USA Today.* http://cgi.usatoday.com/elect/ep/epr/eprbprof.htm (accessed on March 9, 2004).

Buchanan, Patrick J. "A City of Big Ideas and Tiny Minds." *The American Cause.* http://www.theamericancause.org/patacityofbigideas.htm (accessed on March 9, 2004).

The Official Pat Buchanan for President 2000 Archive. http://www.buchanan.org/ (accessed on March 1, 2004).

"One on One: Patrick Buchanan." *Online NewsHour* (October 28, 1999). http://www.pbs.org/newshour/bb/election/july-dec99/buchanan_10-28.html (accessed on March 9, 2004).

"Patrick Buchanan." *Online NewsHour* (September 12, 2000). http://www.pbs.org/newshour/bb/election/july-dec00/buchanan_9-12.html (accessed on March 9, 2004).

Andrew Carnegie

Born November 25, 1835
Dunfermline, Scotland

Died August 11, 1919
Lenox, Massachusetts

Industrialist and philanthropist

Andrew Carnegie stands as a symbol of the idea that immigrants could come to the United States and make a vast fortune. In Carnegie's case, he came to the United States from his native Scotland at age thirteen and worked his way from poverty to one of the great fortunes of the world based on manufacturing steel. In retirement, Carnegie gave away several hundred million dollars, a significant portion of his fortune during his lifetime. He financed public libraries throughout the United States as well as donated money to universities and bought organs for churches.

"Concentrate your energies, your thoughts and your capital. The wise man puts all his eggs in one basket and watches the basket."

The industrial revolution

In one respect, Carnegie shared an experience with countless other Europeans who immigrated to the United States in the nineteenth and early twentieth centuries: His family's livelihood had been seriously affected by the industrial revolution, the historic change from a farm-based economy to an economic system based on the manufacturing of goods and distribution of services on an organized and mass-

Andrew Carnegie. *AP/Wide World Photos.*

produced basis. This meant that new machines powered by steam or running water (streams and rivers) took over the work of many workers using traditional methods. The new machines could do the work of several people in a day and introduced a profound change in European—and especially English—society from about 1760 until about 1940.

Carnegie's family lived in Dunfermline, an ancient capital of Scotland where Scottish national hero and king Robert the Bruce (1274–1329) was buried. There, Carnegie's father William used a hand-powered loom to weave cloth. William Carnegie worked from his small cottage that doubled as the family home, and employed three assistants. The business made the family a modest but fairly comfortable living. William Carnegie was also a local leader of the Chartists. (Chartism was a political movement in Britain between 1838 and 1848 whose members campaigned to obtain the right to vote for working people. At that time in Britain, only relatively wealthy landlords and business owners owned enough property to qualify to vote for members of Parliament. Workers like Carnegie had no way to influence political decisions. The Chartist movement campaigned to let all men vote regardless of wealth.) Andrew Carnegie's mother was Margaret Morrison, the daughter of a shoemaker who also campaigned for political and social reforms.

By 1835, when Andrew Carnegie was born, independent weavers had already been doomed by the industrial revolution. Looms for weaving and machines for spinning yarn from cotton or wool were among the first machines introduced in the long process of industrialization, starting in England in the late 1700s and continuing until the mid-1900s. A power loom, operated by one or two people, could produce more cloth in a day than twenty or more weavers using traditional hand looms. Weavers were forced either to work as employees in new textile factories, where the automated looms were situated, or to find another occupation.

When Andrew Carnegie was eight years old, a new textile mill using looms powered by a steam engine opened in Dunfermline. Any hope that William Carnegie could continue to thrive in his small textile business was wiped out with the arrival of the new factory. Five years later, with the family income steadily declining, Carnegie's mother urged that the family leave Scotland to join relatives living in the

United States. The country was expanding rapidly and held out hope to thousands of families in Europe for a brighter economic future.

Carnegie was thirteen when his family immigrated to the United States in May 1848. They settled near relatives near Pittsburgh, Pennsylvania, a busy, growing city of more than forty thousand people. It seemed to offer many new economic opportunities. At first, Andrew's father tried to recreate the business he had in Scotland, weaving tablecloths on a wooden loom and selling them directly to customers. But the industrial revolution was advancing in the United States just as rapidly as in England, and Carnegie's father had to accept that he could not support his family in the traditional way. Instead, he found a job in the Blackstock Cotton Mill, which made cotton cloth using power-driven looms.

Andrew joined his father in the factory, working as a "bobbin boy," the person who put fresh spools, or bobbins, of yarn onto the rapidly moving looms. It was a job often carried out by child workers, whose nimble fingers seemed well suited to the job.

Father and son both worked twelve hours a day for six days a week. For his seventy-two hours of work, Andrew was paid $1.20 a week (the equivalent of about $25 in the early twenty-first century). Andrew's father thought factory work was depressing and soon quit. But Andrew stayed on. The family lived on his wages, plus whatever his mother could earn sewing shoes for a nearby shoemaker. When Andrew had the chance to move to another factory for $2 a week, he gladly took it. That first change of jobs for more money was just the first of many in Carnegie's long and successful career.

Telegraph messenger

The owner of Carnegie's new factory noticed that his young employee was cheerful and hardworking. He began calling Carnegie away from the factory floor to write business letters, which helped supplement the boy's brief formal education. Carnegie got a major break when an uncle alerted him to an opening as a telegraph messenger. At the time, the newly developed telegraph was an important means of rapid communication for business. Messages came into central telegraph offices, where messenger boys dashed to deliver them to their intended recipients.

Carnegie got the job at the telegraph office, along with another raise to $2.50 a week. The major break was not just the money: before the office officially opened for the day, delivery boys had a chance to practice sending and receiving messages themselves. Carnegie took full advantage of this opportunity and soon became quite adept at this process. This led to a job as a telegraph operator, which earned him $25 a month.

At the time, sending telegraph messages was a highly skilled profession. Operators translated the sound of a series of long and short clicks sent over telegraph wires into letters, using a code developed by American inventor Samuel F. B. Morse (1791–1872). Although the receiving device printed the clicks on paper, Carnegie was able to translate the letters as they came in simply by the sound, which made him especially fast in translating the clicks into messages. So impressive was his work that curious businesspeople would drop into the office, just to see him work. Soon, some customers requested that Carnegie send important messages. One of these was Thomas A. Scott (1823–1881), an executive with the Pennsylvania Railroad.

Working on the railroad

In one of the biggest breaks of his career, the seventeen-year-old Carnegie went to work for Scott as a general assistant in 1853. In this position, Carnegie often traveled along the railroad line between Philadelphia to the east and Pittsburgh to the west to oversee construction and maintenance. On one of his trips, a man named Theodore Woodruff (1811–1892) approached Carnegie about a new invention, the sleeping car. It looked like an ordinary railroad car on the outside, but inside, the car could be converted into a kind of rolling hotel, with sleeping spaces for passengers. Carnegie immediately realized the business potential of the new car for people who traveled long distances and showed it to the head of the railroad, who in turn decided to acquire the sleeping cars for the company. As a reward for bringing the idea to the railroad's attention, Carnegie was allowed to buy shares in the new Woodruff Sleeping Car Company, which earned him more than $5,000 in its first year (the equivalent of over $100,000 in the twenty-first century).

In 1859, Carnegie became superintendent of the Pennsylvania Railroad's western division. He gained a reputation for working hard to keep the trains running on schedule, which required constant maintenance of the cast-iron rails, which were brittle and prone to breaking.

At the outbreak of the American Civil War (1861–65), the focus of Carnegie's responsibilities changed abruptly. His knowledge of both the telegraph and railroads was highly valued, since the Union Army fighting for the northern states depended both on good communications and on the railroads to move its troops and supplies. In addition to working for the railroad, Carnegie also helped the U.S. Military Telegraph Corps.

Henry Bessemer, who invented a method of producing steel that enabled it to be poured and rolled easily, resulting in a more efficient way of building such structures as bridges, rails, and support beams. *Library of Congress.*

Throughout his career, Carnegie invested the money he received from the Woodruff Sleeping Car Company in some of the many companies that were springing up as part of the industrial revolution. Carnegie was twenty-nine when the Civil War ended in 1865, and he already owned shares, or individual small portions of a company into which money is invested, worth a total of almost $40,000 (the equivalent of nearly $480,000 in the twenty-first century) in more than a dozen companies. Consequently, when Carnegie was offered a promotion to general superintendent of the Pennsylvania Railroad, he turned down the offer. He wanted to tend to his investments.

Life as an investor

At first, Carnegie's investments were primarily related to the railroad business, which he knew from experience. When he saw a chance to merge the Woodruff Sleeping Car Company with a rival, he helped make it happen, in the

A steel worker catches a sample of molten steel during the manufacturing process. *John Olson. The Stock Market.*

process becoming the largest single investor in the new Pullman Palace Car Company. Noting that traditional wooden railroad bridges often broke or burned, Carnegie invested in the Keystone Bridge Company to build railroad bridges made of cast iron.

On a trip to England, Carnegie toured a mill making steel with a new process developed by engineer Henry Bessemer (1813–1898). Steel is a form of iron that has been heated to a very high temperature in coal furnaces in order to reduce the amount of carbon and other impurities, such as sulfur, mixed into iron ore when it is mined. The resulting metal is strong, like iron, but not as brittle. Before Bessemer's process, small amounts of iron were converted into steel by heating the metal to the high temperature required. The old process had been slow and expensive, which in turn limited the uses for steel. Bessemer developed a way of injecting oxygen into molten, or melted, iron, burning away the carbon and resulting in steel that could be poured into molds or rolled into thin

sheets. Steel produced using the new process proved to be ideal for building bridges as well as many other products, such as rails, military cannons, and support beams for skyscrapers.

Carnegie acquired the right to use Bessemer's process in a steel mill in the United States. Soon, he was using Bessemer's process to manufacture steel rails for the railroads. Since coal was the principal fuel used to make steel, Carnegie acquired another company that owned coal mines to guarantee a steady supply of coal for his mills. Carnegie also hired scientists to study the chemistry of making steel and did not hesitate to build new plants in order to improve the quality of his product and the efficiency of his operations.

On the one hand, Carnegie treated his workers well, as long as it did not cost too much. On the other hand, he strongly resisted the efforts of his employees to organize into unions. The essential idea of unions was that while a single worker had no influence over a factory owner—one worker could easily be dismissed and replaced by another—all of the factory's workers

Soldiers march past Carnegie Steel during the Homestead Plant violence on July 12, 1892. *Wood engraving by Thure de Thulstrup. © Corbis.*

acting together could unite and disrupt a factory's smooth operation by refusing to work unless their demands were met. A conflict occurred in July 1892, when steelworkers at one of his steel factories, the Homestead Plant on the Monongahela River, 7 miles east of Pittsburgh, went on strike, or refused to continue working, in protest over wages they believed were too low. Homestead was an enormous steel factory, spread over about 150 acres and employing 4,500 men. Three years earlier, the men had negotiated a contract setting their wages, and the contract expired in July 1892. Most workers went on strike until a new agreement was reached.

Right before the workers struck, Carnegie had left on a vacation in his native Scotland and put his newly appointed chief executive, Henry Clay Frick (1849–1919), in charge. Shortly after the strike began, violence broke out between the workers and guards from the Pinkerton Detective Agency, hired by Frick. Several strikers and guards were killed when workers rushed past a fence 4 feet high and 4 miles long that surrounded the factory and attacked guards. Angry workers even tried to use an antique cannon from the town hall to fire on river barges bringing Pinkerton guards up the Monongahela River and into the plant, but the cannon exploded, injuring several strikers.

Frick finally called in troops from the Pennsylvania National Guard to restore order and protect the mill. On July 23, however, Frick was attacked in his office, surviving two gunshot wounds and three stab wounds.

The Homestead strike caused Carnegie great distress. As the mill owner, the public blamed him for the violence and accused him of hiding in Scotland while letting Frick do his dirty work. In truth, Carnegie was furious at the way Frick handled the crisis. Two years later, Carnegie replaced Frick with Charles Schwab (1862–1939) as chief executive. Schwab had begun his career as a common laborer.

Despite the Homestead setback, Carnegie kept building his company. He acquired rights to mine iron ore in the Mesabi Range of Minnesota, where ore could be scooped from just beneath the surface of the mountains at a fraction of the cost of underground mining. He built his own steamboats to carry the ore from Lake Superior to Conneaut, Ohio, on Lake Erie, and then used his own railroad to haul the ore to mills in Pittsburgh.

New uses for steel were literally springing up: steel was used for the columns that supported tall buildings, especially in New York City, for the elevators inside them, and for the elevated tracks on which passenger trains ran. Carnegie's steel company gained a major share of the rapidly expanding steel industry.

By 1900, Carnegie Steel was the largest steel company in the world, producing more steel than all of Great Britain combined. In 1901, banker J. P. Morgan (1837–1913) was trying to assemble a trust, a company that would own a significant portion of the country's steel manufacturers in order to control the price. Rather than face a bruising competition with Morgan, Carnegie began exploring the idea of selling his company. Working through Schwab, the company president, Morgan inquired about Carnegie's asking price. The following day, Carnegie wrote a figure on a slip of paper: $480 million (worth about $10.6 billion in the twenty-first century). Morgan accepted the price on the spot and used Carnegie Steel as the centerpiece of United States Steel.

The philanthropist

For several years before he sold his company, Carnegie began paying more attention to his personal life and philanthropy, benefitting others through charitable gifts. He spent nearly a year traveling around the world. He and his mother also took a sentimental trip back to Dunfermline, Scotland. There, Carnegie donated funds to build a new public library, the first of many libraries Carnegie eventually helped fund. In a special ceremony, his mother, Margaret Carnegie, laid the foundation stone of the new building.

Only after his mother died in 1886 did Carnegie marry. At age fifty-one, he married Louise Whitfield (1857–1946), with whom he had been in love for years. Ten years later, their only child, Margaret, was born.

At age sixty-five, Carnegie started giving away his immense fortune. The project for which he is best remembered was donating funds to build public libraries. In total, 2,811 libraries were built throughout the United States from his donations. The project reflected Carnegie's belief that the best way to help people was to help them help themselves through education. Carnegie donated nearly 5,000 organs to churches in the United States, as well. He also supplied the funds used to build Pittsburgh's Carnegie Technical Schools (which, in 1912, became Carnegie Institute of Technology; and, in 1967, Carnegie-Mellon University, after a merger with the Mellon Institute). Throughout his life, Carnegie remembered friends from Dunfermline, and he later contributed funds to them.

Andrew Carnegie was also a strong advocate of world peace. He was among the first to call for a "league of nations," an organization of nations, as proposed by President Woodrow Wilson (1856–1924; served 1913–21), that would exert moral leadership and help nations avoid future wars. He also built in the Netherlands what he called the Peace Palace, which today houses the principal judicial body of the United Nations, among other institutions. When World War I (1914–18) broke out, Carnegie's wife, Louise, later said that the industrialist's heart was broken. He died five years later, on August 11, 1919, at his vacation home in the Berkshire Mountains of western Massachusetts, one of the most successful immigrants to ever come to the United States.

—James L. Outman

For More Information

Books

Livesay, Harold C. *Andrew Carnegie and the Rise of Big Business.* New York: Longman, 2000.

Meltzer, Milton. *The Many Lives of Andrew Carnegie.* New York: Franklin Watts, 1997.

Wall, Joseph Frazier. *Andrew Carnegie.* Pittsburgh, PA: University of Pittsburgh Press, 1989.

Periodicals

Chernow, Ron. "Blessed Barons." *Time* (December 7, 1998): p. 74.

Web Sites

Carnegie, Andrew. "The Gospel of Wealth." *American Studies at the University of Virginia.* http://xroads.virginia.edu/~DRBR/wealth.html (accessed on March 10, 2004).

Carnegie, Andrew. "The Opportunity of the United States." *Anti-Imperialism in the United States 1898–1935*. http://www.boondocksnet.com/ai/ailtexts/carn02.html (accessed on March 10, 2004).

Lorenzen, Michael. "Deconstructing the Philanthropic Library: The Sociological Reasons Behind Andrew Carnegie's Millions to Libraries." *Michael Lorenzen*. http://www.michaellorenzen.com/carnegie.htm (accessed on March 10, 2004).

"The Richest Man in the World: Andrew Carnegie." *PBS American Experience*. http://www.pbs.org/wgbh/amex/carnegie (accessed on March 10, 2004).

Charlie Chaplin

Born April 16, 1899
London, England

Died December 25, 1977
Vevey, Switzerland

Actor and comedian in the era of American silent films

"Even funnier than the man who has been made ridiculous is the man who, having had something funny happen to him, refuses to admit that anything out of the way has happened, and attempts to maintain his dignity."

Charlie Chaplin. *Library of Congress.*

Charlie Chaplin came to the United States as an English stage actor and became one of the world's best-known and best-loved comic actors in the early days of the U.S. film industry, a time when films were known as "silent movies" because early movies did not contain sound. Chaplin created the figure known as the Little Tramp, who appeared in nearly all of his best-known works. The Little Tramp represented the common man, the ordinary fellow who confronted a loss or setback, got up, and carried on. Even after the era of films with sound, Chaplin used his talents of pantomime, or communicating silently with only hand and body gestures, to create a worldwide audience. But Chaplin fell out of favor with many, as he became involved in a series of marriages, an incident involving child support, and suspicions that he was a communist sympathizer.

Chaplin never became an American citizen, but his great success defined American films in the days before movies had sound, and he contributed to the domination of Hollywood over the motion picture industry worldwide. He was one of the many immigrants who came to the United

States to earn a fortune but kept their original nationality and left after they became successful.

A difficult childhood

Charles Spencer "Charlie" Chaplin's childhood was extraordinarily difficult. His parents, Charles Chaplin and Hannah Harriet Pedlingham Hill, were both stage performers. His mother sang in comic operas under the name Lily Harley. When young Charles was just a year old, his father left the family and was seldom seen afterwards. He died in 1901. For a while after the father left, Chaplin's mother was able to support the family (Charlie Chaplin had an older half brother, Sydney), but from the time Chaplin was six, her career started declining.

Ironically, a difficult and embarrassing incident in his mother's career marked the beginning of her son's career when he was just five. Harley was on stage, trying for a high note, when her voice cracked. "I remember standing in the wings when mother's voice cracked and went into a whisper," Chaplin remembered as an adult. "The audience began to laugh and sing falsetto and to make catcalls…. I did not quite understand what was going on. But the noise increased until mother was obliged to walk off the stage…. She was very upset and argued with the stage manager who … said something about letting me go on in her place…." And so he did, bravely marching on stage and beginning to sing. Not knowing what else to do, he imitated what he had just seen—his mother's voice cracking. The audience roared with laughter.

But this early triumph did not lead directly to fame and fortune. His mother, her career finished, tried to earn a living by sewing. She spent periods of time in hospitals, forcing Chaplin to live in a series of institutions for orphans. He had only four years of formal education, and some of his experiences were brutal. On one occasion, when it was thought he might have ringworm, a highly contagious skin disease, Chaplin had his head shaved and painted with iodine, after which he was put into isolation. On another occasion, he was beaten for misbehavior.

Breaking into show business

Chaplin's older brother became a sailor, leaving his younger brother and mother to cope with living on little money. Chaplin helped earn money by joining a group that performed clog dancing (dancing while wearing heavy wooden shoes called clogs). He also worked selling newspapers, running errands for a doctor, making toys, and working for a printer. When he was not working, Chaplin called on theatrical agencies (companies that find performers for stage producers). At age twelve, he got his first break: a role in a play entitled *Sherlock Holmes.* Then came a number of jobs in stage comedies and a job in another play in London that later went on tour.

On one occasion, Chaplin was playing on stage in the Channel Islands, between Britain and France, where people speak a dialect (a local version) of French. Chaplin realized that his audience could not understand English and therefore did not understand his jokes. But the audience did laugh at pantomime, in which facial expressions and body movements substitute for words.

Chaplin's big breakthrough, as it turned out, was joining the Fred Karno Company, a touring theatrical group that specialized in comedic pantomime. Chaplin portrayed characters who stumble at their jobs—a pianist who loses his music, a magician who spoils his tricks—everyday characters whose misfortunes amused the audience. For Chaplin, the Karno Company was a kind of advanced education in acting that prepared him for his next career in the movies.

First films

Touring America with the company, Chaplin met a movie producer named Mack Sennett (1884–1960), who was making short comedies on film. He offered Chaplin a job making movies for $150 a week. With some reluctance, Chaplin took a chance that pantomime would work on film. His first production, *Kid Auto Races at Venice,* appeared in 1914.

Moving pictures—"the movies"—had become immensely popular. The first films had no sound and thus no script. Music was provided by a pianist or organist in the theater. In Sennett's early films, actors improvised, or thought up on the spot what they would do, with the intent of leading into a chase scene. Sennett later described this set-up as the essence of his comedy. So, too, did Chaplin improvise his most famous character: the Little Tramp.

The Little Tramp

The character of the Little Tramp became instantly recognizable over two decades of filmmaking. It was a character made up by Chaplin spontaneously, or on the spot, while filming *Kid Auto Races at Venice*. He was told to wear something amusing. He took a pair of oversized pants and size fourteen shoes, which he wore on the opposite feet; put on a coat, a collar, and a derby hat; and placed a false mustache trimmed about as wide as the head of a toothbrush under his nose. The costume on the small-statured Chaplin (he was 5 feet 4 inches tall and weighed about 130 pounds) was a satire on a proper little man who has not quite arrived but acts as if he has. Shuffling with his feet nearly sideways was a touch Chaplin added that became part of the character.

In addition to acting in his movies, Chaplin also began directing them, showing other actors exactly how he wanted them to play their parts. Although Chaplin invented the Little Tramp hurriedly for a movie, as his career advanced and he became a director, there was nothing spontaneous about his comedy. Chaplin had a reputation as an exacting director, playing and replaying scenes until he had achieved just the effect he wanted, even it meant wasting vast amounts of film, which was expensive then. The essence of his comedies was to get him into trouble and then give him the chance to attempt, in a very serious way, to appear as a "normal little gentleman." Chaplin once wrote: "That is why, no matter how desperate the predicament is, I am always very much in earnest about clutching my cane, straightening my derby hat and fixing my tie, even though I have just landed on my head."

Chaplin recalled later that his inspiration came from everyday scenes he observed, scenes that his audiences could easily relate to. As he once described the process: "I watch people inside a theater to see when they laugh, I watch them everywhere to get material which they can laugh at."

Pinnacle of success

Chaplin became enormously popular around the world. One theater in New York City played nothing but Chaplin films from 1914 to 1923. He toured London and

Paris and was mobbed. His comedy depended on pantomime, rather than on verbal jokes, which made his films popular even in countries where English was not spoken.

Chaplin made thirty-five short films with Sennett in a year and was paid $150 a week. He then moved to another movie company, Essanay, and made fourteen films in 1915, for which he was paid $1,250 a week. His next move was to the Mutual Company, which paid Chaplin $670,000 a year, nearly one hundred times his salary just two years earlier. Later, Chaplin earned even more money, being paid $1 million to make eight movies over eighteen months by the National film production company (eventually he made nine pictures, but it took five years).

In addition to higher pay, Chaplin also gained control over his films, serving as author and director as well as actor. At age twenty-six, he was reputed to be the world's best-paid performer.

Romances and politics

Chaplin's reputation as America's favorite funny "little guy" was diminished somewhat by a series of marriages to women much younger than he was. In 1918, at age twenty-nine, he married Mildred Harris (1901–1944), age sixteen. They were divorced in two years. In 1924, Chaplin married another sixteen-year-old, Lilita McMurray (1908–1995), an actress. Together, they had two children before they were divorced in 1927. Chaplin's second divorce generated enormous bad publicity, and in some states women's groups successfully demanded that his films be barred.

In 1936, Chaplin married another actress, Paulette Goddard (1911–1990), whom he had met when she was twenty. They were divorced six years later, in 1942, without publicity. In the meantime, Chaplin had met twenty-one-year-old aspiring actress Joan Barry (often mistakenly spelled Berry). She had a daughter and named Chaplin as the father. Chaplin was accused of taking Barry across state lines for immoral purposes, although the charge was later dropped and blood tests showed that Chaplin was not the father of Barry's daughter. Despite the negative test, Chaplin was ordered by a jury to pay Barry to support the child.

In 1943, Chaplin married again. The bride was Oona O'Neill (1925–1991), the eighteen-year-old daughter of playwright Eugene O'Neill (1888–1953). Chaplin was fifty-four years old at the time. Despite the age difference, their marriage proved to be a happy one, and they had eight children.

Charlie Chaplin in a scene from the 1936 film *Modern Times.* © *Bettmann/Corbis.*

Politics is no laughing matter

After World War II (1939–45), the United States experienced a wave of fear of communist influence over politics. (Communists believed in a system of government ownership of land and factories, taken by force if necessary. The government of the Soviet Union was run by a brutal communist dictator, which gave rise to fears of Americans acting secretly to impose a similar system of government in the United States.) Several minor politicians made names for themselves by seeming to hunt down secret communists in the United States.

Chaplin had earlier gained a reputation as a radical, or someone who supports extreme change, by his portrayal of a harassed factory worker in *Modern Times* and his portrayal of German and Italian dictators in *The Great Dictator*. He had also made speeches advocating more aggressive military action against Germany in World War II at a time when Germany was fighting the Soviet Union. These actions made some people think Chaplin might sympathize with communism. Of these charges, Chaplin remarked: "I want to see the return of decency and kindness. I'm just a human being who wants to see this country a real democracy."

Chaplin also became involved in U.S. politics. During the election of 1948, Chaplin protested against sending a former communist out of the country, and he once introduced former U.S. vice president Henry Wallace (1888–1965), the 1948 Progressive Party candidate for president, at a meeting. A senator from Mississippi demanded that Chaplin, who was still a British citizen, be deported for having communist sympathies, and a widely read newspaper columnist took up the cry. Chaplin, who was nearing sixty and already had a successful career behind him, took a vacation to Britain in 1952, and U.S. attorney general James P. McGranery (1895–1962) said Chaplin would not be allowed back into the United States until he proved his "moral worth."

Disgusted, Chaplin went to his estate in Switzerland, where he lived the rest of his life. When he was invited back to the United States to be honored for his pioneering film work, in 1972, he was no longer mentally sharp. The Little Tramp died in Switzerland on Christmas Day, 1977. Two months later, Chaplin's corpse was stolen from his grave. A ransom was demanded for the return of Chaplin's remains, but three months later, Swiss police halted the plot and recovered the body. Chaplin was laid to rest again, in a vault surrounded by cement.

—*James L. Outman*

For More Information

Books

Chaplin, Charles. *My Autobiography*. New York: Simon and Schuster, 1964. Reprint, Plume, 1992.

Lynn, Kenneth S. *Charlie Chaplin and His Times*. New York: Simon and Schuster, 1997.

Milton, Joyce. *Tramp: The Life of Charlie Chaplin*. New York: Harper-Collins, 1996.

Robinson, David. *Charlie Chaplin: Comic Genius*. New York: Harry Abrams, 1996.

Periodicals

Burr, Ty. "Charlie Chaplin: The First Superstar." *Entertainment Weekly* (Fall 1996): p. 20.

"Charlie Chaplin and Oona O'Neill." *People Weekly* (February 12, 1996): p. 172.

Douglas, Ann. "Charlie Chaplin: The Comedian." *Time* (June 8, 1998): p. 118.

Weddle, David. "The Genesis of an Icon: The Creation of the Tramp." *Variety* (special edition on Charlie Chaplin; April 28, 2003): p. S4.

Web Sites

"Charlie Chaplin FBI File." *Fade to Black Magazine*. http://www.fadetoblack.com/foi/charliechaplin/bio.html (accessed on March 10, 2004).

"Comedy and Charlie Chaplin." *Penn State University Integrative Arts*. http://www.psu.edu/dept/inart10_110/inart10/chap.html (accessed on March 10, 2004).

César Chávez

Born March 31, 1927
Yuma, Arizona

Died April 23, 1993
San Luis, Arizona

Migrant workers union leader

"Our lives are all that really belong to us. So it is how we use our lives that determines what kind of people we are."

César Chávez.
© Bettmann/Corbis.

César Chávez was the leader of California farm workers who for three decades helped them achieve improved wages and working conditions as well as a measure of dignity. He also persuaded millions of Americans who may never have been on a farm, or even in California, to stop buying table grapes as a way of supporting the cause of farm workers. Chávez made visible to mothers and fathers in grocery stores across America the symbolic fingerprints left on those grapes by the hands, brown hands mostly, that had picked them. Those brown hands belonged to migrant workers: the families who sometimes spent nights in tin storage sheds or broken-down cars parked under bridges, and spent days picking grapes and other crops for wages that barely sustained life. Chávez grew up traveling from farm to farm harvesting crops, barred from speaking his native Spanish in school, unable to stay in school past the eighth grade, barred from watching a movie in the "whites only" section of a California theater—but able to dream of social justice for those on the bottom of America's social heap: Mexican American migrant workers.

For thirty years, from 1962 until his death in 1993, Chávez was the leader of the United Farm Workers, an organization he formed to improve the lives of farm workers by demanding higher pay and safer working conditions. In this role, Chávez achieved a modest success: for a period in the 1970s and 1980s, his organization managed to force farm owners to pay higher wages and to refrain from using dangerous pesticides, or chemicals used to kill insects, on fields where people were handling the crops. In a larger sense, Chávez inspired the grape boycott, the act of refusing to buy grapes as a statement of support for the migrant workers whom Chávez represented. A public opinion poll in 1970 estimated that seventeen million people observed the boycott, a key to the union's success and an important time in the history of Latino workers in the United States. (Latinos are Spanish-speaking persons in North America descended from early Spanish explorers in the Western Hemisphere. A Latino may have any color skin, from white to brown to black.)

Growing up poor

César Chávez was born near Yuma, Arizona, where his father, Librado, ran a store and worked on the nearby farm owned by César's grandfather. The farm had been owned by the Chávez family since the 1880s, when César's grandfather had immigrated to the United States from Mexico.

In 1937, the Chávez family had to leave their farm. A severe drought had ruined the crop, making it impossible for the family to pay taxes on their land; as a result, the government took possession of the property. The ten-year-old Chávez and his family were forced to join an army of thousands of others in Arizona and California who were in the same position: without land, without money, without jobs. The Chávez family and the other migrant workers traveled from farm to farm in Arizona and California, planting or harvesting crops. When one crop was harvested, the migrants moved to another farm, or another part of the state, to harvest another crop. (An army of migrant workers still moves from place to place in the United States, especially up and down the West Coast. They travel from California to Washington and back, planting or picking crops as the seasons advance, working for low wages, often living in their trucks or vans.)

For the children of migrant workers, attending school meant attending classes for awhile in one school, then moving to another school. Chávez later recalled attending about three dozen schools in just four years, until he finally dropped out of school for good in the eighth grade and began working full-time to help support his family.

Most migrant workers felt they had little to say about their jobs, their pay, or their working conditions. They needed money from week to week in order to live. They usually were not in one place long enough to think about organizing into unions, groups of workers who cooperate in demanding that their employers improve pay and other working conditions. In 1939, when Chávez was thirteen, the Congress of Industrial Organizations (CIO), which represented workers in large manufacturing plants, tried to organize a union among agricultural workers in California who were part of the canned fruit industry. Chávez's father and uncle joined the effort. Although the CIO was not successful in organizing the field workers, Chávez learned from his father and uncle about unions and how they could help workers.

The Chávez family was eventually able to find steady agricultural work near San Jose, California, and move into a small rented house. It was a life of backbreaking labor, of bending over all day to chop weeds with short-handled hoes or picking fruits and vegetables. Life was a struggle to survive—a farm worker's pay was too low to offer hope of a better life.

During World War II (1939–45), Chávez joined the U.S. Navy and spent two years as a sailor in the eastern Pacific. Just before he entered the Navy, Chávez went to a movie in Delano, California, with some friends and sat in a section marked "whites." Told to move from their seats, they refused and the police were called to arrest them. For a teenager who had paid hard-earned money to sit in a seat and watch a movie, it was a humiliating experience that made a deep impression.

A career begins

When the war ended, Chávez left the Navy and resumed his life as a farm worker. In the autumn of 1947, he was harvesting grapes in Delano when workers went on strike (refused to work) in order to get farm owners to negotiate with a newly organized union of farm workers. It was not unusual at the time for local sheriffs, and even U.S. immigration agents, to cooperate with property owners in defeating efforts to organize unions.

During the grape pickers' strike of 1947, sheriff's deputies and federal Immigration Service agents raided the camp of striking workers time after time. The federal agents claimed to be looking for people who did not have a legal right to be in the United States. The effect of their presence was to intimidate the strikers, some of whom were illegal residents and others of whom had relatives from Mexico working in the United States. Two years later, cotton growers near Delano tried to cut the wages of workers, which also resulted in a strike. Both the grape and cotton strikes failed to achieve their objectives, and Chávez decided the fault lay with poor leadership and disorganization among the strike organizers.

Community organizing

In 1951, a Catholic priest, Father Donald McDonnell, who was working among Latino farm workers, introduced Chávez to Fred Ross (1910–), who three years earlier had formed the Community Services Organization (CSO). The CSO was dedicated to helping disadvantaged people help themselves by organizing themselves and exercising their rights as citizens. Chávez spent nights going from door to door, offering migrant workers help with practical problems and giving instructions on how to become American citizens. Registering to vote, in order to influence local government action, was a key aim of the CSO. Community organizing was a technique that became widespread in the 1950s and 1960s, largely influenced by the theories and teachings of Saul Alinsky (1909–1972). Alinsky developed his ideas while organizing poor working people in Chicago, Illinois, to stand up for their rights against a corrupt city government. Soon after their meeting, Ross hired Chávez to work full-time in establishing chapters of the CSO among Spanish-speaking communities in California.

Chávez was highly effective and had become a director of the CSO by 1958. One of the targets of Chávez as leader of the CSO was to attack the practice of hiring Mexican citizens to do farm work instead of American citizens, on grounds that the foreign nationals would work for lower wages. In 1959, the CSO under Chávez filed over eleven hundred complaints with the California government agency whose job was to ensure that growers hire local workers rather than Mexican citizens. Chávez publicized his campaign with marches and newspaper interviews. Later, Chávez would be criticized for trying to win benefits for American farm workers at the expense of equally poor migrant laborers from Mexico.

Organizing farm workers

In the early 1960s, Chávez urged the CSO to establish a branch specifically dedicated to migrant workers. When the organization declined to back his plan, Chávez resigned his position and went off on his own to begin organizing a labor union for migrant farm workers that he called the National Farm Workers Association, starting in the area around Delano, California. It was a difficult challenge. Farm workers often did not stay in once place long enough to establish ties that would encourage them to join a union. Their economic circumstances were so desperate that they could not afford to go without work, in the case of a strike. Farm owners who employed the workers resisted bitterly. For Chávez, progress was slow.

Chávez found an ally, working with a representative of the American Federation of Labor–Congress of Industrial Organizations (AFL-CIO), the main organization representing a variety of labor unions in different industries. Together, they successfully organized agricultural workers to go on strike against owners of grape vineyards around Delano in 1965. The vineyard owners, realizing that a union would eventually lead to higher wages for their workers, at first simply refused to recognize the union as representing the workers and refused to meet its demands.

The grape boycott

Chávez then seized on another idea: the boycott. Chávez appealed to Americans who were sympathetic to the farm workers to refuse to buy California table grapes until the growers signed a contract with the United Farm Workers. Slowly at first and then with greater momentum, millions of Americans responded by pushing their shopping carts past

the grapes. Giving up eating grapes was a way—an easy way—to express sympathy for people, the farm workers, who represented the very bottom of the American economy.

The grape boycott in the 1960s came at a time of significant social upheaval in the United States. African Americans, led by Dr. Martin Luther King Jr. (1929–1968), were using similar tactics, including boycotts, to win equality under the law. Many college students were protesting against the U.S. involvement in the Vietnam War (1954–75). The grape boycott of the United Farm Workers tapped into similar sentiments on behalf of darker-skinned peoples for a taste of economic and political equality.

César Chávez urges citizens to boycott grapes while leading a protest at a grocery store in 1969.
AP/Wide World Photos.

Fasting

Chávez tapped into another proven method of enlisting public support—fasting, or refusing to eat. It was a tech-

César Chávez meets with U.S. senator Robert Kennedy of New York.
Corbis.

nique that had been used successfully by Mohandas Gandhi (1869–1948), the leader of India's movement for independence from British rule. Between February and March of 1968, Chávez refused food for twenty-five days. At the end of his long fast, a Catholic Mass (religious service) was held; among those present was U.S. senator Robert F. Kennedy (1925–1968) of New York, brother of assassinated president John F. Kennedy (1917–1963; served 1961–63) and himself a contender for the presidency in the election of 1968. Senator Kennedy described Chávez as "one of the heroic figures of our time."

Chávez had succeeded in bringing the entire nation's attention to the plight of the people living in extreme poverty in exchange for harvesting the nation's fresh fruits and vegetables. The campaign against the grape growers finally succeeded two years later, in 1970, when grape growers around Delano finally signed an agreement with the United Farm Workers to give grape pickers higher wages.

The struggle continues

The initial victory in the struggle with grape growers did not mark the end of struggles for Chávez and his United Farm Workers. Over the next two decades, the union continued to struggle to gain recognition among farm owners and support among workers and politicians. The results were mixed. In 1970, Chávez called for a consumer boycott of lettuce, which did not attract the same level of support as the earlier grape boycott. The International Brotherhood of Teamsters (known as the Teamsters union), which generally represented truck drivers, started competing with the United Farm Workers union for the support of farm workers. In 1973, when the 1970 agreements with grape producers were due to be renewed, some farm owners signed contracts instead with the Teamsters union without votes by the workers affected. (Some critics accused the Teamsters of a secret agreement to work hand in hand with the growers to defeat the goals of the United Farm Workers.) The new contracts caused a renewed grape strike, which led to widespread violence. Many striking workers were arrested for violating court orders to avoid picketing, or marching in front of a farm or plant with signs, urging customers and workers to stay away. Many workers were beaten. In an effort to stop violence, Chávez canceled the strike and called for a new boycott of grapes, but with less success than the first boycott.

Gradually, a measure of calm was restored. The California legislature passed the Agricultural Labor Relations Act in 1975, which gave farm workers the right to form unions and negotiate with growers. (By contrast, in 1972, Arizona had passed a law barring agricultural workers from going on strike or from organizing boycotts.) In 1977, the United Farm Workers and the Teamsters union negotiated a peaceful end to their competition to represent farm workers, which saw the Teamsters leave the scene. By 1980, the United Farm Workers union had agreements with growers representing about forty-five thousand workers.

In the 1980s, however, the political climate changed. In 1982, a new governor, George Deukmejian (1928–), was elected who was far less sympathetic to the farm workers and more sympathetic to the growers. Soon, the state government reduced efforts to enforce the 1975 farm labor law. Growers refused to renew agreements with the union, leaving agricultural workers where they had been a decade earlier. Chávez, focusing on the issue of chemical poisons sprayed on grapes to combat plant disease and insects, launched a new national grape boycott in 1986, but with far less success than he experienced two decades earlier. Membership in the union declined, and Chávez himself was the target of criticism by those who said he insisted on tightly controlling the organization and did not allow workers a democratic voice in union affairs. Other critics objected to Chávez's insistence on focusing on the rights of American migrant workers, sometimes at the expense of immigrants from Mexico and Central America who also wanted to earn money picking American crops.

In 1991, the government of Mexico honored Chávez with the *Aguila Azteca* (Aztec Eagle), awarded for people of Mexican heritage whose contributions have been made outside of Mexico. On April 23, 1993, César Chávez died peacefully in his sleep. He left a wife, Helen Fabela, and eight children. A week later, forty thousand people marched behind his simple wooden coffin. The mourners included many veterans of the long fight for better pay and conditions in the fields. They also included many politicians and Hollywood celebrities who admired a man who never earned more than $5,000 a year, less than many of his union members, in a lifetime spent trying to improve the lives of migrant workers. In 1994, Chávez's widow received the Medal of Freedom from President Bill Clinton (1946–; served 1993–2001). It is the highest award given to civilians by the U.S. government.

—*James L. Outman*

For More Information

Books

Altman, Linda Jacobs. *Migrant Farm Workers: The Temporary People*. New York: Franklin Watts, 1994.

Ferriss, Susan, and Ricardo Sandoval. *The Fight in the Fields: César Chávez and the Farmworkers Movement*. New York: Harcourt Brace, 1997.

Griswold del Castillo, Richard, and Richard A. Garcia. *César Chávez: A Triumph of Spirit*. Norman: University of Oklahoma Press, 1995.

Matthiessen, Peter. *Sal Si Puedes: César Chávez and the New American Revolution*. New York: Random House, 1969.

Periodicals

Bardacke, Frank. "César's Ghost: Decline and Fall of the U.F.W." *The Nation* (July 26, 1993): p. 130.

"A Great and Good Man." *Commonweal* (June 4, 1993): p. 4.

Jones, Arthur. "Millions Reaped What César Chávez Sowed." *National Catholic Reporter* (May 7, 1993): p. 5.

Matthiessen, Peter. "César Chávez." *The New Yorker* (May 17, 1993): p. 82.

Salandini, Victor. "Threatened by Fasts, Foes, Chávez Held His Peace." *National Catholic Reporter* (May 7, 1993): p. 6.

Web Sites

"The Story of César Chávez." *United Farm Workers.* http://www.ufw.org/cecstory.htm (accessed on March 11, 2004).

Kalpana Chawla

Born July 1, 1961
Karnal, India

Died February 1, 2003
In *Columbia* explosion upon
return to Earth

Astronaut and aeronautical engineer

"You're floating [in space].... Earth is very beautiful. I wish everyone could see it."

K alpana Chawla was the first female astronaut from India. To pursue her dream of flying airplanes and becoming an aerospace engineer, she studied physics, chemistry, and math in high school and excelled at an engineering college in India. She then took on advanced studies in the United States. She joined the American space program in 1995 and traveled millions of miles in space, orbiting Earth hundreds of times on two space-shuttle missions. She was a flight engineer and mission specialist on the space shuttle *Columbia*, which broke up sixteen minutes before it was scheduled to land on February 1, 2003. Chawla and her six fellow astronauts were killed.

Stargazer and trailblazer

Kalpana Chawla was born on July 1, 1961, in Karnal, India, in the farming state of Haryana, 75 miles from New Delhi, India's capital city. Her father, Banarsi Lal Chawla, worked at various odd jobs until he started his own business manufacturing boxes. From there, he started several other

Kalpana Chawla. *AP/Wide World Photos.*

successful enterprises. Her mother, Sanjogta Kharbanda, was the daughter of a doctor. After giving birth to two daughters, Sunita and Deepa, and a son, Sanjay, Chawla's mother wanted another son, she later told *Time* magazine, "but out came Kalpana, who has achieved more than a boy could."

Chawla was captivated by airplanes early in her life. She and her brother Sanjay would watch planes as they flew to and from a local flight school. Throughout her school years, Chawla created projects and wrote papers about stars, planets, and outer space. She decided she wanted to be an aerospace engineer when she was twelve and began focusing on science courses. At Tagore Bal Niketan Secondary School, she specialized in physics, chemistry, and math and also took language courses. When she learned about one of India's first mail-delivery pilots and saw a display of some of his equipment and the planes he flew, Chawla became even more enthusiastic about flying and engineering.

Chawla entered Punjab Engineering College to study aeronautical engineering. She had to contend with and overcome social conventions, or behavior expected by society, about proper studies and professions for young women. Chawla was the only woman in the program. Another example of being tested by social conventions occurred when she accompanied Sanjay to flight school one day. Authorities at the school demanded that she get written consent of her guardian to attend, but her father refused consent.

Chawla graduated with a bachelor of science degree in 1982 and won a scholarship to continue her studies in the

 ## Chawla on Her Early Inspiration

In her official National Aeronautics and Space Administration (NASA) preflight interview for her 2003 *Columbia* mission, Kalpana Chawla reflected on her early interests in flying and aerospace. Her interview is from the Space.com Web site.

When I was going to high school back in India, growing up, I think I was very lucky that we lived in a ... very small town and one of a handful of towns at that time which had flying clubs.... Me and my brother, sometimes we would be on bikes looking up, which you shouldn't be doing, trying to see where these airplanes were headed.... Also growing up, we knew of this person, J. R. D. Tata [1904–1993] in India, who had done some of the first mail flights in India. And also the airplane that he flew for the mail flights now hangs in one of the aerodromes out there that I had had a chance to see. Seeing this airplane and just knowing what this person had done during those years was very intriguing. Definitely captivated my imagination. And, even when I was in high school if people asked me what I wanted to do, I knew I wanted to be an aerospace engineer. In hindsight, it's quite interesting to me that just some of those very simple things helped me make up my mind that that's the area I wanted to pursue.

United States. However, as the deadline drew near for applying to the U.S. college of her choice, the University of Texas in Arlington, her father was away on an extended business trip. As is customary, she needed his approval. Chawla was teaching at Punjab Engineering College when he returned from the trip and learned from his wife about Chawla's recent accomplishments and future hopes. He visited her in the classroom, gave his consent, and helped her to quickly obtain a visa, an official document that allows a noncitizen to attend school or to work in a different country. The date he visited her in the classroom was August 26, and the deadline for applying for classes at the university was August 31: She made it with no time to spare. Her family insisted that Sanjay accompany Chawla to help her get settled in Arlington, Texas.

Learning to fly

Almost immediately in Arlington, Chawla met Jean-Pierre Harrison, a flying instructor who would become her future husband. Chawla earned her master of science degree in aerospace engineering from the University of Texas at Arlington in 1984 and married Harrison that year. Along with a love of flying, the couple shared such hobbies as scuba diving, hiking, reading, and listening to music. Chawla became an experienced pilot, earning commercial pilot licenses for land and sea planes and for gliders. She also earned a flight instructor's license for airplanes and gliders.

After Chawla graduated, the couple moved to Boulder, Colorado, where Chawla began her studies for a doctorate of philosophy degree in aerospace engineering from the University of Colorado. She earned her degree in 1988 and began working for the American space program at the National Aeronautics and Space Administration (NASA) Ames Research Center. Her area of research was powered-lift computational fluid dynamics, the study of airflows encountered by aircraft in flight. Her research included using simulators, or model aircrafts blasted by machine-driven winds, capturing information on two computers about how the aircrafts reacted, and then using the data to predict results of various wind effects on certain kinds of aircraft.

In 1993, Chawla became vice president of Overset Methods Inc., a research firm based in Los Altos, California.

She formed a team of researchers specializing in the development of ways to make the best use of aerodynamics, designs that direct airflow to ease resistance and increase speed. In 1994, Chawla was selected by NASA for astronaut training. In her first assignment, she served as crew representative working on technical issues, including the testing of space shuttle–control software in the Shuttle Avionics Integration Laboratory.

Kalpana Chawla (far left) and fellow *Columbia* crew members Laurel Clark, William McCool, Rick Husband, David Brown, Ilan Ramon, and Michael Anderson take a break during preparations for their January 16, 2003, liftoff. *AP/Wide World Photos.*

Into space

In November 1996, Chawla was assigned as mission specialist and prime robotic arm operator on STS-87 (the space shuttle *Columbia*). She trained for a year leading up to the shuttle launch on November 19, 1997. On the mission, which lasted until December 5, 1997, Chawla flew 6.5 million miles in 252 orbits of Earth. The crew conducted experiments designed to study how the weightless environment of space affects various physical processes and to observe the Sun's

"Space Truckin'"

On her space missions, Chawla carried nearly two dozen CDs, including ones by such artists as Abida Parveen (1954–), Yehudi Menuhin (1916–1999), Ravi Shankar (1920–), and the 1970s progressive rock group Deep Purple. She especially liked the Deep Purple song "Space Truckin'," an up-tempo rocker about cruising in a space ship around the universe, with a chorus inviting listeners to "Come on, Let's go space truckin'." Chawla even exchanged e-mails with band members during one of her space missions.

outer atmospheric layers. Two members of the crew performed a spacewalk to capture a satellite and to test tools and procedures that could be used for assembling a space station in the future.

Chawla made headlines around the world. She was featured on the cover of many magazines, including India's *The Week,* which showed her floating, unrestricted by gravity, in the shuttle. Her personal mission to fly in space had been accomplished. Talking about her experience in space, she told the *News India-Times* about looking out the window and seeing India's Himalayan Mountains: "The Ganges Valley looked majestic, mind boggling." In other interviews, she described how she pointed out New Delhi to the other crew members and said to them, "I lived near there," and of looking out the window just before falling asleep: "You're floating," she said. "The Nile River looks like a lifeline in the Sahara [desert in northern Africa].... Earth is very beautiful. I wish everyone could see it."

Chawla had come a long way from Karnal, India, where she first dreamed of flying, and she did not forget her roots. In 1998, Chawla and her husband established a fund to help support students and education in her hometown. And on her space missions, Chawla carried a white silk banner as part of a worldwide campaign to honor teachers.

On her second flight on *Columbia* in 2003, Chawla was the flight engineer and mission specialist. Working twenty-four hours a day, in two alternating shifts of twelve hours, the crew successfully conducted almost eighty experiments. After her twelve-hour work period, Chawla would eat her dinner (she was a strict vegetarian) and then fall asleep looking out the window while listening to music.

The *Columbia* mission was scheduled to land in Florida at the Kennedy Space Center on Saturday, February 1, 2003, at 9:16 A.M., Eastern Standard Time. As the shuttle

crossed the California coastline, it was traveling through the upper atmosphere at over twenty times the speed of sound. A member of the crew began filming a digital video.

Meanwhile, at Mission Control in Florida, where computers were monitoring the shuttle, engineers noticed a sudden loss of temperature readings on *Columbia*'s left wing. In addition, sensors in the landing gear showed a significant rise in temperature, first by 20 then up to 30 degrees in five minutes. At 8:56 A.M., the temperature dropped off, then the

The *Columbia* crew floats together in a photograph recovered from the shuttle's debris. Clockwise from far left are Kalpana Chawla, David Brown, William McCool, Michael Anderson, Ilan Ramon, Laurel Clark, and Rick Husband. *AP/Wide World Photos.*

A young girl prays at a memorial shrine for Kalpana Chawla in the fallen astronaut's hometown of Karnal, Haryana, India. *Elizabeth Dalziel. AP/Wide World Photos.*

temperature reading stopped. The shuttle crew acknowledged the signal, and the temperature reading losses were not thought to be a problem. At 8:58 A.M., the ship was traveling 13,200 miles per hour—18 times the speed of sound; *Columbia* had descended to nearly 40 miles above Earth, over New Mexico, about 1,400 miles from the Kennedy Center runway and was proceeding as normal. But at 8:59 A.M., with the shuttle over west Texas, ground controllers noticed that *Columbia*'s flight computer was steering the ship to the right. In the last few seconds of recorded computer data, evidence suggests that either shuttle commander Rick Husband (1957–2003) or pilot William McCool (1961–2003) might have attempted to take manual control of the landing process. Something had gone wrong.

Sixteen minutes before the shuttle was scheduled to touch down, Mission Control lost all radio contact and data. The shuttle was over east Texas, and at that time residents in Texas, Arkansas, and Louisiana reported hearing an explosion and witnessing flaming debris in the sky, which fell in parts of Texas and Louisiana. The shuttle had disintegrated, or broken up. Chawla and her six fellow astronauts were killed.

Doing what they loved

Memorial services for the *Columbia* astronauts were held at the National Cathedral in Washington D.C. Kalpana Chawla, known as KC by her friends and colleagues, was considered a role model for Indian girls long before those events. As Jo McGowan wrote in *Commonweal* magazine, "Kalpana Chawla is a household name in India, and a first-name at that. When the space shuttle *Columbia* crashed this month, the headlines here were all full of 'Kalpana,' as if there were no need to identify any further." India renamed its first weather satellite Kalpana-1 in her honor. Found among shuttle wreckage were some of Chawla's music CDs. NASA used them as part of special commemorative plaques honoring the seven astronauts.

Five days after the tragedy, the digital tape the crew was filming shortly before the disaster was found near a town called Palestine in eastern Texas. The tape began at 8:35 A.M. and ended at 8:48 A.M.; eleven minutes later contact with *Columbia* was lost. As the film begins, Chawla asks fellow astronaut Laurel Clark (1961–2003), "We have ten minutes to get gloves on, Laurel, do you need help?" The film shows the astronauts preparing for landing and smiling for the camera. The tape ends four minutes before the first sign of trouble.

CBS News interviewed Charles Figley (1944–), director of the Traumatology Institute at Florida State University, about the tape. (Traumatology is the study of how people and organizations react to tragedy). He said that some might view the found tape as a miracle. "Suddenly here is a postcard of these men and women," Figley said. The video should provide additional peace of mind for the families of the astronauts, he added, "because it shows them happy and doing what they loved."

A year after the tragedy, a series of tests proved how the shuttle was damaged. A piece of foam insulation from *Columbia*'s external fuel tank broke off and hit the left wing of the craft just 81 seconds after the shuttle lifted off on January

16, 2003. The ship was destroyed 16 days later as it cut through Earth's atmosphere in preparation for landing. Hot gases seeped inside the ship's damaged wing, melting the structure from inside and causing it to disintegrate in the upper atmosphere. Similar foam impacts had occurred during prior shuttle launches, but NASA did not believe the foam could cause significant damage.

—Roger Matuz

For More Information

Books

Cabbage, Michael. *Comm Check: The Final Flight of Shuttle Columbia.* New York: Free Press, 2004.

Cole, Michael D. *The Columbia Space Shuttle Disaster: From First Liftoff to Tragic Final Flight.* Rev. ed. Berkeley Heights, NJ: Enslow, 2003.

Gupta, Indra. *Kalpana Chawla: A Fairy Tale Saga with a Tragic End.* New Delhi: Icon Publication, 2003.

Padmanabhan, Anil. *Kalpana Chawla: A Life.* New Delhi; New York: Puffin Books, 2003.

Periodicals

Gibbs, Nancy. "Seven Astronauts, One Fate." *Time* (February 10, 2003): pp. 30–44.

McGowan, Jo. "Impossible Journey: India's Female Astronaut." *Commonweal* (February 28, 2003): p. 8.

Thomas, Evan. "Out of the Blue." *Newsweek* (February 10, 2003): p 22.

Woodmansee, Laura S. "Remembering KC." *Ad Astra* (March-May 2003): pp. 16–19.

Web Sites

"Astronaut Biography: Kalpana Chawla." *Space.com.* http://www.space.com/missionlaunches/bio_chawla.html (accessed on March 11, 2004).

Joseph, Josy. "The Chawlas' Odyssey." *The Rediff Special.* http://www.rediff.com/news/2003/feb/01spec.htm (accessed on March 11, 2004).

"Kalpana Chawla (Ph.D.), NASA Astronaut." *National Aeronautics and Space Administration: Biographical Data.* http://www.jsc.nasa.gov/Bios/htmlbios/chawla.html (accessed on March 11, 2004).

"Reporting Tips: Dr. Kalpana C. Chawla, Astronaut." *South Asian Journalists Association.* http://www.saja.org/tipschawla.html (accessed on March 11, 2004).

Mario Cuomo

Born June 15, 1932
New York, New York

**Governor of New York, lawyer,
and noted speechmaker**

M ario Cuomo was elected governor of New York three times, each time by a wide margin. Yet he is perhaps best known for "the Speech," a nationally televised address he made during the Democratic Party's 1984 presidential convention. The speech was made memorable when Cuomo described the difficult struggles of his immigrant parents to overcome poverty and hardship to provide for their family.

From the family store to center field

Mario Matthew Cuomo was born in 1932 in an apartment above the family store his parents had purchased the year before. His father, Andrea, and mother, Immaculata, had immigrated to New York City from Salerno, Italy, in the late 1920s. Cuomo's parents knew only how to speak Italian, yet they managed to run the store successfully in their mixed ethnic neighborhood, called South Jamaica, in Queens, a borough, or section, of New York City. Before purchasing the store, Cuomo's father saved money by working as a ditchdigger and by cleaning sewers.

"I learned about our obligation to each other from [my parents]. They asked only for a chance to work and to make the world better for their children and they asked to be protected in those moments when they would not be able to protect themselves. This nation and this nation's government did that for them."

Mario Cuomo.
© Bettmann/Corbis.

Cuomo knew only a few English words and phrases, learned from his older brother and older sister, when he began elementary school. He quickly became an excellent student, though. Cuomo was also a fine athlete—good enough to earn a professional baseball contract from the Pittsburgh Pirates organization upon graduating from high school. He was playing as a center fielder for the Pirates' minor league team in Brunswick, Georgia, when his baseball career was cut short after he was hit in the head by a pitch.

After spending a month recuperating in a hospital, Cuomo returned home. Convinced he would not make a career as a baseball player, Cuomo enrolled at St. John's University in New York. He helped pay for his education by playing on a semiprofessional basketball team. (Semiprofessional teams usually play in a local league and recruit a few players who are paid by the team's organizer or by a sponsor. Other players are not paid, but they compete to attract the attention of scouts for professional teams.)

Cuomo earned a bachelor's degree in 1953 and went on to law school at St. John's. He graduated with honors at the top of his class in 1956. While attending St. John's, Cuomo met Matilda Raffa, and they were married in 1954. The Cuomos have five children, three daughters and two sons. Matilda Cuomo became a schoolteacher after graduating from St. John's.

Lawyer and politician

After he graduated from law school, Cuomo served as a clerk for a judge in the New York State of Appeals Court. He soon joined a law firm in Brooklyn, New York. In 1963, Cuomo became a partner in the firm and began teaching law part–time at St. John's. In the mid-1960s, he drew attention in New York City for successfully defending neighborhood groups and small businesses against projects that would tear down homes and displace the people who lived and worked there.

In 1972, New York City mayor John Lindsay (1921–2000) appointed Cuomo to assess the impact of building a large housing project for low-income families in an established neighborhood. The proposed development had become bitterly disputed between residents and other community groups. Cuomo's recommendation for a smaller-scale project that would better integrate new and existing residents and local businesses was accepted with enthusiasm. He wrote about the experience in a book, *Forest Hills Diary: The Crisis of Low-Income Housing* (1977). Presented as a diary, the book records events and shows Cuomo's reactions to people involved in the housing dispute, from politicians to homemakers.

 Cuomo's Political Beliefs

Mario Cuomo called his political philosophy "progressive pragmatism" and a "family kind of politics" in which communities share with and help each other. Those values were formed by his ethnic and religious background as a poor Italian Catholic whose family worked together to improve their lives.

Having established a reputation as defender and an arbiter, or one who helps disputing parties resolve their differences, Cuomo began seeking political office. He was unsuccessful in the Democratic primary, where voters decide on a single candidate to represent a political party, when running for lieutenant governor (second in command) of New York in 1974. Democrat Hugh Carey (1919–), who had attended St. John's and was a friend of Cuomo's, won the governorship. Cuomo later finished second to Edward Koch (1924–) in the election for mayor of New York City in 1977.

Governor Carey appointed Cuomo as New York's secretary of state. In this position, Cuomo won recognition for investigating abuses in state-run nursing homes and for successfully arbitrating land and labor disputes. When Carey ran for reelection in 1978, Cuomo was selected as his running mate. They won the election, and Cuomo quickly emerged as a leader of the New York State Democratic Party. He directed the party's campaign in New York for President Jimmy Carter (1924–; served 1977–81) when Carter ran for reelection in 1980.

When Carey announced he would not seek reelection in 1982, Cuomo entered the race and contended in the Democratic primary with Koch, who had been a widely publicized and controversial mayor of New York City and had strong groups of support. However, Cuomo proved he had equal support in New York City, especially with union members, Hispanic Americans, and African Americans, and earned more votes than Koch outside the city to win the Democratic nomi-

New York governor Mario Cuomo laughs with members of the Jamaica Community Adolescent Program chorus, a drug rehabilitation program in Queens, New York. Governor Cuomo was an advocate for the rights of underprivileged citizens. © Bettmann/Corbis.

nation. Cuomo then defeated his Republican opponent, Lewis Lehrman (1938–), and was sworn into office in January 1983.

As governor, Cuomo championed the needs of citizens less privileged. Cuomo faced opposition for his programs from Republican lawmakers interested in reducing government involvement and the taxes used to finance social programs. Republicans were supported in their efforts by the popularity of President Ronald Reagan (1911–; served 1981–89), who cut federal programs and taxes. Cuomo's efforts were viewed by Democrats as exactly the kind of approach that represented their constituents, or people represented by a political party. He was invited to make the keynote address (the spotlight speech) at the Democratic National Convention, where the party's presidential and vice presidential candidates were to be officially approved for the 1984 election.

Cuomo's skills as an orator were already appreciated in New York. The convention gave him an opportunity to speak on national television and to communicate to Americans about why they should support the Democratic Party's approach. Cuomo admitted to being nervous about making the speech.

Center stage

Cuomo's speech was met with a rousing response at the convention and received rave reviews in the press. In the speech, Cuomo moved away from the typical keynote address, which outlines a party's platform, or how the party stands on various issues, and its political differences with the opposing party. He used a phrase by President Reagan, who described America as a "shining city," to argue that many people were not able to share in the opportunities and wealth of the "shining city." (The title of Cuomo's speech was "A Tale of Two Cities.") To emphasize his view, Cuomo became personal—turning to the example of his parents, who were poor immigrants but achieved through hard and honest work the opportunity to provide for their family. Cuomo argued that in the 1980s those less fortunate were facing additional hardship and challenges because of the policies of the Reagan administration.

The speech became influential. "I remember the effect [the speech] had not only on the delegates, but on the hard-bitten, cynical press corps—men and women … whose profession required them to hear the same speeches with the same messages delivered time and again," wrote Terry Golway in *America* magazine twelve years later. "This speech, however, was different, splendidly written and beautifully delivered." The title of Golway's article, "Blame it on Mario," reflects that after Cuomo's speech, politicians began to routinely use real-life examples to demonstrate the human side of their political programs and the voters they represented.

Staying home in New York

Cuomo's speech at the Democratic Convention gave him national recognition, but he faced challenges in his home state. A growing state budget deficit made it difficult for Cuomo to provide funds for programs to assist those in need.

An Excerpt from Mario Cuomo's "A Tale of Two Cities" Speech

On the evening of July 16, 1984, New York governor Mario Cuomo delivered a rousing speech at the Democratic National Convention in San Francisco, titled "A Tale of Two Cities." A short excerpt follows.

New York governor Mario Cuomo delivered a powerful keynote speech at the 1984 Democratic National Convention.
© *Bettmann/Corbis.*

[The] struggle to live with dignity is the real story of the shining city. And it's a story, ladies and gentlemen, that I didn't read in a book, or learn in a classroom. I saw it, and lived it. Like many of you, I watched a small man with thick calluses on both hands work 15 and 16 hours a day. I saw him once literally bleed from the bottoms of his feet, a man who came here uneducated, alone, unable to speak the language, who taught me all I needed to know about faith and hard work by the simple eloquence of his example. I learned about our kind of democracy from my father. And, I learned about our obligation to each other from him and from my mother. They asked only for a chance to work and to make the world better for their children and they asked to be protected in those moments when they would not be able to protect themselves. This nation and this nation's government did that for them.

And that they were able to build a family and live in dignity and see one of their children go from behind their little grocery store in South Jamaica on the other side of the tracks where he was born, to occupy the highest seat in the greatest state of the greatest nation in the only world we know, is an ineffably beautiful tribute to the democratic process.

His political philosophy, which he named "progressive pragmatism" and a "family kind of politics," called on communities to share with and help each other. His values were formed in his youth as a poor Italian Catholic whose family worked together to improve their lives. He was a very popular governor and was reelected in 1986 and 1990 by wide margins.

Many Democrats wanted Cuomo to run for president in 1988. Cuomo considered running but eventually decided against it. He cited his need to work with the state legislature to solve the financial problems facing New York. The legislature had grown increasingly Republican and resisted many of Cuomo's ideas and programs. Again in 1992, Cuomo was encouraged to run for president and he nearly entered the New Hampshire primary—the first test where voters would select from among several presidential candidates. Cuomo again declined to run after careful thought. As in 1988, he cited his state's fiscal, or financial, problems as work that demanded his full and immediate attention.

New York's financial woes and a preference across the nation for Republican candidates in state and national elections led to Cuomo's defeat when he ran for a fourth term as governor in 1994. He was still a respected national figure—rumored to be the first choice of President Bill Clinton (1946–; served 1993–2001) when a vacancy on the Supreme Court occurred in 1993, and he was considered a candidate when Major League Baseball needed a new commissioner the following year. In an interview with *Newsweek* magazine, Cuomo admitted that he would most enjoy being a Supreme Court justice, "but the place I could do the most good is here and now in New York."

After leaving office, Cuomo remained busy as a popular speaker. He also practiced law and hosted *The Mario Cuomo Show,* a 1996 weekly radio program that was syndicated, or made available for broadcast, across the country. Cuomo abruptly ended the show, however, to campaign for the re-election of President Clinton. He often appeared on news shows and made speeches in support of Clinton. Cuomo's son, Andrew (1957–), served as President Clinton's secretary of housing and urban development.

Cuomo was sixty-four years old when President Clinton was reelected in 1996. Although he began slowing his schedule, he was still interviewed often to represent the Democratic Party's viewpoints on issues, remained a popular speaker on political topics and the practice of law, wrote introductions to books, and authored a children's book, *The Blue Spruce* (1999). He continued being active as well in his local New York community and with cross-denominational religious groups, in which people from different religions socialize and work together in areas of common interest.

—*Roger Matuz*

For More Information

Books

Cuomo, Mario. *The Blue Spruce*. Chelsea, MI: Sleeping Bear Press, 1999.

Cuomo, Mario. *More Than Words: The Speeches of Mario Cuomo*. New York: St. Martin's Press, 1994.

McElvaine, Robert S. *Mario Cuomo: A Biography*. New York: Scribners, 1988.

Miringoff, Lee M., and Barbara L. Carvalho. *The Cuomo Factor: Assessing the Political Appeal of New York's Governor*. Poughkeepsie, NY: Marist Institute for Public Opinion, 1986.

Periodicals

Clift, Eleanor. "The New Mario Scenario. Democrats Fantasize, but Cuomo's Coy as Ever." *Newsweek* (July 23, 1990): p. 20.

Golway, Terry. "Blame It on Mario." *America* (September 14, 1996): p. 6.

Newfield, Jack. "An Interview with Mario Cuomo." *Tikkun* (May-June 1998): pp. 19–24.

Web Sites

Cuomo, Mario. "A Tale of Two Cities." *American Rhetoric*. http://www.americanrhetoric.com/speeches/cuomo1984dnc.htm (accessed on March 11, 2004).

Albert Einstein

Born March 14, 1879
Ulm, Germany

Died April 18, 1955
Princeton, New Jersey

Physicist

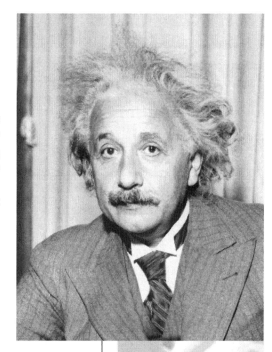

Albert Einstein was already a world-famous scientist when he immigrated to the United States in 1933. Over his lifetime, he had three nationalities: German, Swiss, and American. He also was Jewish, which led him to support the founding of the state of Israel. But as the top physicist in the twentieth century, Einstein in some ways rose above nationalities to become a citizen of the world. His story as a world citizen cast a different light on the larger subject of emigration and migration across national borders.

"The most incomprehensible thing about the world is that it is comprehensible."

Not a promising young student

Albert Einstein was the son of a middle-class Jewish businessman. Einstein was born in Germany, a country that had been unified into a single state only eight years before his birth. Previously, a group of kingdoms, of which Prussia was the largest, had occupied the territory brought together into a single kingdom in 1870. When he was a boy, Einstein's father, Hermann, moved his family to Munich, where he and a brother opened a factory manufacturing electrical equipment.

Albert Einstein. *Getty Images.*

111

The family later moved to Milan, Italy, in 1894, before Einstein had graduated from high school.

Einstein did not have a reputation as a brilliant or even an excellent student. He was regarded as rebellious, a young man who preferred to study topics in math and science that interested him and to ignore assignments that did not. He paid a price for his independent streak in 1895, when the prestigious Swiss Federal Institute of Technology in Zurich rejected his application. Einstein spent a year studying subjects in which he was considered weak. He was finally admitted to the Swiss university in 1896 with the intention of becoming a teacher of physics and math.

Even then, Einstein did not impress all of his teachers. He graduated in 1901 and became a Swiss citizen, but he could not find a teaching job without the recommendation of all his teachers. Instead, Einstein got a job working for the Swiss government, examining applications for patents. (A patent is a claim by an inventor for the exclusive right, during a limited period of time, to use an invention to make money. Applications are examined to make sure the so-called invention really is new.) Einstein's job required technical knowledge, but it is often represented as a low-grade clerical job. It did not enjoy the prestige of a teaching post at a major university, but it did allow Einstein plenty of free time to work on his first love, which was physics, and to enjoy his marriage in 1903 to Mileva Maric of Hungary, a student Einstein had met at the Institute of Technology. The couple had two sons and were divorced in 1919. Einstein later married his widowed cousin, Elsa Einstein, whom he had known since he was a child.

1905: The year of sudden acclaim

The story of Albert Einstein is not one of a scientist working for years to develop a new explanation for the world he sees around him. To the contrary, just a few years out of Zurich, Einstein published a series of scientific papers in a single year—1905—that permanently established his reputation as one of the modern world's great scientists on a par with Galileo Galilei (1564–1642) and Sir Isaac Newton (1642–1727).

One of the papers Einstein published in 1905 was on the topic of what is called Einstein's "special theory of relativity." It was a mathematical demonstration that showed that light moves at the same speed regardless of its source or the motion of the observer. (The speed of an object, on the other hand, is relative to the observer. A car may seem to be moving at 30 miles an hour to someone standing still; to someone moving towards the first car at the same speed, the first car seems to be moving at 60 miles an hour. Einstein's theory said that regardless of whether an observer is moving toward or away from light, the speed of light is always approximately 186,000 miles per second.)

Also in 1905, Einstein published four other papers: on the effects of electric currents; the phenomenon of "Brownian motion" (the random movement of microscopic particles suspended in liquids or gases, which Einstein realized could prove the existence of molecules and atoms too small to observe in the most powerful microscope); the emission and absorption of light; and the inertia of energy (inertia is the quality of matter that keeps objects at rest steady, or keeps objects in motion moving, until some other force acts on them).

Over the next decade, other physicists began analyzing and evaluating Einstein's work, and his reputation soared.

Albert Einstein worked as a professor only after he was recognized for his theory of relativity. *AP/Wide World Photos.*

Scientific recognition

Einstein, who had not been able to get a job teaching physics, became an international scientific celebrity. In 1909, he became a professor of physics at the University of Zurich. Two years later, he became a professor at German University in Prague (now capital of the Czech Republic), and the year after that he became a professor at his own school, the Swiss

Einstein and the Theory of Relativity

Sir Isaac Newton, a pioneer in the study of the nature of objects and of objects in motion (the science of physics), is often credited with "discovering" gravity, when an apple fell from a tree and hit his head. Newton wrote extensively about gravity and its effect on objects. For over two hundred years, Newton was the recognized authority on the subject.

At the beginning of the twentieth century, Albert Einstein challenged Newton's theories. In Einstein's views, things that might seem obvious to the observer are sometimes not. For example, the same clock might tick at a different speed when it is near a giant object, such as the Sun. Light, which is thought to travel very fast (186,000 miles per second) may also be affected by large objects. A second (the unit of time) might be longer or shorter, depending on gravity. In Einstein's view, it is all "relative."

Here is how Professor Alan Lightman (1948–) of the Massachusetts Institute of Technology explains Einstein's theory of relativity on a Web site sponsored by *Nova,* the Public Broadcasting Service (PBS) program that focuses on scientific subjects:

> *What was General Relativity? Einstein's earlier theory of time and space, Special Relativity, proposed that distance and time are not absolute. The ticking rate of a clock depends on the motion of the observer of that clock; likewise for the length*

Federal Institute of Technology in Zurich. In 1913, the Prussian Academy of Sciences in Berlin made Einstein a member of their influential society and invited him to become director of scientific research at the Kaiser Wilhelm Institute. He accepted the offer and moved to Berlin, where he remained for the next nineteen years.

Scientists in other countries also admired his work. In 1919, British scientists traveled to Príncipe Island, off the west coast of Africa, and photographed a total solar eclipse (a shadowing of the Sun when the Moon passes between Earth and the Sun). Their photographs confirmed one of Einstein's startling predictions: that beams of light could be "bent" or "deflected" when passing near a huge mass such as the Sun. Days after the observation, the *New York Times* reported on the observation with the headline: "Lights All Askew In The Heavens. Men Of Science More Or Less Agog Over Results Of Eclipse Observations. Einstein Theory Triumphs."

of a 'yard stick.' Published in 1915, General Relativity proposed that gravity, as well as motion, can affect the intervals of time and of space. The key idea of General Relativity, called the Equivalence Principle, is that gravity pulling in one direction is completely equivalent to an acceleration in the opposite direction. (A car accelerating forwards feels just like sideways gravity pushing you back against your seat. An elevator accelerating upwards feels just like gravity pushing you into the floor.)

If gravity is equivalent to acceleration, and if motion affects measurements of time and space (as shown in Special Relativity), then it follows that gravity does so as well. In particular, the gravity of any mass, such as our sun, has the effect of warping the space and time around it. For example, the angles of a triangle no longer add up to 180 degrees and clocks tick more slowly the closer they are to a gravitational mass like the sun.

Many of the predictions of General Relativity, such as the bending of starlight by gravity and a tiny shift in the orbit of the planet Mercury, have been quantitatively confirmed by experiment.

Einstein's theories are not easy to understand, and indeed he was not explaining events he had witnessed, as Newton did in developing his theory of gravitation. Einstein's theories were just that—ideas generated from his scientific imagination—until the observations of light being deflected during a solar eclipse behaved in exactly the way Einstein had predicted.

Two years later, Einstein was awarded the Nobel Prize for Physics.

Einstein and politics

Physics was not the only subject of interest to Einstein. Far from being a remote professor uninformed about world events, Einstein was a pacifist, one who does not believe in participating in wars. From 1914 to 1918, Europe experienced the most destructive, deadly war fought to that date, World War I. Rather than springing to the defense of his nation, Einstein insisted that it was morally wrong to fight in an army, an attitude that won him widespread criticism at home in Germany.

Einstein was also a strong supporter of Zionism, the idea that Jews deserved their own country situated in Palestine, the land of the Bible. Zionism became a political movement among European Jews starting in the last two decades of the nineteenth century, partly in reaction to continuing religious discrimination.

Einstein the emigrant

In 1933, the National Socialist (Nazi) Party led by Adolf Hitler (1889–1945) won a majority in the German parliament, or legislature, after preaching intense hatred of Jews, whom the Nazis blamed for many of Germany's economic problems. At the time of the election, Einstein and his wife were visiting the United States, and Einstein declared that he would not return to Germany. The scientist was immediately welcomed by other scientists in the United States. Einstein had already agreed to spend part of the year at a newly organized Institute for Advanced Study in Princeton, New Jersey; he was then persuaded by Hitler's rise to power to work full–time at the institute. In the world of science, Einstein's presence added immediate status to the new institute and was a loss to German scientists.

Hitler, who a decade later launched the Holocaust, the mass murder of Jews and others he disapproved of, had based part of his political philosophy on the notion that Germans, as representatives of something he called the "Aryan" race, were superior to other peoples of the world and were therefore entitled to dominate others. In Hitler's views, Jews were distinctly inferior. Of course, in the world of science, the existence of Albert Einstein was living evidence of the inaccuracy of Hitler's racist theory.

During the 1930s, Einstein wrote not only about science but also about politics. He frequently criticized the policies of Hitler in Germany and urged Western nations like the United States to oppose those policies. In 1938, after a breakthrough in physics in Germany, Einstein wrote a letter to U.S. president Franklin D. Roosevelt (1882–1945; served 1933–45) urging government support for research into how to make a bomb using new discoveries about atoms. Einstein himself never participated in the research that resulted in the production of nuclear weapons, and he was shocked and horrified when the United States dropped two such bombs on Japan in August 1945 to end World War II (1939–45) in the Pacific.

In later years, Einstein wrote essays on the desirability of a single world government that would, in effect, do away with individual nations. Although Einstein was always able to attract attention simply on the strength of his name, most of his political ideas were largely ignored.

Although Einstein continued working in the field of physics, his most important works had all been published by 1920. Thereafter, he was a revered figure in science, and he used his position to try to influence politics. During the period of Nazi rule in Germany, Einstein was one of thousands of Jews who successfully fled the country to live elsewhere; an estimated eight million others were not so lucky: they perished in the Holocaust. Whether there were other Einsteins among them will never be known.

Einstein retired from teaching in 1945, although he continued work on his own. In 1952, Einstein turned down an offer to become the president of Israel. The scientist died in Princeton, New Jersey, in 1955 at the age of seventy-six.

—*James L. Outman*

For More Information

Books

Pais, Abraham. *Einstein Lived Here*. New York: Oxford University Press, 1994.

Parker, Barry R. *Einstein's Brainchild: Relativity Made Relatively Easy!* Amherst, NY: Prometheus Books, 2000.

Strathern, Paul. *Einstein and Relativity*. New York: Anchor Books/Doubleday, 1999.

Swisher, Clarice, ed. *Albert Einstein*. San Diego: Greenhaven Press, 2001.

Periodicals

Holton, Gerald. "The Migration of Physicists to the United States." *Bulletin of the Atomic Scientists* (April 1984): p. 18.

Oberbye, Dennis. "New Details Emerge from the Einstein Files; How the FBI Tracked His Phone Calls and His Trash." *New York Times* (May 7, 2002): p. D1 (Science Times).

Web Sites

"Einstein Revealed." *Nova*. http://www.pbs.org/wgbh/nova/einstein (accessed on March 12, 2004).

Lightman, Alan. "Relativity and the Cosmos." *Nova*. http://www.pbs.org/wgbh/nova/einstein/relativity/index.html (accessed on March 12, 2004).

Enrico Fermi

Born September 29, 1901
Rome, Italy

Died November 30, 1954
Chicago, Illinois

Nobel Prize–winning physicist

> "It is no good to try to stop knowledge from going forward. Ignorance is never better than knowledge."

Enrico Fermi. *Los Alamos National Laboratory.*

Enrico Fermi had a long and illustrious career as a physicist. By the age of twenty-five, he had won international recognition for devising a new statistical method for describing atomic particles. After winning the Nobel Prize for Physics in 1938, Fermi and his family immigrated to the United States to avoid growing political oppression in Italy. Immediately after his arrival in America, Fermi was swept up into what President Harry S. Truman (1884–1972) would later describe as "the battle of the laboratories." World War II (1939–45) was underway and scientists in Nazi Germany and the United States were racing to harness atomic power. Fermi was the first scientist to create an atomic chain reaction, which provided a new source of energy and made it possible to build the atom bomb.

Asking questions shows intelligence

Enrico Fermi was born in Rome, Italy, in 1901. His father, Alberto, was a government official with the Italian state railway system and later with the Ministry of Communication. His mother, Ida de Gattis, was a school teacher. Fermi had two siblings, a brother, Giulio, and sister, Maria. Giulio died when Enrico was fourteen, an event that was traumatic for Fermi. The boys had been very close. While grieving, Fermi went into a bookshop one day, bought two volumes on elementary physics, and read through them. Later, he told his sister Maria that he had not even noticed they were written in Latin. Fermi's frequent questions about sophisticated topics in mathematics caught the attention of Adolfo Amidei, a family friend, who guided Fermi's studies. Fermi was an extraordinary student in mathematics and physics. He graduated from secondary school a year early. At the age of twenty-one, Fermi earned a doctorate from the University of Pisa.

Fermi published several scientific papers by the time he graduated from college. He received a fellowship, or a special scholarship, to study in Germany for two years with famous physicists. Fermi knew how to speak German. Fermi already knew how to speak French and Italian, but Amidei had encouraged him to learn German because many advances were being made and written about by German physicists of the period.

Fermi returned to Italy in 1924 and became a professor at the University of Florence. He soon earned an international reputation for what became called Fermi-Dirac statistics. Both he and English physicist P. A. M. Dirac (1902–1984), working independently, were successful in using equations to describe the behavior of heated, subatomic particles. Physicists today use the term "fermions" to identify atomic particles obeying Fermi-Dirac statistics.

Fermi moved to the University of Rome in 1927 to become head of the school's first department of theoretical physics. (Unlike experimental physics, in which experiments can be conducted and results precisely measured, theoretical physics is based on applying theories to explain what cannot be seen, like atomic particles, or what cannot be tested, like the universe.) Fermi formed a group of scholars who worked together on experiments and theories. They published nearly one hundred scientific papers during Fermi's years in Rome, from 1927 to 1938.

In July 1928, Fermi married Laura Capon, the daughter of an Italian admiral. They would have two children.

Brilliance threatened

Fermi became increasingly interested in experimental research in the 1930s. He began focusing on the nucleus of atoms. Following the discovery of artificial radioactivity in 1934, he showed that radioactivity can be made to occur in almost every element. Radioactivity is the energy released when the nucleus of an atom breaks down. It happens naturally in some elements, but it was not until the 1930s that scientists learned how humans could create radioactivity. Fermi formulated a theory of beta decay that was extremely valuable in understanding how an atom functions and predicting how an atom reacts to different kinds of stimuli, like heat. Beta decay is a process through which a neutron in an atomic nucleus breaks apart into a proton and an electron.

While Fermi was making these advances in science, the political and social situation in Italy was becoming dangerous. The country was ruled by a dictator, Benito Mussolini (1883–1945), whose government was exerting control over every aspect of life in Italy and threatening other nations with war. Italy aligned with Germany, another nation that was threatening its neighbors. Germany was controlled by the National Socialist (Nazi) Party of Adolf Hitler (1889–1945). Like Nazi Germany, Italy began imposing laws against certain racial and ethnic groups.

The political situation in Italy affected Fermi's life in two ways: his work life and his family life. The work of scientists in Italy was being increasingly monitored and controlled by government officials. Outside the laboratory, Fermi's family was in danger because Fermi's wife, Laura, was Jewish, and therefore subject to increasingly discriminatory laws and threats from Mussolini's government. The Fermis knew they would have to leave Italy.

In 1938, Fermi was awarded the Nobel Prize in Physics. The prestigious award is given annually, and ceremonies are held in Stockholm, Sweden. The Fermi family traveled to Sweden, attended the ceremonies, and then boarded a ship to the United States. Fermi, who enjoyed using humor in his remarks, would later say that the move was made because he wanted to establish the American branch of the Fermi family.

The Manhattan Project

As Fermi began working in the physics department at Columbia University in New York in 1939, news broke that German physicists were finding success with nuclear fission, the ability to split the nucleus of an atom. Nuclear fission makes it possible to create a chain reaction (one split atom after another in high-speed sequence) that can release enormous amounts of energy. Fermi began working with colleagues at Columbia on experiments in the fission of uranium, a highly radioactive element.

Meanwhile, famous scientists, including **Albert Einstein** (1879–1955; see entry in volume 1), joined to write a letter to U.S. president Franklin D. Roosevelt (1882–1945; served 1933–45) on the importance of nuclear research, which could lead to the creation of a devastating new weapon. They warned that such research was already well underway in Nazi Germany and would pose a grave threat if expansion-minded Nazi Germany were to have such a weapon. In September 1939, Germany invaded Poland, which started World War II. In the United States, a top-secret study on nuclear fission, called the Manhattan Project, was established in 1941.

The surprise attack by Japanese airplanes on Pearl Harbor in Hawaii on December 7, 1941, brought the United States into World War II. Japan was an ally of Germany. Fermi was among several key physicists who were transferred to work at the University of Chicago in Illinois, where all efforts on the Manhattan Project were brought together. Secretly, the scientists worked in a specially constructed laboratory beneath athletic fields. Their job was to create nuclear fission.

On December 2, 1942, Fermi was the first scientist to be successful in creating an atomic chain reaction. This was key to releasing explosive energy and the building of an atom bomb—which would be the most powerful weapon ever created up to that time. A coded phrase was used to communicate to project and government officials, including President Roosevelt, that it was Fermi who created the first self-sustaining chain reaction controlled by humans. That now famous coded phrase read, "The Italian Navigator has landed in the New World."

For the next two years, Fermi conducted further research on nuclear fission at the Argonne National Laboratory

Describing Fermi

J. Robert Oppenheimer, the physicist who headed the Manhattan Project, wrote that Enrico Fermi was not a philosopher. He had, according to Oppenheimer, a "passion for clarity. He was simply unable to let things be foggy. Since they always are, this kept him pretty active."

outside of Chicago. On July 11, 1944, the Fermi family became naturalized citizens of the United States.

The battle of the laboratories

Fermi moved briefly to Hanford, Washington, where he assisted in the design and construction of a plant where plutonium, a radioactive chemical element, would be processed for use in atomic weapons. In September 1944, he joined a group of renowned scientists in Los Alamos, New Mexico, where the final assembly of the first nuclear weapons was to occur. Fermi was in charge of a division charged with solving special problems that arose during construction of the bomb.

The Manhattan Project was so secret that President Roosevelt's vice president, Harry S. Truman (1884–1972), was not informed about it. Truman learned that atomic bombs were being constructed only after he assumed the office of president, after Roosevelt died on April 12, 1945.

The first atomic bomb was detonated at a test site in Alamogordo, New Mexico, on July 16, 1945. Fermi was there, and as always his mind was busy. At the time of the explosion, he was conducting an experiment by dropping bits of paper to estimate the force of the blast. Although miles away from the explosion, he wanted to observe how the paper was affected by the bomb's explosive power. Instead of just falling to the ground—as they had before the blast—they moved backwards and landed behind him. Fermi was able to measure that distance and determine the amount of energy released.

Following the successful creation of the bomb, President Truman debated whether or not to use the powerful new weapon, of which only a few people were aware. Germany had already surrendered, but war between Japan and the United States was ongoing, with no clear end in sight. Truman's secretary of war, Henry Stimson (1867–1950), sought input from a group of scientists working at Los Alamos called the "Interim Committee" (An interim is the time between

A mushroom cloud rises over Nagasaki, Japan, after an atomic bomb was dropped on August 9, 1945.
© Bettmann/Corbis.

one action and another; in this case, the interim was the time between testing the bomb and using it for military purposes.) After deep soul-searching, Fermi and physicists Arthur H. Compton (1892–1962), J. Robert Oppenheimer (1904–1967), and Ernest O. Lawrence (1901–1958) concluded that a technical demonstration of the bomb was not likely to persuade Japan to end the war. The physicists found no acceptable alternative to military use as a way to demonstrate the power of the bomb.

Against the Hydrogren Bomb

Fermi helped unleash the power of atomic energy and assisted in the creation of the atom bomb. However, he was against creating an even more powerful weapon, the hydrogen bomb, a few years later. After a meeting in 1949 of the Atomic Energy Commission, on which he served on the advisory board, Fermi and fellow scientist Isidor Rabi (1898–1988) authored an opinion that was included in a report of the meeting. They stated: "It is clear that such a weapon cannot be justified on any ethical ground.... The fact that no limits exist to the destructiveness of this weapon makes its very existence and the knowledge of its construction a danger to humanity as a whole. It is necessarily an evil thing considered in any light." Nevertheless, the United States and the Soviet Union both developed the weapon and were successful testing it during the 1950s.

An atom bomb was dropped on Hiroshima, Japan, on the morning of August 6, 1945. Japanese strongholds in Manchuria, China, were invaded by the Soviet Union, an ally of the United States in World War II, on August 8. A second atom bomb was detonated over the Japanese city of Nagasaki on August 9, 1945. Following these devastating events, Japan announced its surrender on August 14, 1945, and the surrender became official on September 2, 1945.

Sixteen hours after the bombing of Hiroshima, President Truman made a radio speech to inform Americans about the explosion. He noted that Nazi Germany had been "working feverishly to find a way to add atomic energy to the other engines of war with which they hoped to enslave the world." Speaking of what scientists had accomplished in America by being first to harness atomic power, Truman stated, "The battle of the laboratories held fateful risks for us as well as the battles of the air, land and sea, and we have won the battle of the laboratories as we have won the other battles."

Many honors

After World War II ended, Fermi became a professor at the University of Chicago Institute for Nuclear Studies and served on the general advisory committee of the newly created Atomic Energy Commission. He was elected to the National Academy of Sciences in 1945.

Fermi remained in Chicago for most of the rest of his life. He was a popular lecturer and taught courses at the University of Michigan and Stanford University. In addition to receiving many honorary degrees from universities, Fermi was awarded the Civilian Medal of Merit (from the U.S. Congress) in 1946 for his work on the Manhattan Project and the Franklin Medal from the Franklin Institute (a distinguished science institute) in 1947.

Fermi had many accomplishments as a physicist. In his honor, physicists named a newly discovered element "fermium" and a form of nuclear measurement, the femtometer, was also referred to as a "fermi." He was elected president of the American Physical Society in 1953. When not involved in studies and experiments, Fermi enjoyed walks, mountain hikes, and winter sports.

Fermi began to experience health problems in 1954. Exploratory surgery showed that he had stomach cancer. He continued his research almost to the day he died, November 30, 1954. He was buried in Chicago. Shortly after his death, the Enrico Fermi Award was established by the U.S. Atomic Energy Commission, and Fermi was honored as the first recipient for his life's work.

—Roger Matuz

For More Information

Books

Cooper, Dan. "Enrico Fermi, and the Revolutions of Modern Physics." In *Oxford Portraits in Science*. Oxford: Oxford University Press, 1995.

Fermi, Laura. *Atoms in the Family: My Life with Enrico Fermi*. Chicago: University of Chicago Press, 1954.

Segrè, Emilio. *Enrico Fermi: Physicist*. Chicago: University of Chicago Press, 1970. Reprint, 1995.

Stux, Erica. *Enrico Fermi: Trailblazer in Nuclear Physics*. Berkeley Heights, NJ: Enslow, 2004.

Web Sites

American Experience: The Race for the Superbomb. http://www.pbs.org/wgbh/amex/bomb/index.html (accessed on March 12, 2004).

Rhodes, Richard. *The Time 100: The Most Important People of the Century*. http://www.time.com/time/time100/scientist/profile/fermi03.html (accessed on March 12, 2004).

Millard Fillmore

Born January 7, 1800
Cayuga County, New York

Died March 8, 1874
Buffalo, New York

Thirteenth U.S. president and candidate of the anti-immigrant Know-Nothing Party

"May God save the country, for it is evident that the people will not."

Millard Fillmore became president unexpectedly in 1850 upon the sudden death from a stomach ailment of President Zachary Taylor (1785–1850; served 1849–50). As a conservative politician from New York, Fillmore shared in widespread prejudice against immigration that arose after a large influx of German and Irish immigrants during the 1840s. Some of the anti-immigrant prejudice reflected the fact that Irish immigrants in particular were overwhelmingly Catholics, which aroused long-standing religious prejudices by many American Protestants. In 1856, four years after losing the Whig nomination as the incumbent, or current, president, Fillmore was nominated for president by the anti-immigrant American Party (popularly known as the Know-Nothing Party). But in the election in November, he won a majority of votes in just one state, Maryland. Ironically, Maryland was originally founded in the early 1600s as an English colony where Catholics would be safe to practice their religion.

Millard Fillmore was born in Cayuga County, New York, on January 7, 1800. Fillmore's early life had been guided

Millard Fillmore. © *Corbis.*

by good luck. The son of a poor farmer, Fillmore at age fourteen became an apprentice to a clothing maker. His teacher, Abigail Powers (1798–1853), whom he later married, persuaded him to aim higher, and a friendly county judge helped supervise his study of the law. In the 1820s, Fillmore helped organize a new political party, the Anti-Mason Party, which opposed the supposed political influence of the Masonic Lodge, a secret social organization whose members had included, among others, President George Washington (1732–1799; served 1789–97). (A political party is a group of people with similar ideas and goals who work together to elect like-minded individuals to public office.) At age twenty-eight, Fillmore was elected to the New York state legislature, where he served for three years.

The Anti-Masonic Party never attracted widespread support and soon dissolved. Most of its members, like Fillmore, joined the Whig Party instead. The Whigs were in favor of government policies that helped business owners and promoted the westward expansion of the United States during an era when the "frontier" was still in western Missouri. In 1832, Fillmore was elected to the U.S. House of Representatives from his home district in New York; he served for two years, decided not to run for reelection, then ran again and was elected a representative for three terms in a row. In 1844, he ran unsuccessfully for governor of New York. In 1846, he was elected comptroller (the official in charge of paying government bills) of New York, and was then elected vice president in the election of 1848. Fifteen months later, after President Taylor's death, Fillmore became president.

Social changes in the 1840s

During the 1840s, American society had been undergoing significant changes as a result of immigration, the first such changes since independence from Britain. Until the mid-1830s, most immigrants to the United States came from England or Scotland, which was also the ancestral home of the majority of people already living in the United States (except for African American slaves and a relatively small number of people living in the Hudson River valley of New York, whose ancestors had come from Holland). These English Americans were both white and Protestants, either members of the Church of England (the Episcopal Church in the United States) or members of other denominations such as Presbyterians and Baptists. (Protestants traced their religious ancestry to the movement in Europe during the 1500s called the Reformation, which challenged the supremacy of the pope as head of the Catholic Church.)

Beginning with the flow of German immigrants in the 1840s, more Catholics began immigrating to the United States. The early trickle became a flood in the late 1840s, when the Irish potato crop, a major source of food, was hit by a blight, or plant disease. The failure of the potato crop resulted in widespread starvation and forced desperate Irish farmers to leave the country for the United States. Almost 3 million immigrants, including 1.2 million Irish and over 1 million Germans, came to the United States between 1845 and 1859, an average of about 200,000 per year. The flood of newcomers was unlike anything the United States had experienced before; in the previous three decades, the annual number of immigrants ranged from 10,000 to 100,000. The poor immigrants shocked some residents of cities like Boston, Massachusetts, with public drunkenness and fighting, or gang warfare, while living in poor slums that bred disease. Cities of the era did not have modern sanitation facilities; hogs, or even rats, in the streets were the preferred method of garbage disposal.

The sudden arrival of large numbers of Catholics worried some American Protestants, who feared that Catholics might owe their loyalties to the pope, as head of the Catholic church, instead of the government in Washington, D.C. Although the U.S. Constitution guaranteed freedom of religion and barred declaration of an "official" religion (as had been the case in most European countries), not all states had taken the same position until well into the 1800s. In Massachusetts, for example, taxes supported the Protestant church until 1833; as late as 1877, the constitution of New Hampshire contained a clause disqualifying Catholics from holding public office. Popular sentiment against Catholics had resulted in riots and attacks against churches. In Philadelphia, Pennsylvania, the Catholic bishop ordered that Sunday services not be held on May 14, 1844, for fear of further violence after mobs had attacked several Catholic churches, burning two of them to the ground.

In the mid-1840s, several secret societies sprang up to oppose both immigration and Catholics. The largest of these organizations were the Order of United Americans and the

Order of the Star-Spangled Banner. Their goals were to preserve the United States as a predominantly Protestant country by restricting immigration and preventing immigrants (by which they meant Catholics) from becoming citizens for twenty-one years after they arrived. Conducted in secrecy, the organizations instructed their members to respond to inquiries by replying, "I know nothing." Members thus came to be called "Know Nothings," although there was never an organization with that formal name.

The swelling of immigration after 1845 was not the only change in American society during the 1840s. Prices were rising rapidly, due in large part to the introduction of gold discovered in California in 1848. (More gold in the U.S. economy meant, in effect, that there was more money to spend on goods. The amount of money in circulation increased faster than the amount of goods, resulting in "inflation," a rapid increase in prices.) Industrial enterprises continued to expand, resulting in rapid growth of cities in a country that had been predominantly rural. And the issue of slavery continued to divide the southern states, where it was legal, from the northern states, where it was not. Abolitionists, or people against slavery, in the north pressed for outlawing slavery; southerners, who feared their agricultural economies based on cotton picked by slaves might be ruined if slavery were abolished, strongly resisted.

Fillmore, the accidental president

Fillmore, thrust into the White House in 1850, was immediately confronted with a crisis over the issue of slavery. California had asked to enter the union, threatening to upset the balance of free states and slave states that had been preserved, overall, for thirty years. A bitter debate raged over California's request. Fillmore was more on the side of the south, whereas President Taylor, himself a southerner, had been more firmly on the antislavery side of the debate. Finally, U.S. senator Henry Clay (1777–1852) of Kentucky promised a compromise: California would be admitted as a free state, but the Fugitive Slave Act would make it possible, anywhere in the United States, to recapture slaves who escaped to free states. The large slave market in Washington, D.C., would be abolished, but slavery would still be allowed in the nation's

capital. In addition, Texas, a slave state, would give up its claims to territory reaching all the way to Santa Fe (which later became the capital of New Mexico) in exchange for ten million dollars from the U.S. government to pay the state's debts from its war for independence from Mexico. In effect, Texas was opening the possibility that the territory it gave up could become free states sometime in the future.

When debate over the compromise of 1850 began, Fillmore was still vice president, presiding over the U.S. Senate. While he was in the Senate on the evening of July 8, 1850, Fillmore learned that Taylor had fallen gravely ill in the White House; the next morning, Taylor was dead and Fillmore became president in the midst of the emotional debate. He made no secret of his support for a compromise solution that would avoid a crisis.

A campaign banner for the 1848 Whig Party ticket of Zachary Taylor and Millard Fillmore. *Lithograph with watercolor by Nathaniel Currier. Library of Congress.*

Passage of the Compromise of 1850 with the support of Fillmore made the president popular, but only temporarily. Soon, Southerners regretted the concessions, or points given up in an argument for the sake of reaching an agreement, that they had made, and Northerners grew to hate the Fugitive Slave Act. Fillmore's support evaporated, and in 1852, the Whig Party refused to nominate him as its candidate, turning instead to former Army general Winfield Scott (1786–1866). In the election, the Democratic Party's candidate, Franklin Pierce (1804–1869; served 1853–57) of New Hampshire, won, and Scott came in a distant second. After leaving the White House, Fillmore went home to Buffalo, New York.

Two years later, in 1854, Fillmore reappeared on the political stage in New York, still as a leader of the Whigs and now supported by Know Nothings. The Know Nothings nearly captured control of the legislature in New York, and did capture the state governments of Massachusetts and Delaware, with more limited success in other states. Their campaign was

THE GRAND NATIONAL FIGHT 2 AGAINST 1 FOUGHT ON THE 6TH NOV.1856

presented as an effort to preserve the white, Protestant character of the United States in the face of unregulated immigration by Catholics from Ireland, especially. The campaign was also an effort to draw attention from the issue of slavery.

As the Whig Party continued to disintegrate, badly divided over the issue of slavery, the Know-Nothing movement in 1854 hoped to form a new party and capture the White House in the next presidential election in 1856. The new party, called the American Party, was organized around the anti-immigrant, anti-Catholic principles of the secret societies formed ten years earlier. (The American Party is sometimes referred to as the Know-Nothing Party, but it was never formally known by that name.) Part of the strategy of the party was to focus attention away from the divisive slavery issue, which had destroyed the Whig Party, and onto the twin issues of immigration and religion. But in 1855, at an American Party meeting in Philadelphia, a group of Southerners gained control of the meeting and passed a resolution supporting slav-

A cartoon from the 1856 presidential election shows Millard Fillmore knocked to the ground in a fight with Democratic candidate James Buchanan (left center) and Republican candidate John C. Frémont (right center). *Library of Congress.*

ery, putting the new party in the same position as the fading Whigs. Many Know Nothings from the North did not support slavery, and the next year, when Fillmore was nominated as the presidential candidate of the American Party in the 1856 election, he had no chance of winning.

Although the American Party accounted for 21 percent of the total popular vote in the 1856 election, the party won a majority in only one state, Maryland, with eight electoral votes. The winner of the election was James Buchanan (1791–1868; served 1857–61), who won 45 percent of the popular vote and 174 electoral votes. (In presidential elections, candidates are technically elected by the Electoral College, in which each state has as many votes as the total number of senators and U.S. representatives from that state. Popular votes determine which candidate will receive the electoral votes from each state; usually, but not always, the candidate who wins the most popular votes in a state receives all of that state's electoral-college votes.)

After his overwhelming loss, Fillmore retired to Buffalo and the American Party disappeared. In the next presidential election, the Republican Party swept to power with Abraham Lincoln (1809–1865; served 1861–65) as its candidate. Afraid that the Republicans would move to ban slavery, eleven southern states seceded, or separated, from the United States and formed the Confederacy, leading to the outbreak of the Civil War (1861–65).

During and after the Civil War, Fillmore continued to take what he regarded as a moderate view. After the Union victory over the South, Fillmore supported efforts by President Andrew Johnson (1808–1875; served 1865–69) to moderate the policies of Reconstruction, the policy of punishing the South for the Civil War and aggressively promoting freedom for freed African American slaves.

Fillmore continued to live in Buffalo and never returned to the national political stage. He died in 1874.

—*James L. Outman*

For More Information

Books

Anbinder, Tyler G. *Nativism and Slavery: The Northern Know Nothings and the Politics of the 1850s.* New York: Oxford University Press, 1992.

Grayson, Benson Lee. *The Unknown President: The Administration of President Millard Fillmore.* Lanham, MD: University Press of America, 1981.

Scarry, Robert J. *Millard Fillmore.* Jefferson, NC: McFarland and Company, 2001.

Smith, Elbert B. *The Presidencies of Zachary Taylor and Millard Fillmore.* Lawrence: University Press of Kansas, 1988.

Periodicals

Holland, Barbara. "Millard Fillmore Was My Kind of Guy." *Smithsonian* (October 1989): p. 238.

Wernick, Robert. "The Rise, and Fall, of a Fervid Third Party." *Smithsonian* (November 1996): p. 150.

Web Sites

Holt, Michael F. "Getting the Message Out! National Political Campaign Materials, 1840–1860: The Know Nothing Party." *Abraham Lincoln Historical Digitization Project.* http://dig.lib.niu.edu/message/ ps-knownothing.html (accessed on March 12, 2004).

"Knownothingism." *New Advent.* http://www.newadvent.org/cathen/ 08677a.htm (accessed on March 12, 2004).

"Millard Fillmore." *The White House.* http://www.whitehouse.gov/history/ presidents/mf13.html (accessed on March 12, 2004).

Felix Frankfurter

**Born November 15, 1882
Vienna, Austria**

**Died February 22, 1965
Washington, D.C.**

**U.S. Supreme Court justice, legal scholar,
and defender of civil rights**

"It was a wise man who
said that there is no
greater inequality than
the equal treatment of
unequals."

Felix Frankfurter. *Supreme
Court of the United States.*

Felix Frankfurter came to the United States in 1894 at the age
of twelve, not speaking English but possessed with a lively
imagination. He was part of a great wave of immigrants to the
United States at the end of the nineteenth century. Within
forty years of arrival, he had become a top advisor to the president and was appointed to the U.S. Supreme Court, a living
testament to the promise of opportunity in the United States.

The immigrant on the Lower East Side

Felix Frankfurter was born in Vienna, Austria, on November 15, 1882. His father, Leopold, lived in Vienna, capital
of the immense Austro-Hungarian empire that ruled central
Europe. The Frankfurters were Jewish; Leopold had intended
to become a rabbi but later decided to enter business. His
business did not do well, however, and in 1894 he decided to
bring his family to New York, along with hundreds of thousands of European Jews seeking new opportunities and an escape from ever-present hatred toward their religion throughout Europe.

In New York, the Frankfurters lived on the Lower East Side, a neighborhood of Manhattan largely populated by Jewish immigrants. Young Felix was enrolled in Public School 25, speaking only German, until a teacher, remembered only as Miss Hogan, lay down the law: no speaking in German! Frankfurter learned English quickly, and by 1902, he had graduated from the City College of New York in a combined high school–college program.

From Lower East Side to Harvard

From the Lower East Side, Frankfurter moved to the opposite end of the social and economic spectrum: Harvard Law School. There, the Austrian immigrant who had not spoken English just ten years earlier, was first in his class for three years.

Henry L. Stimson. *Library of Congress.*

Frankfurter had a reputation as a young man of boundless energy and curiosity and with a love for language and the law. After graduating first in his class from Harvard, he was offered a job with Hornblower, Byrne, Miller and Potter, a leading New York City law firm which, by reputation, had never hired a Jewish lawyer before Frankfurter. Frankfurter's religion has been a matter of dispute. Without doubt, his father was Jewish, having considered being a rabbi, but Felix Frankfurter did not practice his religion. Nevertheless, he was a strong supporter of Zionism, the movement launched in the late nineteenth century to establish a country in the Middle East just for Jews. For Frankfurter, religion was more a matter of social ties than of day-to-day religious practice.

Frankfurter did not remain long at Hornblower, Byrne, Miller and Potter. He was offered a job working for Henry L. Stimson (1867–1950), the U.S. district attorney (federal prosecutor) in New York. Frankfurter accepted a 25 percent pay cut to take the job.

The association with Stimson was an important turning point in Frankfurter's life. His new boss, who had been appointed to his position as U.S. attorney by President Theodore Roosevelt (1858–1919; served 1901–9), was prominent in the Republican Party. Initially, Frankfurter handled cases involving antitrust laws (laws barring large companies from having too much influence over their industry) and immigration, an important topic when the flood of immigrants from southern and eastern Europe was still enormous.

Man about town in Washington, D.C.

In 1910, Stimson resigned his position to run for governor of New York. Frankfurter managed his campaign. After Stimson lost the election, he moved to Washington, where President William Howard Taft (1857–1930; served 1909–13) appointed Stimson his secretary of war. Frankfurter followed Stimson to the nation's capital and was given a title of law officer in the Bureau of Insular Affairs, dealing with legal issues involving the War Department and America's possessions overseas. In reality, though, Frankfurter served as an advisor and assistant to Stimson.

It was an exciting time for Frankfurter. Thanks to introductions by a Harvard Law School professor, Frankfurter became friends with U.S. Supreme Court justice Oliver Wendell Holmes Jr. (1841–1935) and future justice Louis Brandeis (1856–1941).

In 1912, Democrat Woodrow Wilson (1856–1924; served 1913–21) was elected president; as a result, Stimson left the government to be replaced by Wilson's choice. But Frankfurter stayed in the department, although his duties did not hold his interest. The Wilson administration was a period of intellectual excitement for Frankfurter. He was one of the first contributing editors to a new magazine, *The New Republic*. The magazine was founded in 1914 as a journal of liberal political opinion during a decade in which the United States faced the dual challenges of social changes brought about by the rise of the industrial economy (economic activity dominated by factories, as opposed to farming), immigration, and a new role for the United States as a world power. Frankfurter was an energetic and active participant in debates about what the future of government policy should be with liberal journalists such as Herbert Croly (1869–1930) and Walter Lippmann (1889–1974), the cofounders of *The New Republic*.

Back to Harvard

It was thus somewhat surprising in 1914 when Frankfurter accepted an offer to become a law professor at Harvard. To some of his friends in Washington, it appeared that Frankfurter was giving up participation in public affairs for an academic life that would be remote and separated from the intense political and policy debates that Frankfurter loved. He proved his friends wrong.

At Harvard, Frankfurter introduced a new approach to teaching law. Instead of limiting courses to reviewing past judicial decisions, as a means of understanding what the law was and how it had been interpreted, Frankfurter included the arguments of lawyers in important cases, the biographies of the judges, and an understanding of how laws were written in Congress and administered by the executive branch. (The executive branch of the federal government is centered on the president and includes the various departments under the president.) As a close friend of Justice Holmes and, later, Justice Brandeis (appointed to the Supreme Court in 1916), Frankfurter recommended top Harvard Law students to be law clerks, or research assistants, to the two justices.

Frankfurter's academic career was interrupted when the United States entered World War I (1914–18) in 1917. He joined the U.S. Army's legal department (called the Judge Advocate General's Corps) and became a member of the president's Mediation Commission, appointed to try to settle labor disputes that might affect the country's war effort. He investigated the forcible removal of one thousand striking copper miners from Arizona to a deserted town in New Mexico and found that the action was unjustified, but he also found that an impartial system was needed to act as a go-between during labor grievances.

As part of the Mediation Commission, Frankfurter was ordered by President Wilson to investigate an incident in San Francisco in 1916, in which a bomb had exploded in a parade marking "Preparedness Day" in anticipation of the

U.S. involvement in World War I. Two radical (in favor of extreme change) labor leaders were convicted of the bombing, but Frankfurter concluded that the public atmosphere in the case had made a fair trial difficult or impossible. Frankfurter was named chairman of the War Labor Policies Board, which tried to settle disputes between companies and workers in order to avoid disrupting the manufacture of supplies needed by the U.S. Army fighting in Europe.

Back at Harvard in 1919, Frankfurter married Marion Denman and resumed his teaching.

Reputation as a radical

Frankfurter continued to be active in affairs outside the university. In 1920, he was among the founders of the American Civil Liberties Union (ACLU), an organization dedicated to protecting the rights of individuals, especially the rights granted under the Constitution's first ten amendments (the Bill of Rights) against government interference.

The early 1920s were a confused time in the United States, especially after communists in Russia established a new government in November 1917. Afraid that communists could start a revolution in the United States, the federal government tried to crack down on activities and speech of which the Republican administrations of Republican presidents Warren G. Harding (1865–1923; served 1921–23) and Calvin Coolidge (1872–1933; served 1923–29) did not approve. According to the ACLU's official history of the organization, "[political] activists were thrown into jail for distributing anti-war literature. Foreign-born people suspected of political radicalism were subject to deportation [made to leave the country]. Racial segregation was the law of the land and violence against African Americans was routine. Moreover, the U.S. Supreme Court had yet to uphold a single free speech claim under the First Amendment." Frankfurter actively defended people arrested by federal agents on suspicion of being communists or otherwise politically dangerous. A federal judge in Boston appointed Frankfurter to help defend immigrants who had been arrested and ordered out of the country, solely on suspicion of their political beliefs.

Perhaps the biggest case in the 1920s involving immigrants and political beliefs was the murder trial of two Italian

immigrants, Nicola Sacco (1891–1927) and Bartolomeo Vanzetti (1888–1927). They were convicted of murdering a Brinks armored-car guard during a robbery in 1920 in Braintree, Massachusetts, near Boston. During their murder trial, the political philosophy of the two men played a prominent role. Both were anarchists, who believed that organized government should be replaced by voluntary associations. They were convicted and sentenced to death. In 1927, while the men awaited execution, Frankfurter closely examined their trial and published an article in the *Atlantic Monthly* magazine that was highly critical of their trial. Frankfurter's focus was on the way the trial had been carried out; he concluded that the procedures, including the introduction of the defendants' political beliefs, had violated their rights. His article attracted widespread attention but did not save the lives of Sacco and Vanzetti, who were executed in 1927.

During the first six years of the administration of President Franklin D. Roosevelt (1882–1945; served 1933–45),

Italian immigrants Nicola Sacco and Bartolomeo Vanzetti. *© Bettmann/Corbis.*

The U.S. Supreme Court, on May 24, 1955: (left to right, seated) Felix Frankfurter, Hugo L. Black, Earl Warren, Stanley F. Reed, and William O. Douglas; (standing) Sherman Minton, Harold H. Burton, Tom C. Clark, and John Marshall Harlan.
© Bettmann/Corbis.

Frankfurter served as an informal advisor to the president. He was influential in forming many programs devised by Roosevelt to combat the Great Depression (1929–41; a period, following a stock market crash in 1929, of depressed world economies and high unemployment), and was the author of the Securities Act of 1933, regulating trading stocks and bonds.

A justice in the making

In 1932, Frankfurter was nominated to serve on the Supreme Judicial Court of Massachusetts, but he turned down the nomination. He also told newly elected president Roosevelt that he did not want to be named solicitor general, who normally argues cases for the federal government before the Supreme Court. Frankfurter instead spent a year from 1933 to 1934 teaching at Oxford University in England.

In January 1939, Roosevelt appointed Frankfurter to the U.S. Supreme Court; he was unanimously confirmed by the

Senate twelve days later and joined his friends Justices Holmes and Brandeis. (The U.S. Constitution requires that when a president nominates someone to become a justice of the Supreme Court, the Senate must vote to approve the nomination before the nomination takes effect; this process is called confirmation.). As a member of the Supreme Court, Frankfurter surprised many observers, who expected that the defender of Sacco and Vanzetti would be an enthusiastic supporter of Roosevelt's proposals for an expanded role of government.

As a justice, Frankfurter was guided by a philosophy called "judicial restraint," which held that judges should be careful not to overrule or conflict with the decisions of the two elected branches of government, Congress and the president. Rather than turning out as a "radical" justice as some thought likely, Frankfurter was a relatively conservative force on the Supreme Court during the period he served (1939–62).

Frankfurter's positions were not really new to him. As early as 1912, he had told a former roommate at Harvard Law School that "precedents [previous legal decisions], not underlying philosophic principles, form our legal habit of thought." On the Supreme Court, Frankfurter felt compelled to observe earlier decisions as his guide on how to proceed with cases that came before him.

Frankfurter retired from the Supreme Court in 1962 following a heart attack and a stroke. He died three years later in Washington, D.C.

—*James L. Outman*

For More Information

Books

Baker, Leonard. *Brandeis and Frankfurter: A Dual Biography*. New York: Harper and Row, 1984.

Cushman, Clare, ed. *The Supreme Court Justices: Illustrated Biographies, 1789–1993*. Washington: Congressional Quarterly, 1993.

Hirsch, H. N. *The Enigma of Felix Frankfurter*. New York: Basic Books, 1981.

Parris, Michael E. *Felix Frankfurter and His Times*. New York: Free Press, 1982.

Urofsky, Melvin I. *Felix Frankfurter: Judicial Restraint and Individual Liberties*. Boston: Twayne, 1991.

Periodicals

Bryer, Stephen J. "Zion's Justice." *The New Republic* (October 5, 1998): p. 18.

Lacayo, Richard. "A Judge's Breach of Confidence: Did Felix Frankfurter Go Too Far to Secure a Famous Victory?" *Time* (April 6, 1987): p. 71.

Web Sites

Frankfurter, Felix. "The Case of Sacco and Vanzetti." *The Atlantic* (March 1927). http://www.theatlantic.com/unbound/flashbks/oj/frankff.htm (accessed on March 14, 2004).

Marcus Garvey

Born August 17, 1887
St. Anns Bay, Jamaica

Died June 10, 1940
London, England

Leader of the Universal Negro Improvement Association, which preached black pride and advocated a return to Africa

M arcus Garvey burst onto the African American scene in March 1916. He had come to Harlem, a black neighborhood in northern Manhattan in New York City, to seek financial support for a school he was trying to establish in his homeland, Jamaica, an island in the Caribbean. He soon went on to promote a mass return to Africa by the descendants of black slaves. Garvey was one of the first effective promoters of black pride, emphasizing the historical dignity of black people.

Marcus Garvey addressed a central issue in American society: the failure, after three hundred years, to include descendants of Africans in a society that prided itself as a "melting pot." (The term "melting pot" refers to a process in which the habits and characteristics of immigrants from many different countries merge together and become a new nationality.) Arriving in New York just after World War I (1914–18), Garvey offered a range of solutions to what he saw as an absence in African Americans of the ancestral pride exhibited by European Americans. The Jamaica-born Garvey was viewed with alarm and suspicion by federal officials in an era when advocates of radical solutions were often turned out of the country.

"I saw before me then, even as I do now, a new world of black men, not peons, serfs, dogs and slaves, but a nation of sturdy men making their impression upon civilization and causing a new light to dawn upon the human race."

Marcus Garvey.

Garvey was not the first person to advocate that African Americans return to their ancestral continent, from which their forefathers had been kidnapped into a life of slavery in both the United States and in the islands of the Caribbean. Similar ideas were floated more than a century earlier by both blacks and whites who doubted that slaves or former slaves would ever achieve justice in the United States. Garvey renewed the idea with a strong sense of drama. He created a large international movement called the Universal Negro Improvement Association for descendants of exiled Africans everywhere.

Out of Jamaica

Marcus Mozaih Garvey Jr. was born in a small town on the island of Jamaica, one of the largest English possessions in the Caribbean. Long after the North American colonies gained their independence from England and formed the United States, the island of Jamaica remained a British possession. Garvey was the son of Marcus Garvey Sr., a stone mason who earned a living cutting large stones from the ground to use in buildings, and his wife Sarah. The senior Garvey was poor—he sometimes had to grow crops to sell for extra money—but he loved to read and kept a small library at home.

Young Marcus dropped out of school after elementary school to serve as an assistant in a printing shop owned by a family friend in Kingston, the island's largest city. From there, Garvey launched a career that would see him engage in publishing newspapers and books and eventually lead him to organize a social movement that spanned several continents and included tens of thousands of followers. Garvey did not stay put in Kingston for long.

In 1910, at the age of twenty-three, Garvey left Jamaica for Costa Rica, in Central America, one of many Jamaicans who hoped to find better opportunities in Central America. During the next few years, Garvey moved around Central and South America, and then moved to England. Everywhere he went, Garvey observed a similar pattern: black people were the subjects of discrimination, treated as inferiors and unable to participate in the political and social life of whatever country in which they lived. The color of their skin made Africans instantly visible and different in appearance from their neighbors.

In England, Garvey did not prosper and was virtually penniless by 1914. He had, however, read *Up From Slavery* by Booker T. Washington (1856–1915). Washington had been born a slave in Virginia and eventually became the leader of the Tuskegee Institute in Tuskegee, Alabama, a school for freed slaves after the American Civil War (1861–65). Washington preached a philosophy of self-reliance, urging former slaves to learn skills needed to succeed in farming. Only by becoming economically self-sufficient, Washington thought, could former slaves hope to achieve political equality with whites. It was a message that Garvey adopted as his own philosophy, in his unique way.

United Negro Improvement Association

In 1914, Garvey returned to Jamaica and founded the United Negro Improvement Association (UNIA). Garvey had no money to build a large organization; the UNIA began as little more than a dream of Garvey's to unite descendants of Africans who were scattered throughout Europe and the Western Hemisphere into a single organization.

Garvey exchanged letters with Washington while organizing educational facilities in Jamaica on the model of Washington's work at Tuskegee, Alabama. The theme of UNIA was what Garvey called "cofraternity"—a global association of people with African ancestors.

In March 1916, Garvey traveled to New York, intending to stay for just five months while raising funds for his activities in Jamaica by making speeches. In fact, he stayed in the United States for eleven years, moving the UNIA to the United States, which had a much larger black population and offered Garvey a wider stage. After a brief tour of the United States and Canada, Garvey set up his new headquarters in Harlem, the center of black cultural life in New York City. There, the colorful Garvey delivered speeches on street corners, and rented a room to hold indoor meetings once a week.

Garvey's message became popular with many African Americans, and UNIA grew rapidly throughout the United

A handbill from 1917 advertising a Marcus Garvey speech. © David J. & Janice L. Frent Collection/Corbis.

BIG MASS MEETING

A CALL TO THE
COLORED CITIZENS

OF

ATLANTA, GEORGIA

To Hear the Great West Indian Negro Leader

HON. MARCUS GARVEY

President of the Universal Negro Improvement Association
of Jamaica, West Indies.

Big Bethel A. M. E. Church

Corner Auburn Avenue and Butler Street

SUNDAY AFTERNOON, AT 3 O'CLOCK
MARCH 25, 1917

He brings a message of inspiration to the
12,000,000 of our people in this country.

SUBJECT:

"The Negroes of the West Indies, after 78 years of Emancipation." With a general talk on the world position of the race.

An orator of exceptional force, Professor Garvey has spoken to packed audiences in England, New York, Boston, Washington, Philadelphia, Chicago, Milwaukee, St. Louis, Detroit, Cleveland, Cincinatti, Indianapolis, Louisville, Nashville and other cities. He has travelled to the principal countries of Europe, and was the first Negro to speak to the Veterans' Club of London, England.

This is the only chance to hear a great man who has taken his message before the world. **COME OUT EARLY TO SECURE SEATS.** It is worth travelling 1,000 miles to hear.

All Invited. Rev. R. H. Singleton, D.D., Pastor.

States, and internationally, in Canada, the Caribbean, Central and South America, England, and West Africa. To promote his cause, Garvey founded a newspaper, *The Negro World*, which circulated internationally. In its pages, Garvey preached his message of economic independence for black people everywhere. Eventually, Garvey thought, black people should return to Africa, to build a unified nation where European colonies had been established in the nineteenth century. In the short run, Garvey encouraged black people to start their own businesses in order to establish economic independence from Europeans.

The Black Star shipping line

Garvey took his own advice. In 1924, he organized what he called the African Orthodox Church, featuring figures of Jesus Christ and Mary as black people. Garvey firmly believed that religion was an important factor in the way people see the world, and that religion should reflect racial pride for descendants of Africans.

Continuing to preach the importance of economic independence for blacks, in 1918 Garvey organized the Negro Factories Corporation. The corporation operated a variety of enterprises: a doll factory, grocery stores, restaurants, and a tailoring company. Eventually the company employed more than a thousand African Americans.

A year later, in 1919, Garvey also organized another company, the Black Star Line. His plan was to acquire passenger ships that would offer passage from the Western Hemisphere (North and South America) to Africa, and allow blacks within the Western Hemisphere to work and travel on ships owned by fellow Africans. It was a grand scheme—Garvey raised over a million dollars, mostly in small amounts from individuals—but it eventually led to Garvey's downfall.

In the meantime, however, the Black Star Line captured the imagination of black people throughout the hemisphere. When a Black Star ship sailed into port in Costa Rica, African workers took a day off and brought flowers and fruit to the ship. In Havana, Cuba there was a similar response, with people rowing out to the ship from shore. A group of African Americans in South Carolina chartered a train to carry them to the port of Charleston, just to see a Black Star ship.

In the meantime, Garvey's ideas were spreading rapidly. He organized an international convention, the first of several, in 1920, which adopted a document titled the "Declaration of Rights of the Negro People of the World." It was a concise statement of Garvey's philosophy of black pride and unity, and the desirability of eventually immigrating to Africa. UNIA adopted as its colors the colors of the flag of

Ethiopia—red, black, and green—and adapted the Universal Ethiopian Anthem as its official song. A combination of paid professionals and volunteers were sent to African communities worldwide to spread the word of UNIA and Garvey.

Garvey's ideas were not the only ones being preached in 1920. Three years earlier, Russian communists had overthrown the czar, or king, of Russia and declared the Bolshevik Revolution (1917) in the name of communism, a political philosophy under which the government owned the land and factories. In the United States, the government was deeply concerned that new ideas, which it regarded as extreme, would take root and challenge the political and economic system. The U.S. attorney general arrested hundreds of "reds" (the term for communists) and, in the case of immigrants, sought to deport them.

Although Garvey was not a communist, he was regarded as another potentially dangerous voice. The government sought a way to get rid of Garvey's influence without sparking widespread sympathy for him. The Black Star Line proved to be the answer.

Garvey and financial fraud

In order to raise money to buy his first ship, Garvey sold shares in the company, chiefly by promoting it through his newspaper and speeches. He wanted the entire company to be financed by small investments from African Americans to further his goal of black economic self-sufficiency. Garvey was not, however, an experienced businessman, nor was he experienced in the business of selling stock to the public, an activity regulated by the federal government. He did not have trouble attracting investments—thousands of African Americans bought shares in the company, usually in small amounts—but this process provided the federal government with an opportunity to attack Garvey's political and social ideas by attacking his business practices.

The government was not the only group opposed to Garvey. Communists opposed him because he preached loyalty to race rather than to the working class. Some African American civil rights leaders, such as W. E. B. Du Bois (1868–1963), leader of the National Association for the Advancement of Colored People, opposed Garvey on the grounds that achieving racial integration and equality in the United States was a better solution to the problems of African Americans.

Consequently, Garvey had few organized supporters in 1923 when the federal government accused him of mail fraud, or cheating, on investors in the Black Star Line. (Federal law prohibits conducting fraudulent, or dishonest, business using the U.S. mail.) Prosecutors charged that he had sold stock in the Black Star Line, even after realizing the company was bankrupt, or without funds. Garvey was convicted and sentenced to five years in prison in 1925. Two years later, President Calvin Coolidge (1872–1933; served 1923–29) shortened Garvey's prison term, on the condition that Garvey leave the country.

Garvey returned to Jamaica to try to reestablish the UNIA and to run for local political office. In the United States, however, his followers split into competing factions. One group was loyal to Garvey as their leader; another group selected other African Americans to run the organization in the United States. The UNIA also inspired some members to set up their own organizations, including the Nation of Islam, whose founder, Elijah Muhammad (1897–1975), became a major force among African Americans in the 1950s and 1960s.

In Jamaica, Garvey organized the People's Political Party in an effort to give blacks representation in Jamaica's government. One of the goals of Garvey and his party was to reform the judicial system, which the courts decreed was contempt, a ruling that led to Garvey's imprisonment once again. Garvey won election to a local office but lost his seat because, as a prisoner, he could not attend any meetings. Upon his release from prison, he won back his seat. Meanwhile, when the seventh UNIA Convention recommended moving its headquarters to England, Garvey agreed. He and his family moved there in 1935. After suffering a series of strokes, he died in 1940.

Impact of Marcus Garvey

Marcus Garvey was not the first person to advocate a reverse migration by black people to the continent where many of their ancestors had been kidnapped and held in slavery throughout the Western Hemisphere. He was, however, one of the most influential proponents, or promoters, of the back-to-Africa movement in the twentieth century. Earlier African American proponents, such as Paul Cuffe (1759–1817), a black sea captain and merchant who actually sailed to Africa (Sierra Leone) with returning natives in 1815, had viewed migration as a solution to slavery. In 1816, the American Colonization Society was given a charter by the U.S. Congress to send freed slaves to Liberia, on the west coast of Africa. The U.S. government even provided funds and assisted in talks with native chiefs for the transfer of land for this purpose. The first settlers landed at the site of Monrovia in 1822. In 1838, the settlers united to form the Commonwealth of Liberia, under a governor appointed by the American Colonization Society.

Garvey's influence was overshadowed by the influence of Du Bois and others who advocated equal rights for all citizens. Ironically, while Garvey never immigrated to Africa himself, Du Bois did. Despairing that equality for people of African ancestry would ever come to America, Du Bois moved to Ghana in 1961 and began writing the *Encyclopedia Africana,* devoted to collecting information about African peoples throughout the world.

—James L. Outman

For More Information

Books

Clark, John H. *Marcus Garvey and the Vision of Africa.* New York: Vintage Books, 1974.

Cronon, Edmund D., ed. *Marcus Garvey.* Englewood Cliffs, NJ: Prentice-Hall, 1973.

Lewis, Rupert. *Marcus Garvey, Anti-Colonial Champion.* Trenton, NJ: Africa World Press, 1988.

Periodicals

DuCille, Michel. "Black Moses, Red Scare; the Clash of Marcus Garvey and J. Edgar Hoover." *The Washington Post* (February 12, 1997): p. H1.

"Remembering Marcus Garvey." *Ebony* (November 1987): p. 138.

Watson, Elwood D. "Marcus Garvey and the Rise of Black Nationalism." *USA Today Magazine* (November 2000): p. 64.

Web Sites

"The Marcus Garvey and Universal Negro Improvement Association Papers Project, a Research Project of the James S. Coleman African Studies Center." *UCLA African Studies*. http://www.isop.ucla.edu/mgpp/ (accessed on March 14, 2004).

PBS. "Marcus Garvey: Look for Me in the Whirlwind." *American Experience*. http://www.pbs.org/wgbh/amex/garvey/ (accessed on March 14, 2004).

Woody Guthrie

Born July 14, 1912
Okemah, Oklahoma

Died October 3, 1967
New York, New York

Folk singer whose songs raised consciousness about the Great Depression and the Dust Bowl of the 1930s

"This land is your land, this land is my land, from California to the New York Island, from the redwood forest to the Gulf Stream waters, this land was made for you and me."

Woody Guthrie was the foremost composer of folk music in twentieth-century America. His hometown of Okemah, Oklahoma, is just the sort of place one would expect him to be from. He once described Okemah as "one of the singiest, square dancingest, drinkingest, yellingest, preachingest, walkingest, talkingest, laughingest, cryingest, shootingest, fist fightingest, bleedingest, gamblingest, gun, club and razor carryingest of our ranch towns and farm towns, because it blossomed out into one of our first Oil Boom Towns."

To fully understand Guthrie's life, it is necessary first to understand two events that took place during the 1930s: the Great Depression and the Dust Bowl.

The Great Depression and the Dust Bowl

In 1929, prices on the New York Stock Exchange fell steeply on October 25, or Black Friday, as it was called later. Overnight, millions of ordinary Americans who had borrowed money to buy shares in companies suddenly found that those shares were worth less than the money they had

Woody Guthrie. *Getty Images.*

borrowed. Many of them had no way of repaying the loans, which meant that banks that had loaned the money became short of cash. When bank customers tried to withdraw their money, they discovered that the banks could not cover their deposits (the source of the loans made by banks). Banks, in need of money to pay depositors, demanded that loans be repaid, driving small businesses out of business.

Black Friday was the start of a long economic depression, a time when businesses failed for lack of customers, when people lost their jobs and could not find another one. Business owners did not want to take a chance on hiring someone for fear that times would get worse and that the dollar saved by not hiring someone would be needed to tide them over. Consumers felt the same way about spending money, which made businesses even more nervous.

On the Great Plains, the Depression was accompanied by a second crisis: drought. The settlement of the plains by so-called dry-land farmers (so named because there was no water for irrigation) was an ecological disaster that became evident during the long dry spell in the 1930s. With the land broken by years of plowing, powerful windstorms swept across the parched soil and raised great clouds of dust unlike anything previously seen by settlers of North America. In April 1935, a particularly powerful storm blew dust for hundreds of miles. The dust buried what crops there were, sometimes reaching as high as fence posts. The top soil that had supported farming was blown off overnight, making more farming impossible. The storm was known as the Great Dust Storm, and the land it affected was called the Dust Bowl.

Time magazine, reporting on the "Great Dust Storm," said: "Originally confined to a 200-mile strip between Canada and Mexico, last week's dust storm suddenly swirled eastward over Missouri, Iowa and Arkansas, crossed the Mississippi to unload on Illinois, Indiana, Kentucky, Tennessee and Louisiana." The clouds of dust snuffed out the last hopes of many still clinging to their farms and homes in the area called the Dust Bowl.

Coming on top of a national economic depression, the drought meant that farmers could not repay loans they had taken out to plant crops or buy their farms. Banks foreclosed, or took possession of the property in order to collect money owed them.

A truck is parked by the side of a road, as a woman and her baby sit on a blanket. The truck is part of an Okie caravan during the 1930s.
Franklin Delano Roosevelt Library.

Thousands of families loaded their meager possessions into old cars and trucks and headed west, for California. The emigrants were known as Okies or Arkies. They came not just from Oklahoma and Arkansas, but from all over the Midwest and as far east as Georgia. They had no money and most had little education. In California, they were feared and unwanted and thus hated. Okies lived in their cars, parked in camps in the countryside, unable to find work or homes. Their story was told by author John Steinbeck (1902–1968) in *Grapes of Wrath*—and by Woody Guthrie, in dozens of folksongs about the poor and dispossessed.

Woody Guthrie's story

Woodrow Wilson Guthrie was born in 1912, named after that year's Democratic candidate (and eventual victor) for president, Woodrow Wilson (1856–1924; served 1913–21). Guthrie's father, Charles, had been a cowboy and then a land speculator and politician in Okemah. Beneath the dirt farms of Oklahoma lay a great pool of oil. With the coming of the automobile, as well as oil-burning machines in factories, the demand for petroleum soared in the first decades of the twentieth century. The year 1897 was important in Oklahoma when oil was discovered in the town of Bartlesville.

In the next decade, more oil was discovered, and still more oil, as drillers sank holes throughout the state in hopes of finding a fortune. Guthrie's father was pushed out of business as Okemah turned into an oil boom town, a place where oil was found and the sudden wealth it created changed the nature of the place.

Guthrie's mother, Nora Belle Tanner Guthrie, began showing symptoms of Huntington's chorea, an inherited brain disease that causes a gradual loss of control—of mental functions, of emotions, and of physical movements. According to Guthrie's biographer Joe Klein, in *Woody Guthrie: A Life,* Guthrie's sister died in a fire at a time when Nora Guthrie could not fully understand what was happening and save her daughter. Later, another fire seriously injured Guthrie's father, and afterwards Nora Guthrie was confined to a mental hospital. Charles Guthrie sent his younger children to live with his sister in Pampa, Texas. Woody, a teenager, stayed behind in Okemah for awhile, living with friends, until he rejoined his family in Pampa.

Guthrie organized a music group in Pampa, the Corncob Trio, and appeared on the radio as well as playing at dances. In 1933, the twenty-one-year-old Guthrie met and married Mary Jennings, the sister of another member of the Corncob trio.

In 1936, the year after the Great Dust Storm, Guthrie left Texas, joining the great crowd of desperate people headed west. He hitchhiked, or rode freight trains, staying with friends or in hobo camps, eventually making his way to Los Angeles. Guthrie was not a displaced farmer, but he moved among many people who were, and gave them a voice through his songs.

Woody Guthrie, migrant singer

In California, Guthrie's musical career picked up. In 1937, he and his uncle Jeff had a radio program playing coun-

A massive cloud of black dust hits Rolla, Kansas, during the Great Dust Storm. Woody Guthrie recorded an entire album of songs based on the Great Dust Storm. *Franklin Delano Roosevelt Library.*

try folk music on station KFVD, with Guthrie commenting on current events in a way that appealed to the many refugees from the Midwest who had migrated to California.

While in Los Angeles, Guthrie became friends with several people who belonged to the American Communist Party. Guthrie himself became committed to communism as a solution to the economic suffering around him. (Communists advocate government ownership and control of businesses and farms, and a nearly equal distribution of income.)

In 1939, Guthrie moved to New York City. There, his songs about Okies were embraced by political activists campaigning for the rights of unions and for democratic government control of the economy. Guthrie promoted the cause of trade unions, organizations of workers who negotiated pay and benefits with their employers as a group rather than as individual workers. He performed in saloons, army camps, and union meeting halls; on union picket lines; and at country fairs, rodeos, and carnivals. He was also a writer for magazines and communist newspapers such as *People's World* and *The Daily Worker.* In 1943, Guthrie published his autobiography, *Bound for Glory.*

Recordings brought Guthrie to a much wider audience than his live performances could have. In 1940, Alan Lomax (1915–2002), who worked for the Library of Congress as assistant director of the Archive of Folk Song, recorded Guthrie's songs as part of a project to capture folk music of the rural South. Victor Records also released recordings of Guthrie in 1940, on an album called *Dust Bowl Ballads.* In 1944, Guthrie recorded over 150 original and folk songs for another recording company that were released under the label "Folkways." One of Guthrie's songs, "The Great Dust Storm (Dust Storm Disaster)," recalled the Great Dust Storm:

> The storm took place at sundown, it lasted through the night,
> When we looked out next morning, we saw a terrible sight.
> We saw outside our window where wheat fields they had grown
> Was now a rippling ocean of dust the wind had blown.
> It covered up our fences, it covered up our barns,
> It covered up our tractors in this wild and dusty storm.
> We loaded our jalopies and piled our families in,
> We rattled down that highway to never come back again.

In 1941, Guthrie got a month-long job in Oregon working for the Bonneville Power Administration, a government agency building dams on the Columbia River to generate electricity. During that month, Guthrie wrote twenty-eight songs, including "Roll On Columbia."

After divorcing his first wife, Guthrie married Marjorie Greenblat Mazia (1917–1983), a dancer with the highly respected Martha Graham (1894–1991) modern dance company in New York, in 1945. Guthrie divorced his second wife and married Anneke Van Kirk in 1953. Altogether, he had eight children by three wives, including contemporary folk singer Arlo Guthrie (1947–), Guthrie's son by Mazia.

Guthrie was associated with (but not a member of) the Weavers, a popular folk music group that was successful until their communist sympathies were discovered. The group was "blacklisted," or put on a list of performers whose recordings were refused by radio stations. Guthrie's long association with communism made it much more difficult for him to find work, or companies that would release his records, from the early 1950s until the late 1960s.

"This Land Is Your Land..."

One of Guthrie's best-known songs begins with the words: "This land is your land, this land is my land, from California to the New York Island, from the redwood forest to the Gulf Stream waters, this land was made for you and me." What seems like a popular and innocent folk song in fact has a political background to it.

In 1940, Guthrie was hitchhiking from Texas to New York. A new song written by Irving Berlin (1888–1988) was sweeping the country: "God Bless America." To Guthrie in 1940, Berlin's song seemed out of touch with the conditions in the country. Guthrie biographer Joe Klein described his reaction: "'God Bless America' … was just another of those songs that told people not to worry, that God was in the driver's seat." To Guthrie, the main point was not that God was in charge, but that people should organize themselves politically and economically to overcome the lingering effects of the Great Depression.

While Berlin's tune eventually became a virtual second national anthem, Guthrie's tune also caught the public imagination, though not to the full extent of Berlin's.

Guthrie's family had not been farmers, and he had not lived the life of an Okie. But his songs reflected their experience. Unlike many country folk songs that tell of lost love, Guthrie's songs told of lost homes. Just as President Franklin D. Roosevelt (1882–1945; served 1933–45) tried to rekindle hope in desperate Americans during the Depression by declaring that "the only thing we have to fear is fear itself," Guthrie counseled collective action. In all, Guthrie wrote an estimated one thousand songs, some of which remain as popular tunes half a century later such as "Roll On Columbia," "So Long, It's Been Good to Know You," and "This Train Is Bound for Glory."

The impact of Woody Guthrie

Sometime in the late 1940s or early 1950s, Guthrie became ill with Huntington's chorea, the inherited ailment that struck down his mother. The onset of Huntington's chorea is not always obvious. Guthrie's behavior changed, and at first it was attributed to drinking too much alcohol.

Victims of Huntington's chorea can become violent and moody. Guthrie spent most of his time in the hospital from 1954 until his death in 1967.

Guthrie's disease had long before removed him from the concert stage, but his songs had never died. One singer in particular who was dedicated to Guthrie in the early 1960s, who imitated Guthrie's style, sang some of his songs, and wrote others in the same style, was Bob Dylan (1941–). During the 1960s, when college students protested against the war in Vietnam, Dylan's songs echoed those of Guthrie a generation later.

Long after his death, Guthrie was honored by the recording industry for his contributions to a style and form of American music, the folk song of protest. In 1971, he was inducted into, or formally listed in, the Songwriters' Hall of Fame. He was made a member of the Nashville Songwriters' Hall of Fame in 1977, and the Rock and Roll Hall of Fame and Museum in 1988. In 1999, he won a Grammy award from the National Academy of Recording Arts and Sciences.

—James L. Outman

For More Information

Books

Guthrie, Woody. *Bound for Glory*. New York: E. P. Dutton, 1943.

Klein, Joe. *Woody Guthrie: A Life*. New York: A. A. Knopf, 1980.

Santelli, Robert, and Emily Davidson, eds. *Hard Travelin': The Life and Legacy of Woody Guthrie*. Hanover, NH: University Press of New England, 1999.

Yates, Janelle. *Woody Guthrie: American Balladeer*. Staten Island, NY: Ward Hill Press, 1995.

Periodicals

Gilgoff, Dan. "On Desolation Row." *U.S. News and World Report* (July 8, 2002): p. 48.

Morthland, John. "Prodigal Son: Left-wing Folk Singer Woody Guthrie Honed His Trade in Pampa, but 67 Years Later, the Town Is Just Beginning to Welcome Him Back Home." *Texas Monthly* (March 2003): p. 78.

Rosen, Jody. "Two American Anthems, in Two American Voices." *New York Times* (July 2, 2000): p. AR1.

Web Sites

"Woody Guthrie and the Archive of American Folk Song: Correspondence, 1940–1950." *Library of Congress: American Folklife Center.* http://memory.loc.gov/ammem/wwghtml/wwghome.html (accessed on March 15, 2004).

The Woody Guthrie Foundation and Archives. http://www.woodyguthrie.org (accessed on March 15, 2004).

"Woody Guthrie's Songs." *Woody Guthrie: Songs & Prose of the Prophet Singer.* http://www.woodyguthrie.de/lyrics.html (accessed on March 15, 2004).

Le Ly Hayslip

Born December 19, 1949
Ky La (now Xa Hoa Qui), Vietnam

Director of the East Meets West
Foundation and author

Le Ly Hayslip experienced and survived the horrors of war. She persevered through many hardships and became a force for uniting once bitter enemies by creating the East Meets West Foundation. Building clinics, schools, and rehabilitation centers in Vietnam with the assistance of American Vietnam War veterans and other donors, the East Meets West Foundation improved life in Vietnam and promoted understanding and respect between people in her native country (Vietnam) and her adopted country (the United States).

Hayslip is also well known for her two memoirs, *When Heaven and Earth Changed Places* (1989) and *Child of War, Woman of Peace* (1993). The first book shows the effects of the Vietnam War (1954–75) from a Vietnamese perspective. The second book covers her life in America beginning in 1970 and her return visits to Vietnam after the war.

"Nourished by God"

Born Phung Thi Le Ly on December 19, 1949, she was the youngest of six children of Phung Trong (her father) and

> "Working together to heal the wounds of war."

Le Ly Hayslip. © *Robert Eric/Corbis Sygma.*

Hayslip as an Infant

In an excerpt from *When Heaven and Earth Changed Places,* Le Ly Hayslip recounted her family's lack of connection to her as an infant:

> *Because villages shun anything that's odd, my family avoided me as an infant and only my mother would hold me and tend to my needs. They said later it was because they did not want to become attached to anything so unlikely to stay in this world.*

Tran Thi Huyen (her mother). The family lived in a village called Ky La (later Xa Hoa Qui) that was near Danang, a port city on the South China Sea. From the beginning of her life, Le Ly faced great challenges. She was born prematurely and weighed only two pounds, but she survived in difficult conditions. Villagers nicknamed her *con troi nuoi* ("she who is nourished by God") as she struggled to live against great odds.

Le Ly was raised in the Buddhist religion and attended a village school. Her studies were cut short by war when she was eight years old. The war conditions made it impossible to hold classes. Vietnam had been a colony of France, but when France abandoned the area in 1954, Vietnam was divided into two countries, communist North Vietnam and democratic South Vietnam. A civil war was being fought in the South, where Le Ly's village was located. Communists of the North were aided in the South by allies called the Viet Cong.

Le Ly's two brothers served with the Viet Cong: Bon Nghe was the leader of a reconnaissance team, or a group of soldiers exploring enemy territory, and Sau Ban was a soldier who was killed after stepping on a mine. In 1961, the United States began sending military advisors to assist South Vietnam. In 1965, the United States entered full-scale war by sending over 150,000 soldiers to Vietnam. By 1967, almost 500,000 American soldiers were fighting in Vietnam.

In her autobiography, *When Heaven and Earth Changed Places,* Le Ly describes how the people of her village were caught in the war between the North and the South. Sometimes they were forced to assist South Vietnamese soldiers by day, and then the Viet Cong by night. Both sides recruited children as spies. As a girl, Le Ly was imprisoned and tortured by South Vietnamese soldiers for having been a lookout for the Viet Cong. When she was fourteen, she received a death sentence by the Viet Cong. Two Viet Cong soldiers were ordered to take Le Ly into the jungle and kill her. Instead, they raped her and left her there.

Le Ly left her village to take a job as housekeeper for a family in Danang. Then, she and her mother traveled to Saigon, the capital of South Vietnam, where her sister Lan was living. Le Ly and her mother found positions as servants to Anh, a wealthy textile factory owner. At sixteen years old, Le Ly became pregnant, and Anh was the father. Before the child, James (Hung), was born in 1967, Anh paid for Le Ly and her mother to return to Danang.

Le Ly's father, Phung Trong, had remained in the village of Ky La to keep watch over ancestral land and shrines. He became depressed over the effect of war on the village and his family and committed suicide.

Returning to Danang, Le Ly worked as a nurse's aide and later as a cocktail waitress. She met and married Ed Munro, a sixty-year-old American construction worker. He promised education for her son and the opportunity to escape from Vietnam. After Le Ly's second son, Tommy, was born, the family left for the United States in 1970.

Between Vietnam and the United States

Munro failed to find work in San Diego, California. The family returned to Vietnam and Munro worked on a construction job in the town of An Khe. When a major battle occurred there in 1972, an American officer helped Le Ly and her children flee An Khe. Soon afterward, the family was reunited and they returned to the United States.

Munro soon died of pneumonia. Le Ly struggled to support her family. She met and married Dennis Hayslip, an American who had served in the Vietnam War. He made a heroic trip to Vietnam to rescue Le Ly's sister, Lan, and her children as South Vietnam fell to the communists in 1975. Le Ly Hayslip's third child, Alan, was born into an unstable home life. Dennis Hayslip had become abusive, and he and Le Ly argued over whether to raise Alan as a Buddhist or as a Christian. After the couple separated, Dennis Hayslip kidnapped Alan, but the child was recovered and a court order banned Dennis from his wife's home. Dennis Hayslip died accidentally in 1982.

After Dennis Hayslip's death, Le Ly Hayslip sought solace in Buddhist rituals. Through community college courses,

workshops, and spiritual retreats, she educated herself and learned business skills. During her years in the United States, she worked in a factory, bought real estate, invested in stocks, started a delicatessen, and then became a partner in an Asian restaurant. While meeting and talking with American veterans who ate at the restaurant, Le Ly realized that many veterans needed emotional healing because of their experiences in Vietnam.

Le Ly Hayslip traveled to Vietnam in 1986 to visit her family. "I wanted desperately to complete some unfinished business: to return to my home village of Ky La—to burn incense at my father's shrine and sleep in the house he had built with his own two hands," she wrote later in *Child of War, Woman of Peace*. Her home region was without access to quality sources of food and medicine. Using money from a trust fund left by Dennis Hayslip, Le Ly established the East Meets West Foundation in 1987. With the help of donors, many of whom were Vietnam veterans, the Foundation purchased medical equipment and supplies and built a clinic in Vietnam's Quang Nam province, her home region.

Books stun American readers

Le Ly Hayslip became nationally famous in the United States when her first book, *When Heaven and Earth Changed Places,* was published in 1989. The book chronicles her experiences as a girl growing up during the Vietnam War. The book was stunning to many Americans, showing how many innocent villagers were oppressed, or persecuted, by both sides during the war.

Hayslip's second book, *Child of War, Woman of Peace*, was published in 1993. It picks up her story upon her arrival in the United States in 1970, showing difficulties she encountered as an Asian wife of an American citizen as well as her work to support her family and improve their opportunities. The book follows her return trips to Vietnam, including one she took with her sons. Her oldest son, Jimmy, was over twenty years old and met his father, Anh, for the first time. *Child of War, Woman of Peace* concludes with Hayslip's triumph in establishing the East Meets West Foundation.

The two books were adapted to film, *Heaven and Earth*, in 1993. Directed by American filmmaker Oliver Stone (1946–), it forms the third film in his Vietnam trilogy, following *Platoon* (1986) and *Born on the Fourth of July* (1989). Stone also helped Le Ly to establish a 20-acre rehabilitation center for homeless and handicapped people at a site called China Beach in Vietnam. This was the place where 3,500 U.S. Marines landed in 1965 to begin the American war effort in Vietnam.

Le Ly Hayslip with director Oliver Stone, who filmed *When Heaven and Earth Changed Places*, the movie version of Hayslip's books. *Wexler Mark/Corbis Sygma.*

Le Ly Hayslip settled in San Francisco, California. In addition to serving as executive director of the East Meets West Foundation, she raises funds through lectures and newsletters. The East Meets West Foundation grew into the largest humanitarian organization in Vietnam. "Working Together to Heal the Wounds of War" is the motto of the foundation.

In the late 1990s, Hayslip wanted to help children in rural areas of Vietnam who were unable to attend school. Their parents made little money working in rice fields and could not afford to buy their children schoolbooks or uniforms. Many of the rural schools were also in poor shape. In 1999, Hayslip formed the Global Village Foundation (GVF) to address that need.

Le Ly Hayslip's best-selling books are used in Asian studies, literature, women's studies, and Vietnam conflict courses at many universities. They have been published in seventeen different languages.

—*Roger Matuz*

For More Information

Books

Hayslip, Le Ly, and James Hayslip. *Child of Peace, Woman of War.* New York: Doubleday, 1993.

Hayslip, Le Ly, and Jay Wurtz. *When Heaven and Earth Changed Places.* New York: Doubleday, 1989.

Ho, Khanh. "Le Ly Hayslip." In *Words Matter: Conversations with Asian American Writers.* Edited by King-Kok Cheung. Honolulu: University of Hawaii Press, 2000.

Periodicals

Klapwald, Thea. "Two Survivors Turn Hell into 'Heaven and Earth.'" *New York Times* (December 19, 1993): p. H22.

Talbot, Mary. "East Meets West for a Good Cause: Group Aids Poor Vietnamese." *New York Daily News* (December 16, 1993).

Web Sites

"Le Ly Hayslip: Author and Philanthropist." *Global Village Foundation.* http://www.globalvillagefoundation.org/thefounder.htm (accessed on March 15, 2004).

"Le Ly Hayslip." *Womens International Center.* http://www.wic.org/bio/lhayslip.htm (accessed on March 15, 2004).

Antonia Hernández

Born May 30, 1948
Torreón, Mexico

Lawyer and activist for Latino causes

A ntonia Hernández has drawn on her experience as an immigrant to forge a career protecting and expanding the rights and opportunities of Latinos. She learned to speak English while attending school as a young girl; as a teenager, she spent summers picking crops; and she survived in tough East Los Angeles. "I grew up in a very happy environment but a very poor environment," she told *Parents* magazine. She became a lawyer and for eighteen years she was president and general counsel of the Mexican American Legal Defense and Educational Fund (MALDEF). Working to support bilingual education and challenging anti-immigrant laws are among the many activist causes Hernández has pursued.

"A solid education levels the playing field for everybody. It's the surest provider of equal opportunity."

Life experience breeds activism

Antonia Hernández was born on May 30, 1948, on a ranch near the town of Torreón in northern Mexico. She was the eldest of six children. Her father, Manuel, was born in the United States and often traveled back and forth between Mexico and the United States wherever work was available. Her

Antonia Hernandez. *Arte Público Press.*

The Value of Speaking Two Languages

Hernández had to learn to speak English or fail in school. She later became an effective advocate, or supporter, of bilingual education. "I made it. But just because I made it cannot be used as an example that it works," she told the *Los Angeles Daily Journal.* "I say, 'Don't look at me, look at all those who didn't make it.' Because you're not judged by whether you made it, whether the minority made it. You're judged by whether the majority makes it."

mother, Nicolasa, raised the children and took odd jobs whenever possible. The family left Mexico in 1956 and settled in east Los Angeles.

Hernández's life experiences prepared her for her role as an activist for Latino causes. She learned to speak English through what she calls the "sink or swim method"—learn to speak English or fail in school. As an adult, she has been a supporter of bilingual education, in which two languages, the child's original language and a new one to be learned, are used in class. Another influence was the example of her father: He described to her how he was one of many American-born Latinos deported to Mexico for no reason during anti-Mexican immigrant hostilities in Texas of the 1930s. Hernández would later campaign against laws in California that threatened or denied rights to recent immigrants. Hernández also had firsthand experience as a migrant worker (a worker who moves from farm to farm, picking crops quickly while they are ripe)—her family often spent summers in the hot, San Joaquin Valley as crop pickers. Among other activities to earn money for the family, Hernández helped sell her mother's homemade tamales (steamed cornmeal dough with filling) in the neighborhood.

In 1998, Hernández told the *Los Angeles Times,* "I strongly believe it is important to find a way of transitioning students from their native language to English.... This country has an immigration policy but they don't have an immigrant policy. To me, bilingual education is a method of teaching kids that integrates them into the American mainstream. It is a process. I firmly believe I am much more valuable because I speak two languages."

By the time Hernández finished high school in the mid-1960s, she was already involved in activist causes for Latinos. Intending to be the first in her family to graduate from college, Hernández enrolled at the University of California, Los Angeles (UCLA). She graduated in 1970, then continued on at UCLA for a degree in law, which she received in 1974.

Meanwhile, she worked at a branch of the California Rural Legal Assistance Office where she helped address the needs of migrant farm workers. It was there, in 1973, that she met her future husband, Michael Stern, who would become a civil rights attorney. Following Hernández's example, all her brothers and sisters earned college degrees; several became teachers.

After completing her law degree, Hernandez worked for nonprofit organizations, including the Legal Aid Corporation. As a legal aid counselor, she realized that "we couldn't help the kids or teachers unless we did something about the laws that were holding them back," Hernández told *Parents* magazine. She began seeking more active roles to fight such laws.

Meanwhile, Stern began working in the federal Public Defender's Office as a court-appointed lawyer for people who could not afford to pay for one. Hernández and Stern were married in 1977 and would have three children.

To Washington and back

An opportunity for a more high-profile use of her legal background came in 1979, when Hernández was recruited to become a staff counsel for the U.S. Senate Committee on the Judiciary. She moved to Washington, D.C. In her role as staff counsel, Hernández was responsible for carefully wording bills, or documents that Congress debates and votes on, created by senators. She also conducted research and provided information to senators on the committee, especially on immigration and human-rights issues. In 1980, she took a brief leave of absence to work in the Southwest on the campaign of U.S. senator Ted Kennedy (1932–) of Massachusetts for the Democratic presidential nomination.

In 1981, Hernández began working for MALDEF as the staff lawyer in its Washington, D.C., office. Two years later, she returned to Los Angeles to serve as the legal affairs director in MALDEF's office on the west coast. She campaigned for greater opportunities for Latinos in federal employment and promoted affirmative action in private- and public-sector jobs. (Affirmative action is a policy for hiring people for jobs based on skill and ethnic or racial characteristics so that the percentage of workers in an organization reflects the ethnic or racial makeup of the larger population.)

The Value of Education

In an interview with *Civil Rights Journal* (Fall 1998), Antonia Hernández talked about the value of education:

> *Without an educated Latino community, our dramatic increase as a percentage of the U.S. population is not going to result in policies that improve our lives as Americans. Wasn't it [author] George Orwell who said, "To be political, you first have to be well informed?" A solid education levels the playing field for everybody. It's the surest provider of equal opportunity.*

Also during this time, MALDEF initiated several lawsuits on behalf of bilingual workers whose ability to speak a second language was a part of their jobs. They were being paid for their physical work but not for use of their language skills, which were necessary for success.

While working for MALDEF in 1983, Hernández also served as an attorney for the East Los Angeles Center for Law and Justice. She was a defense lawyer on criminal and civil cases, including several involving charges of police brutality. The next year, Hernández became directing attorney of the Lincoln Heights office for the Legal Aid Foundation. She led a staff of six attorneys, took part in case litigation, or preparing a case for court, and fought for bills in the state legislature.

Becomes president of MALDEF

Hernández became president of MALDEF in 1985, including its regional offices in San Francisco, California; San Antonio, Texas; Chicago, Illinois; and Washington, D.C. She defined her mission: "to ensure that all Latinos are given the opportunity to participate fully in our society." She directed and managed a $5.2 million budget and a seventy-five-person staff.

During Hernández 's tenure at MALDEF, the organization fought for many causes. In Texas, for example, MALDEF was successful in a court ruling that the Texas legislature had the authority to require wealthier districts to share their wealth with poor districts to create an educational system that provides fair opportunity to all children. In California, Hernández led MALDEF in defeating Proposition 187 in court. The proposition, or proposed law, was passed by California voters to restrict immigration. Through Hernández's leadership, MALDEF helped defeat an immigration bill in the California legislature that would have required Latinos to carry identification cards. MALDEF argued successfully that only the federal government had exclusive power to regulate immigration.

Nationally, MALDEF actively encouraged Latinos to participate in the 1990 and 2000 national census. Following the national census each decade, states can revise their districts, the areas represented by a member of the U.S. Congress. The organization ensured that districts with large Latino populations would have a strong political voice.

After Los Angeles was wracked by riots in 1992, Mayor Tom Bradley (1917–1998) appointed Hernández to the "Rebuild L.A." commission to lead revitalization efforts. Hernández recruited many Latinos to participate in community service to help improve the city.

In 1996, Hernández received the American Bar Association Spirit of Excellence Award. She also worked actively in the community by serving on governing boards for such programs as California Tomorrow, the Quality Education for Minorities Network; California Leadership; the Latino Museum of History, Art, and Culture; and Los Angeles 2000.

Among her many honors, Antonia Hernández (second from right) earned the 1999 Hispanic Heritage Award for leadership. Standing with her (from left to right) are pro football player Anthony Munoz, educator Tina Ramirez, opera singer Placido Domingo, and writer Gary Soto. *AP/Wide World Photos.*

After MALDEF

In December 2003, Hernández resigned from her position as president of MALDEF. She had been with the organization for over twenty-two years, eighteen of them as president. Hernández moved on to become president and chief executive officer of the California Community Foundation in February 2004. "My life's work has been dedicated to making sure everyone has a place at the table," said Hernandez upon leaving, "and I am proud of the progress we have made through MALDEF. Only a rare opportunity like this one that allows me to forge new paths and serve the Los Angeles community in new ways could draw me away."

Begun in 1915, the California Community Foundation partners with its donors to provide funds for nonprofit organizations and public institutions for health and human services, affordable housing, early childhood education, community arts and culture, and other areas of need. Hernández will remain busy with the Foundation and her many other endeavors, which includes membership on the board of trustees for the Rockefeller Foundation, for which she is chairperson and auditor, or financial examiner, of the budget committee that oversees grants of $500 million annually; other national and local boards of such institutions as Harvard University and UCLA; and frequent speaking engagements.

As noted on the *La Prensa San Diego* Web site, Henry Cisneros (1947–), secretary of Housing and Urban Development during the administration of President Bill Clinton (1946–; served 1993–2001), summed up Hernández's efforts: "Few members of our society have contributed what Antonia has contributed to the Latino community. The progress that the Latino community has made over the last twenty years has depended on a legal and civic foundation. And more than any other person Antonia Hernández has been responsible for creating the conditions that are leading to the progress that Latinos are making today. Her courageous and farsighted leadership has paved the way for Latinos to take their place in American society."

—*Roger Matuz*

For More Information

Periodicals

"Antonia Hernández: A Voice for Latinos" (interview). *Migration World Magazine* (September 1999): pp. 51–6.

"Antonia Hernández: The Leading Latina Legal Eagle for Civil Rights." *Civil Rights Journal* (Fall 1998): p. 14.

Chiang, Harriet. "Profile. Antonia Hernández: Mexican American Legal Defense and Educational Fund President." *Los Angeles Times* (August 5, 1985): p. 1.

Groller, Ingrid. "Law in the Family." *Parents* (March 1985): pp. 96–101.

Gross, Liza. "Antonia Hernández: MALDEF's Legal Eagle Hispanic." *Hispanic* (December 1990): pp. 16–18.

Valsamis, Liz. "Barrier Language. Latina Attorney Antonia Hernández Works for Latino Legal Rights." *Los Angeles Daily Journal* (April 23, 2001): p. S20.

Web Sites

"Antonia Hernández." *California Community Foundation.* http://www.calfund.org/3/staff_hernandez.php (accessed on March 15, 2004).

"MALDEF Board Announces the Departure of Longtime President Antonia Hernández." *La Prensa San Diego.* http://www.laprensa-sandiego.org/archieve/december05-03/maldef.htm (accessed on March 15, 2004).

James J. Hill

Born September 16, 1838
Rockwood, Ontario, Canada

Died May 29, 1916
St. Paul, Minnesota

Railroad builder

"Work, hard work,
intelligent work, and
then more work."

James J. Hill's recipe for success

James J. Hill.
© *Bettmann/Corbis.*

Called the "empire builder of the Northwest," James J. Hill founded in 1878 what became the Great Northern Railroad Company, which built a rail line that ran from St. Paul, Minnesota, to Puget Sound in Washington. Hill became one of the wealthiest men of the nineteenth century, but he also shared with other railroad men a reputation as a "robber baron" when the U.S. Supreme Court ruled in 1904 that his railroad and financial system violated antitrust laws (laws designed to punish businesses that dominate a market or industry and are alleged to have stifled competition). His larger reputation rests as a shrewd and visionary businessman, and as a generous philanthropist, one who donates money to worthy causes. Hill was "without peer, the preeminent builder of the frontier economy of the Northwest," according to biographer Michael P. Malone.

Seizes opportunities

James Jerome Hill was born in a log cabin on September 16, 1838, near Rockwood, Ontario, Canada. He was the third of four children of James and Anne Hill. Descendants of both sides of his family had immigrated to Canada from the north of Ireland and were among the original settlers of the Rockwood area, about 50 miles west of Toronto, Ontario. Hill's formal education ended at age fourteen when his father died in 1852. To help support his family, Hill began working in the village store while his mother ran an inn. He continued to read and was tutored in algebra, geometry, literature, and grammar by the Reverend William Wetherald (1820–1898), a local schoolmaster. Hill lost sight in one of his eyes after an accident with a bow and arrow.

Inspired by stories he read about India, China, and Japan, Hill left home at eighteen with plans to go to Asia and make his fortune. Looking for passage by ship, he traveled to Philadelphia, Pennsylvania, and then to Virginia, but found no opportunities. Hill knew he had a better chance of reaching Asia from the West Coast, but much of the American West was still frontier, or open land, in those days. Hill planned to join a group of trappers and traders on their annual westward trip that began in St. Paul, in Minnesota territory (Minnesota was not a state until 1858). He arrived in St. Paul a few days too late to join the last group of the year. While waiting to join up the following year, Hill began to win respect for his business skills.

St. Paul was a trading station on the Mississippi River at that time with a population of less than five thousand. Hill found work as a clerk for a line of steamboats. He helped broaden the company's services by having the steamboats used for shipping groceries, farm implements, fuel, and other items. Hill was put in charge of establishing rates at which to charge customers for shipping. That success led to other opportunities, and Hill gave up on his planned adventure to Asia. When the American Civil War (1861–65) began, the twenty-four-year-old Hill attempted to enlist in the army, but he was refused admission because he was blind in one eye. Instead, Hill helped organize the First Minnesota Volunteer regiment that soon went off to battle.

By 1865, when he was twenty-seven, Hill had held a variety of jobs, including one as an agent for the Northwestern Packet Company: He bought and sold goods and kept inventory, or a list of what is in stock, at a warehouse. In 1867, he was working as a purchasing agent of fuel for the St. Paul

& Pacific Railroad. Recognizing that coal was superior to wood for locomotive fuel, Hill studied resources of coal supplies and markets, made wise purchases, and began to build up a large supply. He began attracting investors as partners for additional purchasing power. With two partners he formed Hill, Griggs & Company. As Hill rose to the top of the local coal business, he began amassing a fortune that would make him among the richest men in America of the nineteenth century.

On August 19, 1867, Hill married Mary Theresa Mehegan, the daughter of immigrants from Ireland. The Hills would have ten children, seven girls and three boys. Meanwhile, by 1872, Hill, Griggs & Company dominated the Twin Cities (Minneapolis and St. Paul) coal market. In 1875, Hill arranged a plan to share the coal market with his competitors, leading to the formation of the Northwestern Fuel Company.

Railroad man

Hill's next vision of opportunity came when he considered ways to link St. Paul with the city of Winnipeg (then called Fort Garry), in the Canadian province of Manitoba. The Red River, which ran from northern Manitoba to central Minnesota, was a common route but slow going. Hill made journeys inland on horseback and snowshoes from points on the river to scout the region. Seeing enormous potential for agricultural development, Hill envisioned a railroad that could bring farmers to the region, as well as shipping in supplies and shipping out food from the harvest. He set his sights on the St. Paul & Pacific Railroad, knowing that it was poorly managed, its tracks needed to be upgraded, and its rail lines were not well integrated. Hill convinced Norman W. Kittson (1814–1888), who had invested in Hill's fuel company, to help him purchase the railroad. Hill and Kittson put up their property and savings and convinced Donald A. Smith (1820–1914), a leader of the Hudson's Bay Company, and George Stephen (1829–1921), then president of the Bank of Montreal, to invest. In 1878, they purchased the St. Paul & Pacific Railroad. It was a risky move, but Hill regarded it as the great adventure of his life: the group purchased the railroad at a bargain price, but the company was burdened with problems.

Hill had already studied the problems thoroughly and was prepared to address them. The company's rail lines were reconstructed, and during the process new connecting lines were built and remote roads were abandoned, improving integration of the system. A line was extended to the Canadian border in 1878, connecting with a Canadian line to Winnipeg. Another line went westward into South Dakota, turned north into North Dakota, and went west to Great Falls, Mon-

Helping a Friend While Stinging a Rival

While many railroads went through boom-and-bust periods during the nineteenth century, the Hill railroad system sustained uninterrupted growth and profits. Through shrewd financial management, Hill was able to keep costs low. He personally supervised construction and carefully chose routes, considering the terrain, nearness to valuable land, and local industries.

Hill also found ways to challenge his competition, directly or indirectly. For example, Hill became involved with the Canadian Pacific Railroad (CPR) in the early 1880s. During debates over what route the railroad should follow across the Canadian West, Hill was among those who successfully championed a route close to the U.S. border. When the plan was accepted, he actively encouraged settlements along the route, helping to populate the Canadian West. At the same time, the CPR competed with Hill's main rival, the recently completed Northern Pacific line that ran along the south side of the American-Canadian border.

tana (completed in 1887). The line was continued from Great Falls over the Cascade Range to Seattle, Washington (completed in 1893). An agreement with the Union Pacific railroad opened up service to Portland, Oregon. During this period, the company was reorganized as the St. Paul, Minneapolis & Manitoba Railway.

As a railroad builder, Hill was innovative and ambitious. He had foreseen coal replacing wood as the primary fuel for locomotives, and for his railroad he used steel rails instead of the traditional iron rails: steel was less expensive, easier to use in construction, and was sturdy enough to last. He made sure that his railroad tracks were near attractive farmland and connected to important towns. Other railroads had been given land grants or governmental financial aid. Hill did not use such assistance. He was therefore free of obligations other than making money for his investors, and they were paid back handsomely. Hill was able to continually attract further investment while taking more control of the company. He had been general manager from 1879 to 1881 and vice president from 1881 to 1882, and he became president in 1882. Hill reorganized the company in 1890 as the Great Northern Railway Company.

All along, Hill planned a railroad that would reach the West Coast from St. Paul. But he built the railroad in increments to take full opportunity of each region. As a portion of 200 miles or so was completed, he recruited homesteaders to settle and establish small towns in the Dakotas and Montana. He ran an experimental farm in North Oaks, Minnesota, to develop superior livestock and crop yields for the settlers locating near his railroads. He wanted to form a population base in an area that would continually use the railway line to

transport goods and to travel. He built feeder lines off of main lines to support mines, logging, and ranching. As the railroad grew nearer to the Pacific Ocean, Hill found buyers in Asia for cotton, wheat, and metals and transported the goods from St. Paul to be loaded on ships heading for Asia. After the goods were removed, the railroad cars would be loaded with timber and minerals from the Pacific Northwest to be taken back and sold in the Midwest, or shipped to other regions via the Mississippi River. In 1900, Hill attempted to develop his own line of steamships to carry goods across the Pacific, but that became one of his few business failures.

Wagons gather on the James J. Hill farm in Minnesota. © *Minnesota Historical Society/Corbis.*

Competition and trustbusting

In the far west, Hill's Great Northern Railway Company was pitted in competition against the Northern Pacific Railroad, which was experiencing financial management problems. Hill grew concerned that the Northern Pacific Railroad would slash its prices to engage in a fare war. An economic downturn in the United States during the early 1890s (called "the Panic of 1893") put the Great Northern in danger of bankruptcy. Hill wanted to assume leadership of the company in a reorganization that would maintain some degree of competition while avoiding a fare war and preventing Northern Pacific from being purchased by another railroad. In 1895, Hill was successful in negotiating a deal to provide financial support; in exchange, the company would reorganize, and Hill and his associates would become a majority on the board of the company.

The agreement met with public opposition and lawsuits. The most damaging lawsuit was filed in Minnesota and was based on a state law that prohibited the consolidation of parallel and competing railroads. A Minnesota court dismissed the case, but it was appealed to the U.S. Supreme Court. An injunction, or court order that stops or bans an event from proceeding further, was granted against the agreement in May 1896. However, there was no law against having individuals invest in a reorganization plan for a company. Hill and his associates acquired a block of Northern Pacific stock.

Then, in 1901, Hill and wealthy banker J. P. Morgan (1837–1913) bought 97 percent of the stock of the Chicago, Burlington & Quincy Railroad. They planned on expanding both the Great Northern and Northern Pacific to Chicago and St. Louis, and to the coal mining region of Illinois. They were countered by another railroad, the Union Pacific group, and its owner, E. H. Harriman (1848–1909). The competition spurred a stock market panic on May 9, 1901, when Northern Pacific stock soared to a thousand dollars a share.

Not the retiring kind

By this time, Hill was over sixty years old and wanted to protect his estate. In 1901, he created the Northern Securi-

James J. Hill (center) stands in front of a train with railroad workers in 1907.
© *Minnesota Historical Society/Corbis.*

ties Company to hold his earnings and to act as a trustee of his properties—separating them from his railroad company, where they were subject to the ups and downs of business. The new company was quickly challenged by the State of Minnesota and the Interstate Commerce Commission. President Theodore Roosevelt (1858–1919; served 1901–9) directed Attorney General Philander C. Knox (1853–1921) to challenge the holding company. In March 1904, the U.S. Supreme Court, by a 5-4 decision, declared that the Northern Securities Company was a trust, an unfair business operation that overwhelmed competition. Hill spent another year appealing the ruling, but it was upheld unanimously by the Supreme Court on March 6, 1905. The victory against Hill furthered Roosevelt's reputation as a "trustbuster."

In 1907, Hill resigned the presidency of the Great Northern and became chairman of the board. He was succeeded as president by his son, Louis W. Hill Sr. (1872–1948). He kept in close contact with the railroad, but he was involved in many other projects. Hill was an early advocate for conservation of natural resources. He wrote a book, *Highways of Progress* (1910), that recounted his experiences and expressed his views on various issues. During 1911 and 1912, he advised a London firm as it formed the Brazilian Iron Ore Company to tap mineral deposits in South America. He was frequently consulted on issues relating to railroad regulation and finance. He retired as Great Northern chairman of the board in 1912. At Harvard University, the James J. Hill Professorship of Transportation, endowed by seventy-four of his friends and admirers, was established in 1915.

In Minnesota, Hill contributed to many institutions, including the St. Paul Theological Seminary, MacAlester College, Hamline University, the College of St. Thomas, Carleton College, and other educational, religious, and charitable organizations. The James J. Hill Library in St. Paul was established in 1921 and houses a world-class collection of business information resources.

In what author Albro Martin called Hill's "last and greatest role," the retired railroad executive worked with J. P. Morgan on the Anglo-French bond drive of 1915. The bonds provided funds for France and England to purchase food and supplies to support their effort in World War I (1914–18). Hill died in his St. Paul home on May 29, 1916. He was "without peer, the preeminent builder of the frontier economy of the Northwest," according to his biographer, Michael P. Malone. "By controlling the transportation structure of the region … he exercised more sweeping economic power than did any other industrialist, even the lumbermen and mining barons."

—*Roger Matuz*

For More Information

Books

Bruchey, Stuart, ed. *Memoirs of Three Railroad Pioneers*. New York: Ayer Company Publishers, 1981.

Comfort, Mildred Houghton. *James Jerome Hill: Railroad Pioneer*. Minneapolis: Denison Press, 1973.

Hill, James J. *Highways of Progress*. New York, Doubleday, Page & Company, 1910. Reprint, Toronto: Books for Business, 2001.

Malone, Michael P. *James J. Hill: Empire Builder of the Northwest*. Norman: University of Oklahoma Press, 1996.

Martin, Albro. *James J. Hill and the Opening of the Northwest.* Minneapolis: Minnesota Historical Society, 1991.

Periodicals

"J. J. Hill's Estate Put at $100,000,000: Empire Builder's Son Files an Inventory Showing Great Holdings of Securities." *New York Times* (October 6, 1916): p. 1.

"James J. Hill" (obituary). *New York Times* (May 30, 1916): p.8.

Web Sites

"James J. Hill House." *Minnesota Historical Society.* http://www.mnhs.org/places/sites/jjhh/aboutjames.html (accessed on March 16, 2004).

"James J. Hill Papers." *James J. Hill Reference Library.* http://www.jjhill.org/History/manuscript/hill_papers.html (accessed on March 16, 2004).

Daniel K. Inouye

Born September 7, 1924
Honolulu, Hawaii

U.S. senator and decorated
World War II hero

"My grandparents came over from Japan as migrant workers in the sugar cane fields. Both were semiliterate ... and obviously, they were impoverished. Who in his right mind would have said their grandson would be sitting here [in the U.S. Capitol]?"

Daniel K. Inouye. *Daniel K. Inouye.*

Daniel K. Inouye was the first American of Japanese descent to serve in the U.S. Congress. A hero from World War II (1939–45), he was awarded several medals for bravery. Inouye was elected the U.S. representative when Hawaii first became a state in 1959. In 1962, he was elected to the U.S. Senate and was reelected six more times. Inouye is best known as a long-time activist for civil rights and for serving on several historic Senate panels, including the nationally televised Senate Watergate Committee Hearings (1973–74). The committee investigated wrongdoing by President Richard Nixon (1913–1994; served 1969–74) and several of his aides that occurred during the president's 1972 reelection campaign.

Go for broke

Daniel Ken Inouye was born on September 7, 1924, in Honolulu, Hawaii. He was the oldest of four children of Hyotaro and Kame (Imanaga) Inouye, who were first-generation Japanese immigrants. Inouye's grandparents had emigrated from Japan and labored as migrant workers in Hawaii's sugar-cane fields. Inouye's father worked as a file clerk to support his family.

As a young boy, Inouye attended both a special Japanese-language school and the Honolulu public schools. Inouye's hobbies during his youth included collecting stamps, doing chemistry and electronics, and raising homing pigeons (pigeons trained to fly away and return to a home base). He was also trained in how to provide emergency medical aid, and he planned on a career in medicine.

Inouye was fifteen years old when World War II began. The United States entered the war two years later following the surprise Japanese bombing of a U.S. naval station at Pearl Harbor, Hawaii, on December 7, 1941. Having had emergency medical training, Inouye was pressed into service following the bombing as the head of a first-aid team. He provided medical assistance for a week in the aftermath of the attack, and, as he noted, "I saw a lot of blood." Inouye graduated from high school in 1942. He then enrolled in the pre-med program (classes that prepare undergraduate college students for demanding medical school courses) at the University of Hawaii.

When the United States became involved in World War II, the government was unsure of how to treat Japanese Americans. The U.S. Selective Service Commission, in charge of drafting men into the armed forces, issued a directive designating all Americans of Japanese ancestry as "4-C," or "enemy alien." On the West Coast of the United States, where Japanese Americans were most prominent, the government sent up internment camps, areas designed to gather and keep Japanese Americans in a single place where they could be observed. In addition to protesting this form of "guilt by association," Japanese Americans petitioned the government to allow them to serve in the armed forces as a means of proving their loyalty to their country.

The U.S. Army formed a special unit, the 442nd Regimental Combat Team, for volunteers of Japanese ancestry. Inouye quit college and enlisted in the army in 1943. He was assigned to the 442nd Regimental Combat Team. Nicknamed the "Go for Broke" regiment, the 442nd fought in Europe. Inouye joined them when Allied forces were fighting in Italy (the United States, Great Britain, the Soviet Union, and others formed the Allied Forces; they fought against the Axis

Japanese American Internment Camps

In a speech in 2002 delivered at the U.S. Military Academy at West Point, Daniel Inouye recalled how Japanese Americans were treated after the bombing of Pearl Harbor on December 7, 1941.

> A few weeks after December 7, 1941, the U.S. Selective Service Commission issued a directive designating all Americans of Japanese ancestry as "4-C," or "enemy alien." It meant that under no circumstance could we of Japanese ancestry serve in the military of the United States. We could not be drafted, nor could we volunteer.
>
> Soon thereafter, Executive Order 9066 was issued by the White House establishing 10 internment camps at which to house all Japanese—citizens and noncitizens—residing on the west coast of the United States. Officially, these locations were designated as concentration camps. None of the inmates had committed any criminal acts, nor were they ever tried in a court of law. Such was the hysteria of war at that time.
>
> And so, we young Americans of Japanese ancestry immediately began petitioning the President of the United States to be permitted to put on the uniform of the land, if only to prove our loyalty and demonstrate our commitment to the essence of your three sacred words: "Duty, Honor, Country."
>
> After several months of consideration, the President of the United States issued another Executive Order establishing a special army combat team consisting of Japanese American volunteers, with words I will remember: "Americanism is a matter of the mind and the heart; Americanism is not, and never was, a matter of race or ancestry."
>
> With that, the 442nd Regimental Combat Team was established, made up primarily of Caucasian-American officers and Japanese-American enlisted personnel. I was one of them.

powers, primarily Germany, Italy, and Japan). Inouye fought for nearly three months in the Rome-Arno campaign—the successful Allied offensive to liberate Rome, Italy.

Bravery and leadership

The 442nd Regiment was then moved to France, which was under control of Germany. The regiment participated in the historic and triumphant Battle of the Lost Battalion (October 1944), where they helped rescue an American battalion surrounded by Germans. Considered one of the most significant military battles of the twentieth century, the Battle of the Lost Battalion turned what appeared to be a German triumph into an Allied victory that helped loosen Germany's grip on France. The D-Day invasion in June 1944, where thousands of Allied troops landed by ships on the beaches of northern France, began a full-scale Allied invasion to liberate Europe and to defeat the Axis powers.

Inouye was back in Italy in 1945 as a platoon leader. In the last days before Germany surrendered and World War II ended in Europe, he was leading his platoon up a slope where German soldiers were controlling an area from machine-gun nests (small, carefully concealed trenches overlooking an open area from which gunmen could easily hit their targets). He was hit in the abdomen by a bullet that came out his back, barely missing his spine. Still, Inouye advanced up a hill toward one of the nests, came to within five yards, and tossed two grenades that blasted the machine gunners. He was able to blow up another nest and was exchanging fire when a grenade exploded and shattered his right arm. He continued exchanging fire before a bullet hit him in the leg and knocked him down the hill. Still, Inouye directed his platoon until the enemy was defeated and his men regrouped.

For his display of bravery and leadership, Inouye was made a captain. He received many honors, including a Distinguished Service Cross (the second highest award for military valor), a Bronze Star, a Purple Heart with cluster, and twelve other medals and citations. In 2000, Inouye was awarded the Medal of Honor, the nation's highest military honor, by President Bill Clinton (1946– ; served 1993–2001).

It took a long time for Inouye to recuperate from his wounds. He lost his right arm. After his wounds were tended to, he was flown back to the United States. He spent twenty

Daniel Inouye pictured during his military service with the 442nd Regimental Combat Team in the 1940s.
Daniel K. Inouye.

An Excerpt from Inouye's Medal of Honor Citation

"With complete disregard for his personal safety, Second Lieutenant Inouye crawled up the treacherous slope to within five yards of the nearest machine gun and hurled two grenades, destroying the emplacement. Before the enemy could retaliate [fire back], he stood up and neutralized a second machine gun nest. Although wounded by a sniper's bullet, he continued to engage other hostile positions at close range until an exploding grenade shattered his right arm. Despite the intense pain, he refused evacuation and continued to direct his platoon until enemy resistance was broken and his men were again deployed in defensive positions."

months in an Army hospital in Battle Creek, Michigan. World War II officially ended in Europe in May 1945 and in Asia in September 1945. On May 27, 1947, Inouye was honorably discharged from the army with the rank of captain. He returned home to Hawaii.

Distinguished political service begins

Inouye re-enrolled in the University of Hawaii on the GI bill, a special program for soldiers that helps finance their education. He studied government and economics and earned a bachelor's degree in 1950. The year before, he married Margaret Shinobu Awamura. They would have one child, Daniel Ken Jr.

Inouye turned his attention to studying law and was accepted at the George Washington University Law School in Washington, D.C. While there, he became editor of the *George Washington Law Review,* and began his political career as a volunteer worker for the Democratic National Committee. Inouye earned his law degree in 1952 and returned with his wife to Hawaii, where he took a position as assistant public prosecutor in Honolulu.

Inouye first ran for public office in 1954. He won election to the Hawaii territorial House of Representatives. At the time, Hawaii, now a state, was still an American territory, with a government similar to that of a state, but having no voting representation in Congress. He won a second term to the territorial house and fellow Democrats voted him as majority leader, the most powerful member of the political party that has a majority of elected representatives. In 1958, he was elected to the territorial senate.

In 1959, Alaska and Hawaii were admitted into the United States as the forty-ninth and fiftieth states, respectively. The two new states would now be represented in the U.S.

Congress. As a very popular politician in Hawaii, Inouye ran and won election to Hawaii's first seat in the House of Representatives in 1959. He served two terms as Hawaii's representative in the House. Inouye was a member of the Banking and Currency Committee and distinguished himself as an outspoken supporter of civil rights. As a member of the House Agriculture Committee, he was able to support sugar and pineapple growers, crucial to the economy in Hawaii.

Among the hundred most important Americans

In 1962, Hawaii's first senator, Oren E. Long (1889–1965), announced he was retiring, and he endorsed Inouye to succeed him. Inouye swept through a primary election to become the Democratic Party's nominee. He defeated his Republican opponent in the general election by a 2-1 margin. Also in 1962, Inouye was selected as one of the hundred most important Americans by *Life* magazine, among the most widely read magazines of the time.

In the Senate, Inouye was an enthusiastic supporter of the programs of President John F. Kennedy (1917–1963; served 1961–63). After Kennedy was assassinated in 1963, Inouye supported the programs of Lyndon B. Johnson (1908–1973; served 1963–69), Kennedy's successor as president. Inouye continued his civil rights activism. The civil rights movement was gaining momentum, leading up to the famous "March on Washington" in 1963 and the passage of the Civil Rights Act in 1964. The act outlawed all discrimination on the basis of race, religion, or ethnic origin, and it covered employment, education, housing, and public accommodations.

Inouye also supported the Johnson administration's social welfare policies, called the Great Society. Johnson proposed to use America's wealth to fight a war on poverty. Far-reaching legislation was passed from 1965 to 1968 to improve economic opportunities and education; to provide help for citizens against rising medical costs; to ensure fair housing and labor practices; and to reform immigration laws that had favored immigrants from Europe for many decades.

Inouye's support for these pieces of legislation won him increasing power in the Senate and national recognition.

He was chosen to be the keynote speaker at the Democratic National Convention in 1968. The keynote speaker makes the first major speech at a convention or gathering, setting the tone for activities that will follow. Inouye focused his speech on the need for racial harmony.

Despite civil rights legislation and advances in opportunities for nonwhites, social unrest was common in the 1960s. There were race riots in several cities, most notably in the Watts area of Los Angeles, California, in 1965, when thirty-five people died, and in Detroit, Michigan, in 1967, where over forty people died. In addition, demonstrations against the Vietnam War (1954–75) became commonplace after 1965, including a massive peace march on Washington, D.C., in 1967. Outside the Democratic National Convention in Chicago in 1968, rioting and other civil unrest broke out. Young people who gathered to protest were met with aggressive resistance by the Chicago police force.

Inouye supported America's growing involvement in the Vietnam War, which was being fought between communist North Vietnam and democratic South Vietnam. Military advisors were sent by the United States beginning in 1961, and in 1965 American troops were sent. Over five hundred thousand troops were stationed there by 1968. The toll of death on distant battlefields combined with violence at home—most notably the assassinations of civil rights leader Dr. Martin Luther King Jr. (1929–1968) in April and presidential candidate Robert F. Kennedy (1925–1968) in June—made 1968 an especially turbulent year.

President Johnson gave up his reelection bid early in 1968, and the Democrats, led by Vice President Hubert Humphrey (1911–1978), would lose the general election in November to Republican Richard Nixon. Inouye, meanwhile, won reelection to the Senate seat with 83 percent of the vote. During his second Senate term, Inouye reversed his support for American involvement in Vietnam, believing too many lives were being lost in a conflict that seemed to have no end. But American involvement continued until 1975. To avoid another Vietnam-like conflict in the future, Inouye cosponsored the War Powers Act of 1973. This bill was intended to limit a president's power to commit American military forces without congressional approval but has had only modest success.

High-profile Senate committees

In 1973 and 1974, Inouye served on the Senate Select Committee on Presidential Campaign Activities, known commonly as the Senate Watergate Committee. The committee was formed to investigate allegations that members of President Nixon's administration, and perhaps the president himself, had authorized and covered up for individuals engaged in illegal activities for Nixon's 1972 reelection campaign. Watergate was the name of a Washington, D.C., hotel where burglars raided an office of the Democratic Party.

As the investigation deepened, a series of dramatic revelations provided evidence that the president himself knew about the burglary and authorized a cover-up, an attempt to conceal information about a crime. To provide the public with as much information as possible, the committee began nationally televised hearings in which witnesses were called to testify. The committee helped uncover clear evidence of the president's involvement, which led in 1974 to President Nixon becoming the first president to resign from office. Inouye was one of several senators, including Sam Ervin (1896–1985), a Democrat from North Carolina, and Howard Baker (1925–), a Republican from Tennessee, who distinguished themselves in front of a national audience and won high ratings (over 80 percent approval) in polls taken at the conclusion of the hearings.

In 1987, Inouye was appointed chairman of a committee looking into abuse of power at the executive level. The Senate Select Committee on Secret Military Assistance to Iran and the Nicaraguan Opposition, popularly known as the Iran-Contra Committee, investigated reports that members of the National Security Staff of President Ronald Reagan (1911–; served 1981–89) had sold arms to Iran. Such an act was in violation of international law and official American policy. Additionally, profits from the arms sale were allegedly used to secretly finance a band of resistance fighters seeking to force out the government of Nicaragua. Foreign aid was supposed to be subject to congressional approval. The nationally televised hearings of this committee revealed that some members of the Reagan administration were acting without supervision, and two officials were found guilty of illegal activities.

Inouye also chaired the 1976 Senate Select Committee on Intelligence. The Committee was established to set up regulations for undercover operations abroad and internal operations against American citizens by the intelligence community. The regulations were a response to revelations that U.S. intelligence organizations had engaged in assassination plots and other international conspiracies.

Long Senate tenure

When Inouye won election in 1998 to the Senate for a seventh time, he became one of the top ten senators in length of service in American history. During his seventh term, he continued his long-standing support for abortion rights, consumer rights, gun control, and public works programs to create jobs for the unemployed. His civil rights activism continued in his position as chair of the Committee on Indian Affairs, and his committee work included such areas as defense, commerce, science, transportation, and communications. Continuing to serve the interests of Hawaii, Inouye helped the National Park Service acquire over 100,000 acres of the Kahuku Ranch in Kau, to protect rare and endangered bird and mammal species, as an expansion of Hawaii Volcanoes National Park.

In 2002, Inouye was honored with the Sylvanus Thayer Award, given annually since 1958 by the Association of Graduates of the U.S. Military Academy at West Point, New York. The award honors "an outstanding citizen of the United States whose service and accomplishments in the national interest exemplify personal devotion to the ideals expressed in the West Point motto, 'Duty, Honor, Country.'"

In his acceptance speech at West Point, Inouye noted, "In a sense, this is a homecoming for me. Fifty-seven years ago [when Inouye enlisted in the army], I was advised that I would be traveling to West Point to begin my studies as a cadet. But circumstances of war brought about a sudden change."

The Hill, The Capitol Newsletter interviewed Inouye in his Senate office in 1999, forty years to the day since he was first elected to Congress. "My grandparents came over from Japan as migrant workers in the sugar cane fields," Inouye noted. "Both were semiliterate [having a limited ability to read and write]. They were not scholars or great leaders, and obviously, they were impoverished. Who in his right mind would have said their grandson would be sitting here?"

—*Roger Matuz*

For More Information

Books

Chang, Thelma. *I Can Never Forget: Men of the 100th/442nd.* Tucson, AZ: Sigi Productions, 1991.

Goodsell, Jane. *Daniel Inouye.* New York: Crowell, 1977.

Marvis, Barbara J. *Contemporary American Success Stories: Famous People of Asian Ancestry.* Hockessin, DE: Mitchell Lane Publishers, 1994.

Nijya, Brian, ed. *Encyclopedia of Japanese American History: An A to Z Reference from 1868 to the Present.* Updated ed. New York: Facts on File, 2000.

Web Sites

Eisele, Albert. "Sen. Inouye Biography." *The Hill, The Capitol Newsletter.* From *Kauai Economic Development Board.* http://www.kedb.com/news/1998-2000/inouye/ (accessed on March 16, 2004).

"Thayer Award Speech." *AOG: Association of Graduates, USMA, West Point.* http://www.aog.usma.edu/AOG/AWARDS/TA/01speech.htm (accessed on March 16, 2004).

Helen Hunt Jackson

Born October 14, 1830
Amherst, Massachusetts

Died August 12, 1885
San Francisco, California

Writer and activist for
Native American rights

"Oh, write of me, not
'Died in bitter pains,' But
'Emigrated to another
star!'"

Helen Hunt Jackson.
Library of Congress.

M
ost widely remembered as an activist for Native American rights, Helen Hunt Jackson also wrote poetry, essays, novels, and children's stories. She used her writing talent to publicize the mistreatment of Native Americans, particularly the Mission Indians of Southern California. This dedication to Indian reform earned her a place in American history.

A life of tragedy

Helen Hunt Jackson was born Helen Maria Fiske in Amherst, Massachusetts, on October 14, 1830. Her parents were Nathan Welby Fiske, a professor and minister, and Deborah Vinal, a writer. The Fiske household was religious and scholarly, and undoubtedly, Helen's later career was influenced by her parents' intellectual interests. One of four siblings, Helen's two brothers died in infancy, leaving only her sister, Anne. While still a young girl, Helen's mother died of tuberculosis, an infectious and fatal lung disease common in the nineteenth century. Her father's death followed three years later. Before his death, however, Nathan Fiske saw to it that Helen received a good education. At a time when most females were not given the opportunity for formal learning, Helen attended the highly regarded Ipswich Female Seminary and the Abbott Institute, a reputable boarding school. There she met Emily Dickinson (1830–1886), who would later become one of America's most distinguished poets. Their friendship lasted a lifetime.

At the age of twenty-one, Helen married Edward Hunt, a graduate of West Point Academy. Their eleven years together were marked by great tragedy, beginning with the death of their infant son Murray in 1854, who died of a brain disease. Then in 1863, while experimenting with a submarine of his own inventing, Edward Hunt was accidentally killed. Two years later, Helen buried her second and only remaining son, nine-year-old Rennie, who had contracted diphtheria, an infectious bacterial disease that produces a poison and results in high fever, weakness, and ultimately, suffocation. (The development of a preventive vaccine in 1923 reduced the death rate to 10 percent.) By this time, the American Civil War (1861–65) had just ended, and Helen was alone, too grief-stricken to celebrate. In 1866, she decided to leave behind her military life of mobility and settled down in Newport, Rhode Island, where she and her husband had once been stationed. Here, she began to write.

At first, Helen devoted her literary efforts to children's stories, essays, poems, and travel sketches. As was customary during this time, she wrote under pseudonyms, or false names: most often H. H., but sometimes with the name Saxe Holm. Women writers of that time typically created pseudonyms so that readers would not know their gender, a custom that illustrated society's general view of women as second-class citizens. At first, Helen's writing was typical of the emotional content that was most popular among female readers. She wrote about all things domestic—family life, marriage, keeping a home. Her published pieces brought her great success, and her work appeared in such prominent publications as *Nation, Atlantic,* and *New York Independent.*

A reformer is born

During this time, Helen got back in touch with her childhood friend, Emily Dickinson. Because of the uprooted life she had led while married to a military man, Helen's correspondence with Dickinson had become infrequent. The two women writers supported one another in their literary endeavors, and never again would they lose touch. Helen repeatedly pleaded with her old friend to share her poetry with her "day and generation."

Helen was not a woman of robust health. After dealing with the stress and grief of the deaths of her husband and children, she took her doctor's advice and moved west, hoping to take advantage of the health-restoring powers of the Rocky Mountains. Always curious, she chose the new town of Colorado Springs as her new home, and she moved there in 1893. Two years later, she married William Sharpless Jackson, a banker and railroad executive. Marrying a prominent citizen allowed Helen to focus on her writing without the added worry of wondering where she would get the money to pay bills.

Though she loved the West and eagerly called it home, Jackson often traveled to the East. In 1879, while visiting Boston, Massachusetts, she attended a lecture about the plight of the Ponca and Omaha Indians. This lecture opened her eyes to the injustice suffered by the tribes at the hands of the U.S. government, and she left that reception a transformed woman.

Westward Movement pushes out Native Americans

In the mid-1800s, many European immigrants were attracted to the United States by the promise of free land and the opportunity for prosperity. The reality was a far cry from the dream, however. When they reached the shores of New York, they found instead a hard life in overcrowded conditions. Unable to make a living, let alone prosper, or get ahead, many of the immigrants listened to the advertisements announcing the "promised land" of the West. Wide open prairies, free land, limitless opportunity—this and more was promised to those courageous enough to make the trek west. Thousands of men, women, and children heeded the call. Thus began what is known as the Westward Movement.

These hopefuls met in St. Louis, Missouri, to form wagon trains, or large groups of covered wagons. They took with them only what could fit in the wagons. In many cases, families were forced to leave behind precious heirlooms, furniture, and other valuables. They faced many obstacles on their trip: harsh weather, sickness and disease, broken wagon wheels, attacks from hostile Native Americans, no facilities for women giving birth. Many, many immigrants died on this coast-to-coast journey west, but those who did survive needed somewhere to live once they reached their destination. The "free land" they were promised was not actually free; it was the home of thousands of Native Americans.

Federal government mistreats Native Americans

The immigrants and Native Americans were unable to live together peacefully. The differences in their cultures and beliefs proved to be too great to overcome, and the U.S. government was more concerned with settling the immigrants than with guaranteeing the rights of the Native Americans. White miners devastated the land, robbing the Native Americans of their food sources. As a result, they were forced to raid local towns for food just so they and their tribes could survive. In return, miners hunted Native Americans and abused them. The U.S. government passed the Indenture Act in 1855, which legally allowed white people to enslave the Native Americans and sell them at auctions. White trappers also caused many hardships for the Native Americans, as they destroyed the fur-bearing animal population, a natural resource that kept the Native Americans fed and clothed throughout the seasons. The Native Americans were left little choice but to raid settler towns to get the items necessary to survive.

The U.S. government quickly realized they had a major crisis on their hands, and their response was to rid the land of Native Americans rather than to work out a peaceful resolution. The government's goal was to relocate the Native Americans to lands that were not overcrowded by immigrants.

One tribe in particular, the Ponca, was treated especially badly. When a representative from the government informed the Ponca that they would need to relocate from their home in Nebraska to Oklahoma, they refused. In 1878, the Ponca sent ten chiefs, under the leadership of Chief Luther

Standing Bear (c. 1868–c. 1939), by train to Oklahoma. They wanted to investigate the area to determine if they could happily live there. But the chiefs were not used to the climate and weather in that region, and they became ill. As a result, they refused to give in to the government's order; they would not allow their people to move to Oklahoma only to die. As punishment, the government abandoned the chiefs, and they were forced to journey the 500 miles home on foot. They had no money, no food, and just one blanket for each person. The trip took two months, and when they got home, U.S. troops were waiting for them. The Ponca were forced into a line and made to walk to Oklahoma under the supervision of U.S. soldiers. While they made their journey, some of the soldiers stayed behind to steal what they could of the Native Americans' tools and household goods. Many of the Ponca died during the trip; the elderly, the children, and the sick were hit the hardest. The tribe had no immunity to the diseases that were being introduced to them by both their new surroundings and the American soldiers, and 158 of the 730 Ponca had died by the end of 1878.

Native American rights become a public issue

Chief Standing Bear was at the reception attended by Jackson in 1879. His plea for help struck a chord with Jackson, and she made it her mission to assist the Native Americans in their fight for justice. The result of her dedication was a book published in 1881, *A Century of Dishonor.* The book exposed the government's mistreatment and abuse of Native Americans. It publicized for the first time the countless broken treaties and corrupt behavior by federal representatives as well as politicians themselves. At her own expense, she sent a copy of her book to every member of Congress. Inside the cover, she handprinted this statement: "Look upon your hands: They are stained with the blood of your relations."

The U.S. Department of the Interior hired Jackson and a translator to investigate the condition of the Native Americans then referred to as the Mission Indians—those living in the three southernmost counties of California. Jackson was then given the title and responsibility of special commissioner of Indian affairs in 1882. Sadly, her fifty-six-page report on the state of Native American affairs and her request for some sort of atonement, or payback for past wrongdoings, was completely ignored by the government.

Ramona becomes an instant bestseller

Jackson refused to be silent, despite the lack of response from her country's government officials. Because *A Century of Dishonor* did not bring about the reform she had hoped for, Jackson decided the best way to help the Native Americans in their fight for justice was to reach Americans through writing the public would consider "less serious." So she wrote *Ramona*, a novel depicting the Native American experience. She began writing in a New York City hotel room in December 1883, and the book was completed just three months later. As she explained to a friend, "As soon as I began, it seemed impossible to write fast enough."

Helen Hunt Jackson brought the issue of Native American rights to the American public through her writings.
© *Bettmann/Corbis.*

Although the book was sold as a novel, Jackson claimed that every incident she wrote about was true. She admitted that *Ramona* was inspired by *Uncle Tom's Cabin,* a novel written by friend Harriet Beecher Stowe (1811–1896). *Uncle Tom's Cabin* brought to the public's attention the plight of the African American slaves, and it remains today as an American classic. Said Jackson, "If I can do one hundredth part for the Indian that Mrs. Stowe did for the Negro, I will be thankful." Although satisfied with the sales of the book, Jackson was disheartened by the reviews. Positive though they were, they focused not on the politics of Native American affairs, but on the charm of the setting and the romance between a half-breed girl and a Native American forced from his tribal lands.

Death comes too soon

Jackson planned to write a children's story on the Native American issue, but she died in San Francisco of cancer on August 12, 1885, less than one year after the publication of *Ramona*. She died disappointed that her novel did not have the impact she was hoping for, which makes the enduring influence of *Ramona* something of a tragedy in that the author never lived to understand the impact her novel has had on California heritage. *Ramona* has inspired a number of films and a 1920s hit song of the same name. Throughout Southern California, the name Ramona can be found on street and commercial establishment signs. An annual pageant called *The Ramona Pageant* is held for three consecutive weekends spanning April and May in Riverside, California. The event includes a stage adaptation of the novel featuring a four-hundred-member cast. It is the largest and longest-running outdoor play in the nation.

—*Rebecca Valentine*

For More Information

Books

Jackson, Helen Hunt. *A Century of Dishonor*. New York: Harper & Brothers, 1881. Multiple reprints.

Jackson, Helen Hunt. *Ramona: A Story*. Boston: Roberts Bros., 1884. Multiple reprints.

Mathes, Valerie Sherer. *Helen Hunt Jackson and Her Indian Reform Legacy*. Austin: University of Texas Press, 1990.

Mathes, Valerie Sherer, ed. *The Indian Reform Letters of Helen Hunt Jackson, 1879–1885*. Norman: University of Oklahoma Press, 1998.

May, Antoinette. *Helen Hunt Jackson: A Lonely Voice of Conscience*. San Francisco: Chronicle Books, 1987.

Phillips, Kate. *Helen Hunt Jackson: A Literary Life*. Berkeley: University of California Press, 2003.

West, Marc I., ed. *Bits of Colorado: Helen Hunt Jackson's Writings for Young Readers*. Palmer Lake, CO: Filter Press, 2000.

Whitaker, Rosemary. *Helen Hunt Jackson*. Boise, ID: Boise State University, 1987.

Web Sites

Greenstein, Albert. "Helen Hunt Jackson." *Southern California History*. http://www.socalhistory.org/Biographies/hhjackson.htm (accessed on March 17, 2004).

"Helen Hunt Jackson." *Colorado Women's Hall of Fame*. http://www.cogreatwomen.org/jackson.htm (accessed on March 17, 2004).

"Helen Hunt Jackson Biography." *Colorado College Tutt Library.* http://www2.coloradocollege.edu/library/SpecialCollections/Manuscript/HHJbio.html (accessed on March 17, 2004).

"New Perspectives on the West." *PBS.com.* http://www.pbs.org/weta/thewest/ (accessed on March 17, 2004).

"The Ponca Indians." *PageWise, Inc.* http://www.wawa.essortment.com/poncaindians_ruci.htm (accessed on March 17, 2004).

Al Jolson

Born May 26, 1886
Seredzius, Lithuania

Died October 23, 1950
San Francisco, California

Vaudeville entertainer

"You think that's noise—
you ain't heard nuttin'
yet!"

Al Jolson was arguably the biggest star on Broadway in the early to mid-1900s, with a career that spanned four decades (1911–40). He starred in the first commercially successful "talking" movie (film with sound, as compared with the "silent" films in which all dialogue was printed on the screen), *The Jazz Singer,* in 1927, and that is the role for which he is best remembered. Jolson was the first Jewish star to publicly acknowledge his Jewish heritage. He is credited with almost single-handedly introducing African American music such as jazz and ragtime to white audiences. He was known in his day as "The World's Greatest Entertainer."

A young Russian Jew makes his way

Al Jolson was born Asa Yoelson on May 26, 1886, in the Lithuanian village of Seredzius, located in Russia. This date cannot be proved to be Jolson's birthday, as no formal birth certificate exists. At that time, Imperial Russia was run by anti-Semites, or people who are racist against Jews, and the authorities did not feel the birth of another Jew was worth recording.

Al Jolson. *Getty Images.*

Asa was the youngest of four siblings born into a strict Jewish family headed by Moshe Yoelson, a cantor, or male singer who leads prayers in a synagogue (a place of worship for Jews). Both Asa and his brother were expected to become cantors. They were trained to sing using matchsticks to hold open their mouths as encouragement to sing loud and clear.

When Yoelson's father became a rabbi (a Jewish religious official), he headed for America in hopes of escaping the oppression that marked Imperial Russia. Without reason, Jews were routinely brutalized by the Russian government, often to the point of death. Jewish families were split up, and their businesses forced to close. Moshe wanted a better life for his family, and he became the rabbi of a congregation in Washington, D.C., in 1894. He sent for his wife and children, and the family began a new life. Tragedy struck in 1895, however, when eight-year-old Asa's mother became ill and died suddenly. Having been his mother's favorite child, and raised solely by her for the past four years, Asa became withdrawn and suffered from the traumatic experience of watching his mother die. The world as he knew it had been destroyed. It was an event that was to have a powerful impact on the rest of his life.

Although Moshe tried to raise his children in traditional Jewish ways, his efforts were largely unsuccessful, at least where they concerned Asa and his older brother Hirsch. The brothers worked as newsboys, a job that kept them on the streets and took them into the less reputable establishments of the day. In their travels, they learned the ragtime songs heard on the streets and in the saloons of Washington, and they came to know the musicians. This new life intrigued them, and they embraced the culture despite their father's pleas. Asa soon became Al, and Hirsch became Harry. The two boys ran away from home a number of times, and Al even endured a brief stay in an orphanage.

Having already been musically trained, the brothers soaked up the ragtime tunes that surrounded them. They quickly learned the music and styles of other immigrant cultures in the city as well as the dance steps created by the African American (called Negro in those days) boys who brought their talent to the streets. Al took any job available to break into show business. After heading to New York City, he sang in a traveling circus. Then it was on to burlesque (a type of show in which actors and singers imitated other famous characters in humorous ways) and vaudeville (a stage show that includes dance, comedy, singing, acting, and even acrobatics). He and his brother Harry eventually formed a comedy act. It was at this time they changed their last name to "Joelson" in an effort to appear less "ethnic," or Jewish. Shortly after that, it became Jolson. The Jolson brothers found minor success with their act, but Al was self-conscious about his performance, which often relied on crude (unrefined, often considered in bad taste) humor. The solution to this problem would prove to be the very thing that brought the eighteen-year-old Jolson fame.

With blackface, a star is born

In 1904, the Jolson brothers teamed up with comic Joe Palmer on the vaudeville circuit. While the act known as Jolson, Palmer, and Jolson was performing at Keeney's Theatre in Brooklyn in 1904, Al Jolson began wearing blackface as a way to give him freedom in his acting. Blackface is exactly what it sounds like it is: a face painted black. Cork was burned and the residue was smeared on the face. Lips were then painted white, and the result was clownlike. Although today blackface is considered racially offensive, that attitude had not taken hold in the early 1900s. It had been common for white men to imitate African Americans on American stages since the 1830s, and the practice was not interpreted as racist or insulting. In fact, Jewish entertainers used blackface not only as a means of entertainment but as a way of keeping in touch with the oppression, or persecution, they had suffered throughout history. For Jolson, blackface was a mask behind which he could hide, which gave him a confidence he had long ago lost with the death of his mother.

Jolson's blackface routine became an instant hit, and soon he was booked in some of the best vaudeville houses in the country. At this point, Harry moved on in hopes of finding success with a solo career. Fame eluded him, however, and he was never able to escape being "Al Jolson's brother." Palmer continued with Al Jolson a bit longer, but bowed out when he felt he was holding Jolson back from stardom.

In 1906, Al Jolson began billing himself as a "singing comedian." Every performance included vocal scales as well as a whistling routine that sounded very much like a hyperactive birdcall. He became known for his dramatic facial expressions, made all the more obvious because he outlined his lips in white. In 1908, he joined a minstrel show, a comic variety show in which all participants wore blackface. Jolson wanted to perform the kinds of music he grew up with—jazz, ragtime, and blues—but the minstrel shows of this era were focused on the music of the American Civil War (1861–65). Unhappy with this limitation, he quit the minstrel shows and began performing solo.

As always, hiding behind the mask of blackface gave Jolson a freedom rarely seen in vaudeville, and he was celebrated for the depth of emotion he conveyed. Drawing upon his orphaned childhood, the spirituality of the synagogue, and the soulfulness of the black music he loved, Jolson gave his audience performances they could not experience elsewhere. In fact, despite an overall acceptance that rock-and-roll singer Elvis Presley (1935–1977) was the first performer to include below-the-waist movements in his performances, it is actually Jolson who deserves this credit. At a time when African American entertainers would have been putting themselves in danger by such a performance, and white performers would have been labeled scandalous, Jolson not only got away with it, but became famous because of it. He also performed several songs in a female persona, thereby crossing not only racial lines, but those of gender as well.

To Broadway and beyond

Having traveled to California during the early years of his solo career, Jolson returned to New York in 1911 to star in *La Belle Paree,* a vaudeville revue that established him as the biggest star on Broadway. By this time, he had married Henrietta Keller, a young dancer he met while in California. Despite Henrietta's wishes that Jolson take a break and start a family, he forged on to star in several more musical revues, many of them produced by the Shubert Brothers (Lee [c. 1873–1953], Samuel [c. 1875–1905], and Jacob [c. 1879–1963]). Although he played the same character in every show, audiences loved the long-suffering blackface underdog, and Jolson took advantage of that loyalty. He incorporated new songs into his performances whenever possible, and he was instrumental in the careers of famous musical composers George Gershwin (1898–1937) and George M. Cohan (1878–1942).

The Shubert Brothers recognized a good thing when they saw it, and Jolson was it. At his request, the Shuberts built a runway that reached out into the Winter Garden auditorium (one of the most popular theaters of the day). Jolson used this runway to dance and sing out into the middle of the audience, something never before done. The audience went wild for Jolson, and his fifteen-minute time slot often ran over into forty minutes or more.

In 1913, Jolson starred in the Broadway production *The Honeymoon Express*. Although he had costars, Jolson soon turned the musical into a one-man show, and he received top billing for the first time in his career. On opening night, Jolson stopped in the middle of an act, turned to the audience, and asked, "Do you want to hear the rest of the story, or do you want me?" The audience's shouts gave him all the encouragement he needed, and he turned the show into a concert of the songs he was most famous for performing. Although no Broadway performer before (or since) had ever had the daring to pull such a stunt, it became Jolson's trademark. The Shubert Brothers banked on Jolson's innovative performances, and in 1921 they built a sixteen-hundred-seat theater, aptly named Jolson's 59th Street Theatre.

Personal life not so glorious

While Jolson's professional life dazzled with fame, he paid a price in his personal life. His wife Henrietta filed for divorce in 1918, and despite Jolson's attempts at reconciliation, she would have nothing to do with him. She had suffered physical abuse at his hands and had been publicly humiliated over his countless affairs. Jolson's desire to be seen as a "man's man" led to a serious gambling addiction, a condition that would haunt him throughout his life. In 1922, Jolson married one of the many chorus girls with whom he came into contact, Ethel Delmar. She turned to alcohol as comfort from the abuse and long absences of her husband, and in 1926 the couple divorced. Ethel never recovered from her alcoholism, and she was committed to private nursing facilities on Long Island, where she died in 1976.

Star of the silver screen and *The Jazz Singer*

Although Jolson had appeared in several silent movies, he had not achieved any notoriety for them. In 1927, all that changed when Warner Studios offered him the role of Jack Robin in the first successful sound movie, *The Jazz Singer*. The story closely resembled Jolson's own life: Stage singer Jack Robin rises to stardom despite the disapproval of his Orthodox, or traditional, cantor father. Although the film was initially to use sound only for a handful of songs, Jolson improvised, or made up, dialogue along the way and that, too, was inserted into the picture. The debut of *The Jazz Singer* marked the end of the silent film era. Moviegoers wanted nothing but "talkies," and Jolson was the sensation's first star.

Al Jolson as he appeared in *The Jazz Singer.* *AP/World Wide Photos.*

Jolson starred in numerous films after that, including *The Singing Fool* (1928) and *Say It with Songs* (1929). These movies were sentimental tearjerkers, as nearly all of his stage and screen productions had been. But the tastes of the era were changing, and by the time Jolson made his final movies in 1930, he was no longer king of Hollywood. In 1929, he married his third wife, a young woman more than half his age by the name of Ruby Keeler (1909–1993). A chorus girl who grew up on the streets of New York, Ruby was unlike Jolson's previous wives in that she refused to endure his abuse quietly. As a result, their rocky marriage was highly publicized in the gossip columns. But Ruby remained Mrs. Al Jolson as long as she had a career to keep her busy. The couple even adopted a boy and renamed him Al Jolson Jr. As Ruby spent more time at home as a mother to their son, she found herself less willing to put up with her husband's abusive behavior. She divorced him in 1939, and their adopted son was eventually adopted again by Ruby's next husband.

A return to Broadway and a venture into radio

Jolson did not worry about his loss of power in Hollywood. Instead, he returned to Broadway. His timing was not the best, however, as the Great Depression (1929–40; a period of intense poverty as a result of the stock market crash of 1929) prevented people from having the extra cash to spend on entertainment. Seats were left empty, and Jolson became depressed, often missing performances.

Jolson experimented with radio appearances in 1932. He did not enjoy the experience, though, and quit after less than four months. After several more unsuccessful attempts at Hollywood, Jolson flip-flopped back to radio in 1936, this time with his own series. In 1940, he returned to Broadway in *Hold On to Your Hats*. With this production, he won the kind of recognition that had eluded him for years. His health began failing shortly after his most recent divorce, however, and he decided to close the show despite high ticket sales.

Jolson performed for American troops during World War II (1939–45). Although he continued to make radio appearances, his focus was on the troops—that is, until he met Erle Galbraith. In 1944, Galbraith was a twenty-one-year-old X-ray technician in a Georgia military camp. Jolson met her while touring, and he immediately offered her a screen test based on her good looks and Kentucky drawl. Jolson's relationship with Galbraith intensified, and they were married in 1945. This marriage was unlike Jolson's others from the start. Galbraith would simply walk out on Jolson when his temper and attitude became too much, and Jolson developed a respect for her that was lacking in his previous marriages.

Recovery and return

While recovering from a bout of malaria, Jolson starred in the George Gershwin film *Rhapsody in Blue* (1945). The 1946 movie, *The Jolson Story*, put the entertainer back in the public eye. The film became an overnight sensation largely because it included renditions of twenty-four of Jolson's lifetime hits, sung by none other than the star himself. Although he did not play himself in the autobiographical movie, he did appear in one short scene. Jolson was sixty-one years old.

With a renewed energy for life, Jolson and his wife adopted two infants, Asa Jr. and Alicia. Although Asa Jr.

would grow up to lead an industrious life, Alicia was mentally impaired and was institutionalized, as was common in those days. Little is known of her.

Jolson recorded a number of hit songs during this time and began filming a sequel to the movie that made him a comeback. *Jolson Sings Again* was released in 1949. Again, Jolson contributed renditions of the songs that made him famous, sixteen of them this time. As a result, movie and television offers began pouring in. Jolson, ever the patriot, put his plans on hold so that he could travel to Korea and entertain American soldiers fighting in the Korean War (1950–53). After paying for the travel expenses himself, Jolson gave more than 160 concerts.

Homage to the comeback king

While preparing for an appearance on entertainer Bing Crosby's (1904–1977) radio show on October 23, 1950, Jolson complained of indigestion while playing cards with friends in his hotel room. Doctors arrived when it seemed the problem was more serious, and it was at that time that Jolson felt for his own pulse and quietly claimed, "Oh, I'm going." He died moments later. Broadway turned off its lights for ten minutes that day to honor Jolson's passing. He was buried in Culver City, California.

Controversial, influential, forgotten

Despite his having been openly Jewish, Jolson made a life for himself by exploiting elements of minority cultures. He used blackface, which today is considered obviously racist. He mimicked—often times in an unflattering, exaggerated way—the behaviors and speaking patterns of immigrants from all backgrounds and encouraged Americans to laugh at them. Yet he did more than that. He brought to the forefront these differences and allowed Americans to weave them into the ever-changing scene that was becoming American culture. He introduced African American music and dance to white America and made it something to celebrate. Through his art, he inspired white America to accept and at times to embrace the unique qualities of the immigrants who were flooding the eastern shores. His role was not merely to entertain but to help Americans understand their changing world.

Despite his controversy and influence, Jolson is largely a forgotten figure in the twenty-first century. There exists today no statue or sign in New York honoring the entertainer. He has been given no formal recognition for his role in making America a mixture of many different people and cultures—a true melting pot.

—*Rebecca Valentine*

For More Information

Books

Alexander, Michael. *Jazz Age Jews*. Princeton, NJ: Princeton University Press, 2001.

Cohen, Adam Max. "Al Jolson." In *St. James Encyclopedia of Popular Culture*. Detroit: Gale, 2002.

Erdman, Harley. *Staging the Jew: The Performance of an American Ethnicity, 1860–1920*. New Brunswick, NJ: Rutgers University Press, 1997.

Goldman, Herbert G. *Jolson: The Legend Comes to Life*. New York: Oxford University Press, 1988.

McClelland, Doug. *Blackface to Blacklist: Al Jolson, Larry Parks, and the Jolson Story*. Lanham, MD: Rowman & Littlefield, 1987.

Melnick, Jeffrey Paul. *Right to Sing the Blues: African Americans, Jews, and American Popular Song*. Cambridge, MA: Harvard University Press, 1999.

Web Sites

Hanan, Stephen Mo. "Al Jolson: The Soul Beneath the Mask." *Tikkun*. http://www.tikkun.org/magazine/index.cfm/action/tikkun/issue/tik9809/article/980923.html (accessed on March 17, 2004).

International Al Jolson Society. *Al Jolson*. http://www.jolson.org (accessed on March 17, 2004).

Kenrick, John. "Al Jolson: A Biography." *Musicals 101*. http://www.musicals101.com/jolsonbiopf.htm (accessed on March 17, 2004).

Mary "Mother" Jones

Born May 1, 1830
County Cork, Ireland

Died November 30, 1930
Silver Spring, Maryland

Fierce advocate for the rights of working
people, especially coal miners

Like many immigrants to the United States, Mary Harris Jones led a hard life. She experienced the economic hardships that were common to factory workers in the middle of the nineteenth century. But it was as a campaigner for coal miners that she gained her nickname, Mother Jones, and a national reputation for making trouble for mine owners. Jones was symbolic of the struggle waged by workers to achieve better lives in the face of unyielding opposition by business. Her willingness to fight against the wealthy class was an attitude that she brought with her from her native Ireland.

"Pray for the dead, and fight like hell for the living."

The spirit of a rebel

Mary Harris Jones was born Mary Harris in Cork, Ireland, the daughter of Richard and Mary Harris, on May 1, 1830. But although that was the date she gave in her autobiography, she may have altered her birthday to coincide with the date marking the anniversary of a riot in Chicago that pitted the police against workers who were on strike, or refusing to work until their employer met their demands, for an eight-

Mary "Mother" Jones.
Library of Congress.

hour work day. One of Jones's biographers, Elliot Gorn, insists that she was born on August 1, 1837, and that by claiming May 1 as her birthday, she meant to add to her image as the mother of union organizers. What does not seem in dispute is that her father's family had long been campaigners for the rights of Irish people while Ireland was ruled by the English, and when many Irish farmers led a poor, miserable existence working for English landlords. In 1835, Richard Harris was forced to flee Ireland to Canada, to escape arrest for his political activities. Three years later, he brought his family to Toronto, Ontario, Canada, where he worked as a laborer on the railroad.

Mary Harris Jones had an ordinary childhood, attending public school and graduating from high school at age seventeen. She found a job as a teacher at a Catholic school in Monroe, Michigan. In the 1850s, the United States did not restrict immigration, and it was easy to move from Canada, or from other countries, to find work in the United States. Harris Jones disliked the strict atmosphere in the Catholic school and decided to move to Chicago. She found work as a seamstress, sewing clothes, curtains, and furniture coverings for the city's wealthy families. But it was hard to make an adequate living as a seamstress, and in 1861 Harris Jones decided to resume her career as a teacher.

Harris Jones moved to Memphis, Tennessee, after hearing about teaching jobs there. She began work in the fall. In Memphis, she met George Jones, an iron worker who also spent much of his time trying to persuade his fellow workers to join a labor union. Many workers thought they could improve their lives by joining together; members of a labor union then negotiated with employers as a group for higher wages and better conditions. If employers refused, the workers threatened to strike.

Jones and Harris Jones were married in the summer of 1861 and eventually had four children. Mary Harris Jones taught school, and her husband became a full-time organizer for his union. His position drew Mary Harris Jones close to the labor movement, which was just getting started in the United States as new industrial enterprises employed increasing numbers of workers. Then, in 1867, disaster struck. Yellow fever, a disease carried by mosquitoes and for which no cure was known, struck Mary Jones's family. One by one, all four of her children, and then her husband, died from the disease in the space of a few months.

Mary Jones returned to Chicago and resumed her work as a seamstress. In 1871, just four years after losing her family to yellow fever, a large fire swept whole neighborhoods in Chicago, destroying Jones's modest business. In the chaos that followed the event, still known as the Great Fire, Jones tried to help other victims, while noticing that her wealthy customers did not seem to care what happened to people living in poor neighborhoods. At the same time, Jones began attending meetings organized by the Knights of Labor, an early labor union trying to organize workers in Chicago's fast-growing factories. Many of the workers in Chicago were, like Jones, immigrants who had come to the United States looking for better lives. Some of the immigrants had been recruited in Europe to fight in the U.S. Army during the American Civil War (1861–65). After the war, they drifted to Chicago and other large cities looking for work. By listening to speakers at Knights of Labor meetings, Jones developed a talent for delivering fiery speeches of her own on behalf of the labor union, combining a sharp tongue with an image of a middle-aged mother campaigning for social justice. Soon, she began working full-time for the Knights of Labor, giving up her dressmaking work for the vocation that would make her name a household word over the next six decades.

Life as an organizer

The period of Jones's life as a labor organizer coincided with the period of mass immigration to the United States. Millions of Europeans, especially from southern and eastern Europe, flowed into the United States, seeking jobs and opportunities during a period of industrial expansion. For most of the period between 1870 and 1920, the United States experienced rapid industrial growth. The opportunity to work attracted millions of Europeans, many of them poor farm laborers, to cities like New York, Pittsburgh, Cleveland, and Chicago. It was a period when enormous fortunes were built by businessmen like John D. Rockefeller (1839–1937) in petroleum, and **Andrew Carnegie** (1835–1919; see entry in volume 1) in steel manufacturing. It was also a period when millions of Americans worked for very low wages and lived in tiny quarters—whole families were often jammed into one or two rooms in urban apartment houses that lacked fresh air and indoor plumbing. These conditions gave rise to efforts by workers to improve their conditions, by joining labor unions or by supporting political reforms that promised to halt the powers of business owners and even to take over businesses to be run by the government.

Jones was often in the midst of the most vicious, even violent, struggles between workers and company owners who strongly resisted efforts by their workers to demand higher wages. For most of her career as a labor organizer, Jones was most closely associated with the United Mineworkers Union, which represented coal miners. Coal was the principal source of energy that provided power to industrial enterprises. The coal was either burned directly to fuel steam engines (the coal heated water to create steam, which instantly expanded, driving machinery such as railroad locomotives) or burned to generate electricity. Coal miners were, as a group, strong men who did not shy away from violence if they were confronted by force. At the same time, coal miners typically lived in "company towns," in shacks built by mine owners to house their workers near the mines. Miners were often paid in "script," a form of money that could only be spent in company-owned stores, where mine owners could charge workers whatever high prices they wanted.

Starting in 1874 and lasting fifty years, Jones was often found at the site of the longest, most bitter labor conflicts involving miners. Among the highlights of her career:

- 1874: Jones was sent by the Knights of Labor to Pennsylvania, where coal miners were on strike for over a year. There, Jones found that workers' families, living without pay, were living in misery, unable to buy food and other goods at company stores. Jones focused her attention on keeping up morale. It was during this strike that Mary Jones got the nickname "Mother Jones." Among striking miners were Irish immigrants organized into a secret group called the Molly Maguires, who sometimes resorted to violence to achieve their goals. The Molly Maguires were infiltrated, or secretly joined, by company agents, and several members were arrested, charged with murder, and executed. Fear of company police agents was another obstacle that union organizers had to overcome.

- 1877: A national railroad strike centered in Pittsburgh resulted in U.S. president Rutherford Hayes (1822–1893; served 1877–81) calling out troops to protect railroad property—or to support the railroad owners, in the view of labor sympathizers. Jones was in Pittsburgh to support the strikers and their families.

- 1886: In May 1886, during a labor rally held at Haymarket Square in Chicago to support a strike against the McCormick-Harvester Company, a bomb exploded, killing several policemen. The police in turn fired guns into the crowd, killing eleven. Jones attended the rally but was not present during the violence. Eight anarchists, or people who believe in replacing government institutions with voluntary associations of workers, were accused of killing the police, and seven were sentenced to death. Four of the men were later hanged, one killed himself in jail, and the last three were eventually set free by the governor of Illinois. There was little or no evidence that any

A painting shows policemen entering the scene during the Haymarket Square Riot of May 1886. *Library of Congress.*

of the eight had been involved in the bomb that killed the police, and the Haymarket Square incident became a symbol of injustice for the labor movement.

- 1891–1903: Jones became an organizer for the United Mine Workers Union, working among coal miners in Pennsylvania. Jones, sometimes in disguise, toured the mining area to organize workers and sometimes organized miners' wives to help patrol mine entrances and discourage strike breakers. Jones often favored a tougher negotiating position than the president of the union, John Mitchell (1870–1919). Jones resigned from the United Mine Workers in 1903 after the union agreed to settle a coal strike in Colorado that gave white miners in one location what they wanted but gave nothing to Spanish-speaking miners at another location. Jones's stand on behalf of Mexican miners made Jones a labor heroine in Mexico, where she became known as *Madre Yones* ("Mother Jones," in Spanish).

- 1903: Jones led a march of four hundred children, many of them crippled by industrial accidents, from Philadelphia to New York to publicize the need for limitations on employing children in factories. U.S. president Theodore Roosevelt (1858–1919; served 1901–9) refused to meet Jones at his home in Oyster Bay, New York, on Long Island, but the march attracted tremendous publicity for the cause of child laborers. In a letter to Roosevelt published in newspapers, Jones told the president: "These little children, raked by cruel toil beneath the iron wheels of greed, are starving in this country which you have declared is in the height of prosperity—slaughtered, ten hours a day, every day in the week, every week in the month, every month in the year, that our manufacturing aristocracy [ruling class] may live to exploit more slaves as the years roll by." The next year, the Pennsylvania legislature passed regulations to protect the health and welfare of children working in factories.

- 1912: Back with the United Mine Workers after the resignation of Mitchell, Jones was arrested during a West Virginia strike and sentenced to twenty years in prison by a military judge. Later, evidence showed Jones was carried onto property controlled by the military during the strike, and she was pardoned by the governor of West Virginia.

• 1913: During another coal strike near Ludlow, Colorado, Jones, by now over eighty years old, was arrested and held in the basement of the courthouse without being charged. Troops guarding the mine and trying to clear away families of strikers shot and killed two women and eleven children, resulting in a public-relations disaster for the mine's owner, John D. Rockefeller, and freedom for Mother Jones.

Despite her advancing age, Jones continued to be an active voice in the American labor movement. She supported striking subway workers in New York City in 1915 and 1916 and striking steelworkers in 1919 and 1920, when she was ninety. Her autobiography, published in 1925, showed that even at age ninety-five, she had lost none of her passion for social justice. At the age of one hundred, in 1930, she went on the radio to call on working people to continue their struggle for social and economic justice.

Industrial Workers of the World founder Mary "Mother" Jones meets with U.S. president Calvin Coolidge on September 27, 1924. © *Corbis.*

Mother Jones as a symbol

A demure, grandmotherly woman on the outside, Irish immigrant Mary "Mother" Jones was a fierce, effective campaigner for the rights of working people, especially coal miners, in the late nineteenth and early twentieth centuries. Through her work, she symbolized the struggle waged by workers, many of them immigrants, to achieve economic well-being and security. It may be that her own birthday was changed, in her writing, to add to the symbolism. Her white hair, her prim, modest appearance covered an underlying passionate personality determined to fight for higher pay, shorter hours, and safer working conditions on behalf of working men, especially miners, and their families.

When her father had brought young Mary Harris to North America as an immigrant, he also brought a tradition of resistance against economic power that mistreated workers, whether it was held by English landlords or American business owners. It was a tradition that lived a century. Mary Harris Jones died on November 30, 1930, just past her one hundredth birthday.

—*James L. Outman*

For More Information

Books

Currie, Stephen. *We Have Marched Together: The Working Children's Crusade*. Minneapolis: Lerner Publications, 1997.

Gorn, Elliott J. *Mother Jones: The Most Dangerous Woman in America*. New York: Hill and Wang, 2001.

Jones, Mary Harris. *The Autobiography of Mother Jones*. Chicago: C. H. Kerr, 1972.

Whitman, Alden, ed. *American Reformers*. New York: H. W. Wilson Company, 1985.

Periodicals

Gorn, Elliott J. "Mother Jones: The Woman." *Mother Jones* (May 2001): p. 58.

Gustaitis, Joseph. "Mary Harris Jones: 'The Most Dangerous Woman in America.'" *American History Illustrated* (January 1988): p. 22.

Web Sites

Hawse, Mara Lou. "Mother Jones: The Miners' Angel." *Illinois Labor History Society*. http://www.kentlaw.edu/ilhs/majones.htm (accessed on March 17, 2004).

Jones, Mary Harris. "Mother Jones: The Woman." *MotherJones.com.* http://
www.motherjones.com/news/special_reports/2001/05/motherjones_
gorn.html (accessed on March 17, 2004).

Chief Joseph

Born Spring 1840
Wallowa Valley, present-day Oregon

Died September 21, 1904
Nespelem, Oregon

Leader of the Nimitu (Nez Perce) tribe and famous orator

"It is cold and we have no blankets. The little children are freezing to death. I want time to look for my children, and see how many of them I can find. Maybe I shall find them among the dead. Hear me my chiefs. I am tired; my heart is sick and sad. From where the sun now stands, I will fight no more for ever."

Chief Joseph. *Library of Congress.*

C hief Joseph endures as a symbol of dignity—as a tribal leader who exhausted all efforts to find a peaceful means to secure the homeland of his tribe, and as an eloquent spokesman who won a good measure of public sympathy for the plight of the Nez Perce tribe. His attempts to avoid war, his skillful military strategy when confronted by larger and better-equipped U.S. forces, his care for the defenseless people in his tribe, and his noble surrender when victory proved impossible became legendary during his lifetime.

Two traditions

Chief Joseph was born in a cave during the spring of 1840 in the Wallowa Valley of present-day Oregon. His father, Tuekakas (c. 1790–1871), had been baptized earlier that year by a Presbyterian missionary minister named Henry Spalding (1803–1874) and had taken the name Joseph. When his son was born, the father became known as Joseph the Elder and the son Young Joseph. His mother was named Khapkahponi-mi. Up until age seven, Young Joseph was schooled in Christian teachings by Spalding, who called him Ephraim.

Young Joseph was also raised in traditional Nez Perce customs and was given the name Hin-mah-too-yah-lat-kekht (Thunder Rolling Down the Mountain). Like other boys of the Nez Perce, he participated in a ritual at age nine through which he attained a "Wyakin," or guardian spirit. While growing up, Young Joseph followed the typical migratory pattern of the Nez Perce—spending winter and early spring in the Wallowa Valley, moving to the prairie and woodlands in the summer months, and fishing mountain streams for salmon in late summer and autumn. He helped gather food, such as wild root crops (vegetables that grow underground, like wild potato, which the Nez Perce called *keh-keet*) and fruit (including many varieties of berries) as well as pine nuts and sunflower seeds. He hunted for large game animals, especially deer and elk, small game animals, and birds.

But as Young Joseph was growing up, the lands around him were undergoing great change. In 1843, the first wagon trains with white settlers passed through the region and formed what would be called the Oregon Trail. Three thousand settlers came to the region in 1845, and another four thousand came in 1847. That year, an epidemic of measles, an infectious disease, spread from settlers to the nearby Cayuse tribe and resulted in many deaths. The angered Cayuse engaged in a three-year war with settlers and the soldiers protecting them. Joseph the Elder and the Nez Perce did not participate in the war. They remained in the Wallowa Valley, which remained free of white settlers.

In 1853, Washington Territory was established, and two years later the governor of the territory, Isaac Stevens

How the Nimipu Became Known as the Nez Perce

Archaeological evidence in the land of the Nez Perce shows the area was inhabited for thousands of years. Not much was known about the Nez Perce until the mid-1700s, when they began acquiring and herding horses and their warriors went on hunting trips. The first record of them by Americans occurred during the Lewis and Clark expedition, a group of explorers, led by Meriwether Lewis (1774–1809) and William Clark (1770–1838), sent by U.S. president Thomas Jefferson (1743–1826; served 1801–9) in 1804 to reach the Pacific Ocean and explore lands acquired in the Louisiana Purchase of 1803. In his journal, Lewis referred to the Nez Perce as the Chupunnish, which was probably taken from their word *Tssup-nit-palu* (meaning "Walking People," because they migrated with the changes of seasons). Lewis wrote that the tribe had "among the most amicable men we have seen. Their Character is placid and gentle, rarely moved to passion."

English explorers called the tribe the Pierced Noses, because some of the Nimipu decorated their noses with dentalium shells (narrow, tubular, conical shells from mollusks found in the ocean). French explorers adopted that name in its French form, *Nez percés,* from which it was Americanized to Nez Perce.

(1818–1862), negotiated a treaty with the Nez Perce that reserved 7 million acres for the tribe. The U.S. Congress ratified the treaty in 1859. Joseph the Elder, who supported peace with white settlers, helped develop the treaty, which included land set aside for the Nez Perce in present-day Oregon, Washington, and Idaho. In 1860, gold was discovered on Nez Perce land, bringing many more white frontiersmen to the area. The treaty of 1855 was soon rescinded, or taken back and canceled, and a new one was negotiated. Joseph the Elder refused to sign the new treaty, but a chief from a different band of the Nez Perce agreed to a financial settlement that turned over more than 6 million acres back to the United States in 1863. Joseph the Elder tore up what he called "the Thief Treaty" and declared that he was no longer a Christian. Young Joseph, then fifteen years old, followed his father's example. The "Thief Treaty" was ratified, or approved, by the U.S. Congress in 1867. In 1868, the first white settlers began arriving in the Wallowa Valley.

Negotiations fail

When his father died in 1871, Young Joseph was elected by the tribe to succeed him as chief. U.S. government officials tried to force Chief Joseph's band from the Wallowa Valley to a small reservation in Idaho. But Chief Joseph worked with sympathetic officials from the U.S. government's Bureau of Indian Affairs (BIA) to help secure support for his people. He seemed to have accomplished that in 1873, when an executive order from President Ulysses S. Grant (1822–1885; served 1869–77) recognized the Wallowa Valley as Nez Perce territory. Two years later, however, Grant rescinded the order after pressure by the BIA to permit the building of a wagon road that would bring more settlers into the valley.

Many in his tribe wanted war against the settlers, but Chief Joseph pacified them while he continued to try to convince officials about the right of his people to the valley. In January 1877, after many meetings, Joseph's band was again ordered to move to a reservation at Lapwai, Idaho. They were supposed to move by April 1, 1877, but in May, Chief Joseph was still attempting to negotiate. American military leaders of the region threatened to remove the Nez Perce by force. To show they were serious, they took as prisoner one of the Nez Perce, a chief named Toohoolhoolzote. He was soon released, and the Nez Perce began their journey to the reservation in Idaho.

As the Nez Perce neared the reservation following a difficult crossing of the Snake River in Idaho, a member of Joseph's band killed four white settlers who were known as Indian-haters as revenge for his father's murder years before. This act ignited a war, and Chief Joseph had to turn from diplomacy to military strategy.

Long journey for survival

The Nez Perce won an early battle against an American cavalry unit (horses and riders) where they were outnumbered one hundred fighting men to sixty. As the Nez Perce moved to a safer position, their scouts reported that another American unit was approaching. Chief Joseph decided to lead his tribe to Canada. The year before, Chief Sitting Bull (c. 1831–1890) of the Sioux had escaped to Canada after winning the Battle of Little Big Horn against George Armstrong Custer (1839–1876; the battle is also known as Custer's Last Stand), and Chief Joseph believed that moving to Canada would save his people. From June to October in 1877, Chief Joseph and his tribe managed to stay ahead of the better armed American forces, to pick advantageous times to engage in battles, and to defend their position successfully.

Their journey took them across Idaho and into Montana, where the Nez Perce had to cross the Bitteroot Mountains and pass near a fort containing over 250 armed soldiers and volunteers. In a daring move, Chief Joseph led men, women, children, and animals along a narrow route on a cliff side above the fort, where they were too far away to be hit with gunfire and artillery from the fort.

Instead of heading due north to Canada, the Nez Perce went south along the mountains, where they could trade with Native Americans of the Crow tribe. But their camp was attacked in the Battle of Big Hole by an Indian fighting unit, and many Nez Perce women and children were killed. Still, Nez Perce marksmen were so skilled that they stopped a cavalry assault, forced it into retreat, and then moved on while the unit regrouped.

Reaching the southwest corner of Montana, the Nez Perce turned east and passed through Yellowstone National Park in Wyoming. (Yellowstone had become a national park in 1872.) Meanwhile, two new U.S. regiments were pressed into service and waiting near the famous Mammoth Hot Springs in Yellowstone.

Chief Joseph changed course, however, after first having his people and animals moving in different directions to confuse trackers. He selected a narrow mountain path wide enough for only two people, and the tribe moved along the path slowly and in silence. Regiments looking for them were not able to see, hear, or track them. The Nez Perce were able to leave Yellowstone safely and entered Montana for a long journey to Canada. In Montana, they learned that other tribes were tired of war with the United States and were not going to help the Nez Perce.

The Nez Perce successfully fought off an assault by the U.S. Seventh Cavalry at Canyon Creek, Montana, on September 13, 1877—four months after having begun their journey. While the cavalry regrouped, the Nez Perce moved on, blocking the path behind them with boulders and fallen trees. The cavalry returned to Fort Keogh in eastern Montana. Over the next ten days, the Nez Perce traveled most of the width of Montana and reached the Missouri River. Seventy years earlier, the Lewis and Clark expedition had passed on the river at that point on their way to the Pacific Ocean, on the journey where they would record the first meeting between U.S. citizens and the Nez Perce.

"I will fight no more forever"

Colonel Nelson Miles (1839–1925), meanwhile, left Fort Keogh with over 380 fighting men to head off the Nez Perce before they reached Canada. On the morning of September 30, 1877, at Bear Paw, Montana, just 40 miles south of the Canadian border, Miles led an assault that successfully divided the Nez Perce camp into two sides. Nez Perce warriors went for their weapons and defensive positions, separated from defenseless women and children. Chief Joseph would recall later: "About seventy men, myself among them, were cut off. My little daughter, twelve years of age, was with me. I gave her a rope, and told her to catch a horse and join the others who were cut off from the camp." Meanwhile, Nez Perce marksmen were able to drive back Miles's forces and took a defensive formation.

The battle turned into a siege—where one side (the Nez Perce) remains, or is trapped, in a defensive area or structure and the other side (Miles's forces) batters the place with steady gunfire and artillery, larger weapons like cannons. Five inches of snow fell on the first night, with the Nez Perce digging trenches either for their soldiers to form a defense or for warmth and protection for their nonfighters. Over the next few days the siege continued, with a few failed assaults by Miles's men. Meanwhile, Chief Joseph and Miles began discussing terms of surrender. Chief Joseph was assured by Miles and his superior, General Oliver Otis Howard (1830–1909), that his people would be allowed to return to the reservation in Idaho after spending the winter in Yellowstone, where the wounded could be tended to.

Chief Joseph then handed his rifle to Howard as a symbolic gesture of surrender. Howard politely deferred the honor to Colonel Miles. Then, Chief Joseph made his famous speech of surrender. Chief Joseph said, "Tell General Howard I know his heart. What he told me before (about returning to the reservation), I have in my heart, I am tired of fighting. Our chiefs are killed. Looking Glass is dead. Toohoolhoolzote is dead. The old men are all killed…. It is cold and we have no blankets. The little children are freezing to death. I want time to look for my children, and see how many of them I can find. Maybe I shall find them among the dead. Hear me my chiefs. I am tired; my heart is sick and sad. From where the sun now stands, I will fight no more for ever."

By that time, Chief Joseph was leading about five hundred people, less than a hundred of whom were fighting men. They had traveled nearly 2,000 miles—a distance nearly equal the length of Europe, and longer than the distance from Paris, France, to Moscow, Russia. In over three months, the band of about seven hundred, fewer than two hundred of whom were warriors, fought two thousand U.S. soldiers and volunteers in four major battles and numerous smaller skirmishes.

Colonel Miles respected the Nez Perce. "Exceedingly self-reliant, each man seemed to be able to do his own think-

ing and to be purely democratic and independent in his ideas and purposes," Miles noted. Miles called Chief Joseph "the boldest and best marksman of any Indian I have ever encountered. And Chief Joseph was a man of more sagacity [perception] and intelligence than any Indian I have ever met."

Trail of broken promises

At the end of Chief Joseph's long journey to save the Nez Perce, he began another long struggle on their behalf. The terms of surrender were not honored, despite pleas to American officials from Colonel Miles. Instead of being allowed to live on their reservation in Idaho, or their homeland in the Wallowa Valley, the Nez Perce were marched eastward to Bismarck, North Dakota, for a temporary stay. In Bismark, they were greeted by many townspeople. The story of Chief Joseph and the Nez Perce was already beginning to spread across the United States. From North Dakota, the Nez Perce were moved to a reservation near Fort Leavenworth, Kansas. This was a flat, hot, and swampy area, not at all like their lush homeland. Many of the Nez Perce contracted malaria. The Nez Perce were then moved to a similarly flat and unsuitable reservation in Oklahoma.

As the leader of his Nez Perce tribe, Chief Joseph defended the dignity of his people. © *Corbis.*

Chief Joseph continued to be very active for his people, working with the BIA with the support of many army officers, including General Howard and Colonel Miles. Because he spoke so eloquently and his reputation had spread far in the United States, Chief Joseph was invited to visit Washington, D.C., in 1879. He met with President Rutherford B. Hayes (1822–1893; served 1877–81), but he was unsuccessful in having his land returned. Chief Joseph's stature grew even more, however, when he explained his cause in speeches, including one during his visit to Washington, D.C., and in an article he wrote for the *North American Review,* one of the leading magazines of the nineteenth century. In his speeches and his writings, Chief Joseph often used terms Americans identify with, like "The earth is mother of all people, and all people should have equal rights upon it," that form the basis of American democracy.

The Nez Perce finally won the right to return to the Pacific Northwest in 1885, but instead of going to the Wallowa Valley, they were settled on a reservation at Colville, Oregon. They had to contend with white farmers, foresters, and miners and to try and live in a manner different from the way in which they had prospered for many years.

Chief Joseph continued to plea the case of the Nez Perce. He traveled to New York City and Washington, D.C., in 1897 to attend the dedication of a tomb for former general and president Ulysses S. Grant. He stood in company with Howard and Miles, who still believed Chief Joseph deserved the chance to live in Wallowa. Still, he could not win back the land of his people. In 1899, he returned to the Wallowa Valley for the first time in twenty-two years. The valley had changed, but much was still as it had been. He visited his father's grave. Chief Joseph was back in Washington, D.C., in 1903, speaking with President Theodore Roosevelt (1858–1919; served 1901–9), but Roosevelt took no effective steps to secure the return home of the Nez Perce.

In 1904, Chief Joseph suffered a heart attack. He was sitting by a fire, next to the tipi in which he lived—continuing to live in the manner of his people. He died and was buried in Nespelem, Oregon, where a monument marks his grave.

—*Roger Matuz*

Chief Joseph, Famous Speaker

In a speech made in January 1879 at Lincoln Hall, Washington, D.C., Chief Joseph spoke of equal rights:

> *If the white man wants to live in peace with the Indian he can live in peace. There need be no trouble. Treat all men alike. Give them all an even chance to live and grow…. The earth is mother of all people, and all people should have equal rights upon it. You might as well expect the rivers to run backward as that any man who was born a free man should be contented penned up and denied liberty to go where he pleases….*
>
> *I have asked some of the great white chiefs where they get their authority to say to the Indian that he shall stay in one place, while he sees white men going where they please. They can not tell me.*

For More Information

Books

McAuliffe, Bill. *Chief Joseph of the Nez Perce: A Photo-Illustrated Biography.* Mankato, MN: Bridgestone Books, 1998.

Shaughnessy, Diane, and Jack Carpenter. *Chief Joseph: Nez Perce Peace-keeper.* New York: PowerKids Press, 1997.

Taylor, Marian W. *Chief Joseph: Nez Perce Leader.* New York: Chelsea House, 1993.

Warren, Robert Penn. *Chief Joseph of the Nez Perce.* New York: Random House, 1983.

Web Sites

"Chief Joseph: As Remembered by Ohiyesha (Charles A. Eastman)." *American Indian Resource Directory.* http://www.indians.org/welker/joseph1.htm (accessed on March 11, 2004).

"Chief Joseph." *PBS: New Perspectives on the West.* http://www.pbs.org/weta/thewest/people/a_c/chiefjoseph.htm (accessed on March 11, 2004).

Where to Learn More

Books

Adovasio, J. M., with Jake Page. *The First Americans: In Pursuit of Archaeology's Greatest Mystery.* New York: Random House, 2002.

Barrett, Tracy. *Growing Up in Colonial America.* Brookfield, CT: Millbrook Press, 1995.

Brogan, Hugh. *The Longman History of the United States of America.* 2nd ed. London and New York: Addison Wesley Longman, 1999.

Ciongoli, A. Kenneth, and Jay Parini. *Passage to Liberty: The Story of Italian Immigration and the Rebirth of America.* New York: Regan Books, 2002.

Clark, Jayne. *The Greeks in America.* Minneapolis: Lerner Publications, 1990.

Daley, William W. *The Chinese Americans.* New York: Chelsea House, 1996.

Daniels, Roger. *Coming to America: A History of Immigration and Ethnicity in American Life.* New York: HarperCollins, 1990.

Davis, William C. *The American Frontier: Pioneers, Settlers, and Cowboys, 1800–1899.* New York: Smithmark, 1992.

Dezell, Maureen. *Irish America: Coming into Clover.* New York: Doubleday, 2000.

Dolan, Sean. *The Polish Americans.* New York: Chelsea House, 1997.

Dubofsky, Melvyn. *Industrialism and the American Worker, 1865–1920.* 3rd ed. Wheeling, IL: Harlan Davidson, 1996.

Fagan, Brian M. *Kingdoms of Gold, Kingdoms of Jade: The Americas Before Columbus*. London: Thames and Hudson, 1991.

Ferry, Steve. *Russian Americans*. Tarrytown, NY: Benchmark Books, 1996.

Fitzhugh, William W. "Puffins, Ringed Pins, and Runestones: The Viking Passage to America." In *Vikings: The North Atlantic Saga*. Edited by William W. Fitzhugh and Elisabeth I. Ward. Washington and London: Smithsonian Institution Press in association with National Museum of Natural History, 2000.

Fixico, Donald L. *Termination and Relocation: Federal Indian Policy, 1945–1966*. Albuquerque: University of New Mexico Press, 1986.

Freedman, Russell. *In the Days of the Vaqueros: The First True Cowboys*. New York: Clarion Books, 2001.

Frost, Helen. *German Immigrants, 1820–1920*. Mankato, MN: Blue Earth Books, 2002.

Gernand, Renée. *The Cuban Americans*. New York: Chelsea House, 1996.

Gonzalez, Juan. *Harvest of Empire: A History of Latinos in America*. New York: Viking, 2000.

Grossman, James R. *Land of Hope: Chicago, Black Southerners, and the Great Migration*. Chicago: University of Chicago Press, 1989.

Hawke, David Freeman. *Everyday Life in Early America*. New York: Harper & Row, 1988.

Hertzberg, Arthur. *The Jews in America: Four Centuries of an Uneasy Encounter*. New York: Simon and Schuster, 1989.

Hoobler, Dorothy, and Thomas Hoobler. *The Chinese American Family Album*. New York: Oxford University Press, 1994.

Hoobler, Dorothy, and Thomas Hoobler. *The German American Family Album*. New York and Oxford: Oxford University Press, 1996.

Hoobler, Dorothy, and Thomas Hoobler. *The Scandinavian American Family Album*. New York and Oxford: Oxford University Press, 1997.

Howe, Irving. *World of Our Fathers: The Journey of the East European Jews to America and the Life They Found and Made*. New York: Simon and Schuster, 1976.

The Irish in America. Coffey, Michael, ed., with text by Terry Golway. New York: Hyperion, 1997.

Jackson, Robert H., and Edward Castillo. *Indians, Franciscans, and Spanish Colonization: The Impact of the Mission System on California Indians*. Albuquerque: University of New Mexico Press, 1995.

Johnson, Paul. *A History of the Jews*. New York: Harper & Row, 1987.

Kitano, Harry. *The Japanese Americans*. New York: Chelsea House, 1996.

Kitano, Harry H. L., and Roger Daniels. *Asian Americans: Emerging Minorities*. Englewood Cliffs, NJ: Prentice Hall, 1995.

Kraut, Alan M. *The Immigrant in American Society, 1880–1921*. 2nd ed. Wheeling, IL: Harlan Davidson, 2001.

Lavender, David Sievert. *The Rockies*. Rev. ed. New York: HarperCollins, 1975.

Lee, Lauren. *Japanese Americans*. Tarrytown, NY: Marshall Cavendish, 1996.

Lehrer, Brian. *The Korean Americans*. New York: Chelsea House, 1996.

Loewen, James W. *Lies My Teacher Told Me: Everything Your American History Textbook Got Wrong*. New York: Touchstone Books, 1996.

Magocsi, Paul R. *The Russian Americans*. New York: Chelsea House, 1996.

McLynn, Frank. *Wagons West: The Epic Story of America's Overland Trails*. New York: Grove Press, 2002.

Middleton, Richard. *Colonial America: A History, 1565–1776*. 3rd ed. Oxford, UK: Blackwell, 2002.

Monos, Dimitris. *The Greek Americans*. New York: Chelsea House, 1996.

Nabokov, Peter, ed. *Native American Testimony*. New York: Thomas Crowell, 1978.

Odess, Daniel, Stephen Loring, and William W. Fitzhugh. "Skraeling: First Peoples of Helluland, Markland, and Vinland." In *Vikings: The North Atlantic Saga*. Edited by William W. Fitzhugh and Elisabeth I. Ward. Washington and London: Smithsonian Institution Press in association with National Museum of Natural History, 2000.

Olson, Kay Melchisedech. *Norwegian, Swedish, and Danish Immigrants, 1820–1920*. Mankato, MN: Blue Earth Books, 2002.

Palmer, Colin A. *The First Passage: Blacks in the Americas, 1502–1617*. New York: Oxford University Press, 1995.

Petrini, Catherine. *The Italian Americans*. San Diego: Lucent Books, 2002.

Phillips, David, and Steven Ferry. *Greek Americans*. Tarrytown, NY: Benchmark Books, 1996.

Piersen, William D. *From Africa to America: African American History from the Colonial Era to the Early Republic, 1526–1790*. New York: Twayne, 1996.

Pitt, Leonard. *The Decline of the Californios: A Social History of the Spanish-Speaking Californians, 1846–1890*. Berkeley: University of California Press, 1966.

Portes, Alejandro, and Rubén G. Rumbaut. *Immigrant America: A Portrait*. 2nd ed. Berkeley: University of California Press, 1996.

Press, Petra. *Puerto Ricans*. Tarrytown, NY: Benchmark Books, 1996.

Schmidley, A. Dianne. *U.S. Census Bureau, Current Population Reports, Series P23-206, "Profile of the Foreign-Born Population in the United States": 2000*. Washington, DC: U.S. Government Printing Office, 2001.

Scott, John Anthony. *Settlers on the Eastern Shore: The British Colonies in North America, 1607–1750*. New York: Facts on File, 1991.

Shannon, William. *The American Irish*. Amherst: University of Massachusetts Press, 1990.

Stegner, Page. *Winning the Wild West: The Epic Saga of the American Frontier, 1800–1899*. New York: The Free Press, 2002.

Suro, Roberto. *Strangers Among Us: How Latino Immigration Is Transforming America*. New York: Knopf, 1998.

Takaki, Ronald. *Strangers from a Different Shore: A History of Asian Americans*. Boston: Little, Brown, and Company, 1989.

Tonelli, Bill, ed. *The Italian American Reader: A Collection of Outstanding Fiction, Memoirs, Journalism, Essays, and Poetry*. New York: William Morrow, 2003.

Wepman, Dennis. *Immigration: From the Founding of Virginia to the Closing of Ellis Island*. New York: Facts on File, 2002.

Williams, Jean Kinney. *The Mormons: The American Religious Experience*. New York: Franklin Watts, 1996.

Wood, Peter H. *Strange New Land: African Americans, 1617–1776*. New York: Oxford University Press, 1996.

Periodicals

Hogan, Roseann Reinemuth. "Examining the Transatlantic Voyage." Parts I and II. *Ancestry Magazine* (Part 1: November/December 2000): vol. 18, no. 6; (Part II: March/April 2001): vol. 19, no. 2. These articles can be found online at http://www.ancestry.com/library/view/ancmag/3365.asp and http://www.ancestry.com/library/view/ancmag/4130.asp (accessed on April 1, 2004).

Peck, Ira. "How Three Groups Overcame Prejudice." *Scholastic Update* (May 6, 1998): vol. 6, no. 17, p. 12.

Rose, Jonathan. "Organized Crime: An 'Equal-Opportunity' Employer; Every American Ethnic Group Has Had Its Fingers in Organized Crime—a Fact That the Dominance of Italian-American Crime Rings Tends to Mask." *Scholastic Update* (March 21, 1986): vol. 118, p. 12.

Web Sites

"About Jewish Culture." *MyJewishLearning.com*. http://www.myjewishlearning.com/culture/AboutJewishCulture.htm (accessed on April 1, 2004).

"Africa: One Continent, Many Worlds." *Natural History Museum of Los Angeles*. http://www.nhm.org/africa/facts/ (accessed on April 1, 2004).

"The American Presidency State of the Union Messages." *The American Presidency*. http://www.polsci.ucsb.edu/projects/presproject/idgrant/site/state.html (accessed on April 1, 2004).

"American West: Transportation." *World-Wide Web Virtual Library's History Index*. http://www.ku.edu/kansas/west/trans.htm (accessed on April 1, 2004).

"Austrian-Hungarian Immigrants." *Spartacus Educational*. http://www.spartacus.schoolnet.co.uk/USAEah.htm (accessed on April 1, 2004).

Bernard, Kara Tobin, and Shane K. Bernard. *Encyclopedia of Cajun Culture*. http://www.cajunculture.com/ (accessed on April 1, 2004).

"A Brief History of Indian Migration to America." *American Immigration Law Foundation.* http://www.ailf.org/awards/ahp_0203_essay.htm (accessed on April 1, 2004).

Chinese American Data Center. http://members.aol.com/chineseusa/00cen.htm (accessed on April 1, 2004).

"Coming to America Two Years after 9-11." *Migration Policy Institute.* http://www.ilw.com/lawyers/immigdaily/letters/2003,0911-mpi.pdf (accessed on April 1, 2004).

"French Colonization of Louisiana and Louisiana Purchase Map Collection." *Louisiana Digital Library.* http://louisdl.louislibraries.org/LMP/Pages/home.html (accessed on April 1, 2004).

Guzmán, Betsy. "The Hispanic Population: Census 2000 Brief." *U.S. Census Bureau, May 2001.* http://www.census.gov/prod/2001pubs/c2kbr01-3.pdf (accessed on April 1, 2004).

"Haitians in America." *Haiti and the U.S.A.: Linked by History and Community.* http://www.haiti-usa.org/modern/index.php (accessed on April 1, 2004).

"A History of Chinese Americans in California." *National Park Service.* http://www.cr.nps.gov/history/online_books/5views/5views3.htm (accessed on April 1, 2004).

Immigration: The Living Mosaic of People, Culture, and Hope. http://library.thinkquest.org/20619/index.html (accessed on April 1, 2004).

"Landmarks in Immigration History." *Digital History.* http://www.digitalhistory.uh.edu/historyonline/immigration_chron.cfm (accessed on April 1, 2004).

Le, C. N. "The Model Minority Image." *Asian Nation: The Landscape of Asian America.* http://www.asian-nation.org/model-minority.shtml (accessed on April 1, 2004).

Logan, John R., and Glenn Deane. "Black Diversity in Metropolitan America." *Lewis Mumford Center for Comparative Urban and Regional Research, University at Albany.* http://mumford1.dyndns.org/cen2000/BlackWhite/BlackDiversityReport/black-diversity01.htm (accessed on April 1, 2004).

Lovgren, Stefan. "Who Were the First Americans?" *NationalGeographic.com.* http://news.nationalgeographic.com/news/2003/09/0903_030903_bajaskull.html (accessed on April 1, 2004).

Mosley-Dozier, Bernette A. "Double Minority: Haitians in America." *Yale–New Haven Teachers Institute.* http://www.yale.edu/ynhti/curriculum/units/1989/1/89.01.08.x.html (accessed on April 1, 2004).

RapidImmigration.com. http://www.rapidimmigration.com/usa/1_eng_immigration_history.html (accessed on April 1, 2004).

The Scottish History Pages. http://www.scotshistoryonline.co.uk/scothist.html (accessed on April 1, 2004).

Simkin, John. "Immigration." *Spartacus Educational.* http://www.spartacus.schoolnet.co.uk/USAimmigration.htm (accessed on April 1, 2004).

Spiegel, Taru. "The Finns in America." *Library of Congress: European Reading Room.* http://www.loc.gov/rr/european/FinnsAmer/finchro.html (accessed on April 1, 2004).

"The Story of Africa: Slavery." *BBC News.* http://www.bbc.co.uk/world service/africa/features/storyofafrica/9chapter9.shtml (accessed on April 1, 2004).

Trinklein, Mike, and Steve Boettcher. *The Oregon Trail.* http://www.isu.edu/%7Etrinmich/Oregontrail.html (accessed on April 1, 2004).

"U.S. Immigration." *Internet Modern History Sourcebook.* http://www.fordham.edu/halsall/mod/modsbook28.html (accessed on April 1, 2004).

Virtual Museum of New France. http://www.civilization.ca/vmnf/vmnfe.asp (accessed on April 1, 2004).

Index

Baker, Howard, *1:* 191
Bakewell, Lucy, *1:* 44
"The Ballad of John and Yoko"
    (Lennon), *2:* 277
Bank of China Tower, *2:* 286
Barenboim, Daniel, *2:* 328,
    333–34, 334 (ill.)
Barry, Joan, *1:* 80
Bartholdi, Frédéric Auguste, *2:*
    247, 363–66, 364 (ill.), 368,
    373
Bartsch, Paul, *1:* 45
Bastille Day, *2:* 293
Batman and Robin, 2: 343
Battle of the Little Big Horn, *1:*
    223
Battle of the Lost Battalion, *1:*
    186
Beame, Abraham, *2:* 262
Beatles (musical group), *2:*
    273–74, 276–77
Beaumont, Gustave de, *2:* 383–84,
    388
Bedloe's Island, *2:* 364
Bell, Alexander Graham, *1:* 49
    (ill.), **49–56,** 51 (ill.)
Bell, Alexander Melville, *1:* 49
Bell, Elisa Grace Symonds, *1:* 50
Bell Telephone Company, *1:* 52
La Belle Paree, 1: 205
Berdahl, Andrew, *2:* 325
Berdahl, Jennie Marie, *2:* 323–24
Berlin, Irving, *1:* 158
Bessemer, Henry, *1:* 69 (ill.), 70
Beta decay, *1:* 120
Beyond the Melting Pot (Moynihan
    and Glazer), *2:* 259, 263–64
Bilingual education, *1:* 168, 170
Birds, *1:* 43–48, 45 (ill.), 47 (ill.)
Birds of America (Audubon), *1:* 43,
    46–47, 47 (ill.)
Black Friday, *1:* 152–53
Black, Hugo L., *1:* 140 (ill.)
Black Panther Party, *2:* 240
Black pride, *1:* 143
Black Star Line, *1:* 147, 148–49
Blackface, *1:* 204, 209
Blacks. *See* African Americans
Blaskó, Béla Ferenc Dezsö. *See* Lu-
    gosi, Bela
The Blue Spruce (Cuomo), *1:* 109
Bodybuilding, *2:* 339–40
Bonaparte, Louis-Napoléon, *2:*
    364, 382–83

Bosnia, *2:* 352, 353
Bottoms, 2: 275
Bound for Glory (Guthrie), *1:* 157
Bowmar Instruments, *2:* 399
Bradley, Tom, *1:* 171
Brandeis, Louis, *1:* 136, 137
Braun, Alexander, *1:* 14
Braun, Cecile, *1:* 14
Brazilian Iron Ore Company, *1:*
    182
Bridges, *2:* 312, 314–15, 316–19,
    317 (ill.), 318 (ill.)
British East India Company, *1:* 36
Broadway
    Jolson, Al, on, *1:* 206, 208
    Lugosi, Bela, on, *2:* 252–53
Brooklyn Bridge, *2:* 317 (ill.),
    318–19, 318 (ill.)
Brothers, Shubert, *1:* 205
Brown, David, *1:* 97 (ill.), 99 (ill.)
Brown, Moses, *2:* 358, 360
Brownian motion, *1:* 113
Browning, Tod, *2:* 255
Brzezinski, Zbigniew, *1:* 20
Buchanan, James, *1:* 131 (ill.),
    132
Buchanan, Pat, *1:* 57 (ill.),
    57–64, 59 (ill.)
Bureau of Indian Affairs, *1:* 222
Burlesque shows, *1:* 203–4
Burton, Harold H., *1:* 140 (ill.)
Bush, George
    Buchanan, Pat, and, *1:* 60–61
    Kissinger, Henry, and, *2:* 234
    Schwarzenegger, Arnold, and,
        2: 342, 342 (ill.)
    Shalikashvili, John, and, *2:* 352

C

Cables, suspension bridge, *2:* 316,
    339
Cage, John, *2:* 274–75
Calculators, electronic, *2:* 399
California
    Agricultural Labor Relations
        Act, *1:* 91
    farm workers in, *1:* 91–92
    Okies to, *1:* 154
    Proposition 49, *2:* 343–44
    Proposition 187, *1:* 170

F

Factory workers, child, *1:* 216
Farm workers
    Chávez, César, and, *1:* 84–85, 87–92
    Hernández, Antonia, and, *1:* 169
Fasting, *1:* 89–90
Fathers, immigrant, *1:* 6
Fermi, Enrico, *1:* 118 (ill.), **118–25**
Fermi-Dirac statistics, *1:* 119
Fermions, *1:* 119
Figley, Charles, *1:* 101
Filipinos. *See* Philippines
Fillmore, Millard, *1:* 126 (ill.), **126–33,** 130 (ill.), 131 (ill.)
Films. *See* Movies
Final Solution, *2:* 405. *See also* Holocaust
Fishes, fossil, *1:* 11–12
Fishes of Brazil (Agassiz), *1:* 11
Fiske, Nathan, *1:* 194–95
Fluxus movement, *2:* 275
Fly (Ono), *2:* 277
Football, *2:* 304, 305–11
Ford, Gerald, *1:* 60; *2:* 229, 233
Forest Hills Diary (Cuomo), *1:* 105
Forrester, Jay W., *2:* 398–99
Fort Astoria, *1:* 37, 37 (ill.)
Fossil fishes, *1:* 11–12
Four Horsemen, *2:* 309
442nd Regimental Combat Team, *1:* 185–88; *2:* 238
The Four Winners (Rockne), *2:* 310
Fourth World Conference on Women, *1:* 22
Fragrant Hill Hotel, *2:* 286
France
    French Revolution, *2:* 293, 366–67, 382–83
    Great Debate, *2:* 383
    Statue of Liberty and, *2:* 363–64, 368
    Third Republic of, *2:* 364
Frankenstein, *2:* 255
Frankfurter, Felix, *1:* 134 (ill.), **134–42,** 140 (ill.)
Franklin, Benjamin, *2:* 289, 291
Fred Karno Company, *1:* 78
Freed slaves, *2:* 391
Freedom of religion. *See* Religious freedom

Freedom of speech, *1:* 138
Freedom Rides, *2:* 239
Frémont, John, *1:* 131 (ill.)
French Revolution
    Delacroix, Eugene, and, *2:* 366–67
    English Dissenters and, *2:* 293
    Tocqueville, Alexis de, and, *2:* 382–83
Frias, Miguel, *1:* 27
Frick, Henry Clay, *1:* 72
Fricke, David, *2:* 279
Fugitive Slave Act, *1:* 129–30; *2:* 391
Fur trade, *1:* 33, 34–38, 35 (ill.), 37 (ill.)

G

Galbraith, Erle, *1:* 208–9
Galleon Award, *2:* 270
Garvey, Marcus, *1:* 143 (ill.), **143–51**
Gays, *2:* 404
Gaza Strip, *2:* 330, 332
General relativity, *1:* 115
German immigrants
    1830, after, *2:* 384
    1840s–50s, *2:* 244
    national identity of, *2:* 263–64
Gershwin, George, *1:* 206, 208
Gestapo, *2:* 404
Giants in the Earth (Rölvaag), *2:* 325–26
Gipp, George, *2:* 307–9
The Gipper, *2:* 308–9
"Give Peace a Chance" (Lennon), *2:* 277
Glaciers, *1:* 10, 14–16, 15 (ill.)
Glazer, Nathan, *2:* 259, 263–64
Global Village Foundation, *1:* 166
"God Bless America" (Berlin), *1:* 158
Goddard, Paulett, *1:* 80
Gold Rush. *See* California Gold Rush
Golden Age of Television, *2:* 377
The Golden Girls, *2:* 379
Golway, Terry, *1:* 107
Gordon, William, *1:* 29–30
Gorn, Elliot, *1:* 212
Gould, Jay, *2:* 300

N